PRISONERS of JAN SMUTS

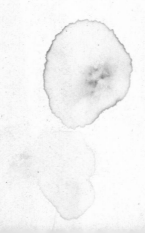

PRISONERS
OF JAN SMUTS

Italian Prisoners of War
in South Africa in WWII

KAREN HORN

JONATHAN BALL PUBLISHERS
JOHANNESBURG & CAPE TOWN

Originally published in South African in 2024 by
JONATHAN BALL PUBLISHERS
A division of Media24 (Pty) Ltd
PO Box 33977
Jeppestown
2043

ISBN 978-1-77619-284-7
ebook ISBN 978-1-77619-285-4

jonathanball.co.za
x.com/JonathanBallPub
facebook.com/JonathanBallPublishers

Cover by Sean Robertson
Design and typesetting by Johan Koortzen
Set in Adobe Garamond Pro 11 on 15pt

Printed by **novus print**, a Novus Holdings company

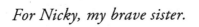

For Nicky, my brave sister.

Contents

Author's note

I care not where my body may take me as long as my soul is embarked on a meaningful journey. – Dante Alighieri

My first book, *In Enemy Hands: South African POWs in WWII* (2015), was based on research about South African soldiers who were captured in North Africa during the war and their experiences as prisoners of war (POWs). These men were held captive in Italy, and later in German-occupied territories, and they returned home in 1945 only after the Allies defeated the German forces in April of that year.

Decades after the war, these veterans welcomed me into their homes and shared their stories. As captives, they sat on the sidelines as their friends fought on in the war, yet their isolation from the battlefront did not diminish their suffering. Upon reflection, I realised that it is not the hardship these men endured that fascinated me but their ability to live, hope, love and laugh during times of suffering – and even to turn out better men at the end of it.

As the Second World War spread across the globe between 1939 and 1945, hundreds of thousands of Italian conscripts were captured in East and North Africa. The Allies, especially Britain, decided that many of them should spend the war in POW camps in British Dominions, including South Africa. Prime Minister Jan Smuts agreed, and as a consequence between 60 000 and 100 000 Italian POWs were sent to the Union of South Africa.[1]

So, while homesick South African POWs whiled away their time in camps across Europe, Italian POWs did the same in the Zonderwater Prisoner-of-War Camp near Pretoria. It was, therefore, to Zonderwater that my focus then shifted.

A POW is someone who is captured and incarcerated by enemy forces during battle. Once a soldier raises a white flag to surrender, the rules of battle no longer apply. The Geneva Convention regulated the treatment of war prisoners to some extent, yet POWs remained largely at the mercy of their captors. Mental and physical survival depended on each man's ability to develop new skills and to adapt to life in a POW camp. Their responses were diverse: many of them struggled with this process, but others thrived. Camp commanders and guards responded with a range of emotions, ranging from mild irritation to intense exasperation, depending on the POWs' level of ingenuity in making their experience more bearable.

Colourful anecdotes about the Italian POWs persisted during the decades that followed the war and stories abound of their creativity, their technical skills – especially in construction projects – and also their convivial and romantic outlook on life. While there is truth to many of these stories, others are marked by exaggeration. The POWs' presence also left tangible marks, such as the roads, mountain passes and churches they built, the crops they helped to harvest, the forests they helped to maintain and the enterprises they later embarked upon. Many South Africans remain fascinated by these foreign visitors and hold them in high regard. There is no doubt that they made a valuable contribution to South Africa during the war, but at what cost to themselves both emotionally and socially? Some even stayed in South Africa to forge careers and left indelible imprints here: if you have ever wondered where the Italian-styled Gatti's ice cream derived its name, or attended any of the erstwhile Cape Performing Arts Board (CAPAB) operas in Cape Town directed by maestro Gregorio Fiasconaro, you would have been experiencing the fruits of their ingenuity and labours.

To try to write about the experiences of tens of thousands of prisoners of war would force one to generalise and to overlook the nuances and complexities of individual experiences. There is also the danger of 'mythologising' the Italian POW episode. I believe that a focus on individual stories will make the experiences of POWs more real and relatable to a modern audience and that is why I have decided to focus on five main characters.

My long research journey began in 2016, though by that time war veterans' memories were fading and many had passed away. Most of the Italian POWs who spent time in South Africa returned to Italy after the war and my research funding did not allow me to undertake the long journey to interview them there.

At a certain point, though, I heard about Paolo Ricci. A former captive in the Zonderwater camp, he decided to remain in South Africa when the war came to an end. Born in 1920, Paolo was already 97 when I interviewed him in Pretoria in 2017.

I also visited Emilio Coccia at the Zonderwater Museum, where he is the chairman of the Zonderwater ex-POW Society and, through him, I came to hear about the memoirs that were available on the Zonderwater website. The life-changing events of the war and of captivity motivated many former POWs to document what they remembered. I was fortunate to happen upon these memoirs, even if they were all in Italian, a language I had no knowledge of at that time. Through the *Società Dante Alighieri* (Dante Alighieri Society), an organisation that promotes the Italian language and culture around the world, I was introduced to Tiarè Totaro. A professional translator, she patiently and accurately translated numerous, often long-winded texts into English, conveying the meaning and context. This process was essential to the book – without Tiarè, this indispensable resource would not have been accessible to me.

The memoirs of Raffaello Cei were one of those that had been translated by Tiarè. Raffaello had written down his story because, in his words, he wanted the youth to know the importance of peace. By a happy coincidence, I discovered that Raffaello was at that time still alive and well and living in Italy. We became Facebook friends and he shared many of his POW experiences directly with me via email. His assistance and kindness in helping me with my writing were invaluable and I shall never forget him.

Another memoir that I asked Tiarè to translate was Pietro Scottu's recollections of the war and his time in South Africa. He was an adventurous man who had no regard for barbed-wire fences. Pietro and I exchanged several emails and in one he wrote that he looked forward to seeing this book in print. Living in Genoa, he wrote that he missed the beaches of the Eastern Cape and considered his time in South Africa to have been the 'longest holiday of my life'.[2]

Luigi Pederzoli was not a soldier but an administrator in an Italian colony on the African continent. Upon his capture, he became known as POW 18962. His daughter, Emily Spenser (also known as Emilia Pederzoli), became a friend of mine, albeit from afar, and I am enormously grateful to her for her willingness to share Luigi's experiences.

Then there is Giovanni Palermo, a man of conviction who never surrendered his beliefs in his leaders, causing him to endure harsher conditions in captivity. His son was gracious in letting me use Giovanni's war memoirs.

These five men – Paolo, Raffaello, Pietro, Luigi and Giovanni – are the main characters in this book about the Italian POWs in South Africa. It is through their eyes that we gain an understanding of what it was like to be a prisoner at Zonderwater and Pietermaritzburg or in a remote work camp – or what it meant to be on the run from the authorities. Each of these five men had a unique and distinct experience in South Africa. Their stories cover different aspects of the Italian prisoner-of-war experience in the Union; and while they can never be completely representative, their accounts offer greater insights into the realities of being a captive in a foreign land.

Memories fade and when working with memoirs it quickly becomes clear that there is no such thing as historical accuracy, regardless of how hard one tries to verify information. Many of the experiences that were written about in the prisoners' memoirs can be verified, to some extent, by archival documents, but not all. In such instances, I analysed, interpreted and imagined as accurately as I could. That said, I wrote from the perspective of a South African historian, fully aware that objectivity is an elusive goal.

If, on the pages of this book, the reader does not always find the same happy story they have come to know about the Italian POWs in South Africa, I ask that they bear in mind that I stayed true to the evidence I found in archival documents. After all, it is also the historian's responsibility to confront the myths of the past.

I am immensely grateful to the veterans and their families for allowing me to tell their stories. Emilio Coccia's willingness to share information and his many years of devoted work at the Zonderwater Museum have provided me with a crucial link to the past. The museum is situated where the Zonderwater POW camp used to be. Today, verdant grass and tall trees bring a sense of calm to the cemetery where some of those POWs were laid to rest.

At the South African National Museum of Military History (NMMH), Phindile Madida searched for and scanned hundreds of photographs for this book. Her professional approach and her friendly emails brightened my writing days. In Italy, Elisa Longorato of the Zonderwater Block ex-POW Association and daughter of a former POW sourced many photos for me and these add immense value and interest to this book. Emilia Pederzoli, the daughter of Luigi, also provided many photographs. I am endlessly thankful to all of them for sharing these priceless mementoes of that period. More photographs came from the archives of the International Red Cross and I appreciate their having given me permission to republish them.

I found most of the archival material at the archives of the Department of Defence's Documentation Centre in Centurion. I am thankful to Steve D'Agrela and his colleagues, who supplied me with box after box of documents. To my fellow military historians, especially Ian van der Waag, Anri Delport, Evert Kleynhans, David Katz and Jacques de Vries, thank you for your continuing support. I also reserve a special word of thanks to Bill Nasson, whose writing remains a source of inspiration.

My gratitude also goes to my colleagues at the International Studies Group at the University of the Free State, especially Ian Phimister, who motivates and encourages all of us who are fortunate enough to be associated with this group.

To my publisher, Annie Olivier: you are a wise woman and it is a joy to work with you. Thank you. My thanks also goes to everyone at Jonathan Ball Publishers who worked hard to get this book on the shelves.

André, without you this book would have been completed either sooner or later, but it would have been written without joy, so thank you.

In writing about war, my aim is to find examples of the many ways in which humanity prevails in times of conflict and strife. I hope that you, the reader, will find abundant examples of this in these pages.

INTRODUCTION

THE YEAR 1922 was a good one for Benito Mussolini – that was the year he transformed himself into a dictatorial Fascist leader. Previously, he had worked as a part-time teacher, an author and a newspaper editor, but he found it more rewarding to instigate controversy and practise subversion.

To ensure his success in taking political power, he assembled his own private army. These men became known as the Blackshirts[1] and their devotion and loyalty to Mussolini was unmatched, no matter how many times he changed his ideas on politics or how many friends he declared to be his enemies. The Blackshirts carried out his orders without thinking and they engendered fear and intimidation and even murdered fellow Italians as they went about their business of placing Mussolini on a pedestal.

Towards the end of 1922, Mussolini was ready to take power and decided to march on Rome. He wanted to become the hero, the one who had liberated the Italian people from the monarchy, the socialists and the anarchists. On the way to Rome, the Blackshirts violently seized control of villages as they ransacked their way towards Rome, although their leader stayed away from the dirty work, travelling to Rome by train instead. As the Blackshirts gathered to confront the government's military, Victor Emmanuel III, King of Italy, lost heart and appointed Mussolini as the country's new Prime Minister.

And so began Mussolini's dictatorship in Italy. Setting the country on a Fascist path, he made sure that the ideology reached every corner of the country. In essence, a Fascist state is one that is ruled by a dictator who does not tolerate opposition and turns the country into a one-party state. With no elections, individual and cultural liberty fall away and the state controls every aspect of life. Any resistance is dealt with brutally – Fascist states are known for their reliance on aggressive militarism to suppress any form of opposition. Fascists are extreme nationalists: They place their country's interests above those of all others and, on this basis, they also justify their use of military aggression against neighbouring countries.

In most ways a typical strong man, Mussolini would not admit to any faults or failures; the march on Rome became a propaganda tool to warn those who dared to stand in the way of heroes on their way to carrying out their destiny. Inspired by the Caesars of ancient Rome, Mussolini wanted to create a new Roman Empire that could carry his ideas across the world. To do this, though, he needed a larger area over which to rule and a population that would obey him without question. He probably knew that he could not fully rely on the older generations for support, as they had seen him change political direction on more than one occasion in the past.

Those who had followed Mussolini's career would have known him initially as a socialist but at the start of the First World War he abandoned that ideology in favour of militarism. The older generation, Mussolini knew, would have to be subjugated through laws and disciplinary action. If anyone were to have taken a closer look at his personal life, they would have noticed that Mussolini apparently did not care much for any political ideology, at least not when it came to personal relationships, as he had had affairs and a string of children with women who were known to be socialists and communists.

It was among the First World War veterans and the youth that Mussolini found his support: he could bend the young generation to his will and exploit the frustrations of the veterans to inspire loyalty.

Young and impressionable, the youth became the main target of Mussolini's Fascist indoctrination. Even so, Italian children did not become Fascists overnight: it was through fear and intimidation, on the one hand, and love and loyalty, on the other, that the Fascists gained a fan base among the younger generations. Youth programmes and a formal education system instilled with Fascist propaganda helped to build Mussolini's idea of the perfect Fascist.

The Italian youth of the early 1920s grew up mostly without knowing the joys of personal freedom. Italy was a poor country and most children worked to help make ends meet. For most of them, the idea of individual free will was irrelevant as the pressures of daily life took their toll.

Furthermore, the children did not know any political system other than the one they were born into and so most of them obeyed the state and its leader without question. By the time the young boys became adolescents, ideas of war dominated their education and most young men became willing conscripts ready to die for Mussolini's ideals.[2]

Obedience and conformity formed the basis of Fascism, a political ideology that became a way of life and one which permeated all aspects of Italian society. Of course, there were exceptions, but even among those who opposed Fascism, there was no way out in the case of military conscription: every young man had to do military service, first in the outlying Italian colonies in Africa and later when the country was dragged into the Second World War. Although Mussolini could not have predicted that a war would start in 1939, his emphasis on militarism prepared the young men and women for such an event. Those who were infants and toddlers when Mussolini marched on Rome in 1922 were just the right age to fight and die on the battlefields in the Second World War.

Since 1880, Italy had been competing with other European powers in the so-called Scramble for Africa. When he took power, Mussolini continued with his grand plan to re-establish the ancient Roman Empire. It was also an opportunity for him to put the theory of his Fascist and militaristic ideology into practice.[3] For example, the day before his Blackshirt brigades invaded the East African country of Abyssinia,[4] Mussolini reminded all Italians that Abyssinia was a 'barbarian country' and the inhabitants were 'unworthy of ranking among civilized nations'.[5]

While most applauded Mussolini's speech, not everyone who listened to him that day was convinced that he was right, but they were warned that the invasion of African colonies was a matter of 'one heart alone! One will alone! One decision!'[6] The Blackshirts carried out their orders to the letter: the level of brutality with which they did so is still being written about today.[7] By the time the Second World War began in 1939, Italy had colonised Eritrea, Ethiopia and Italian Somaliland in East Africa, in addition to Cyrenaica and Tripolitania, which were unified to form Italian Libya, in North Africa.

But whereas the colonies did much for Mussolini's ego, they drained his economy. Still owing First World War debts to the United States and Britain, Italy declared a *de jure* default on its US debt.[8] The economic situation in Italy was worsened by a growing population and an inability to produce enough food. Even though most Italians were engaged in agricultural production, they were forced to import essential foodstuffs that they could ill afford.[9]

With his nation struggling to cope, Mussolini had to tighten his grip to manage the growing discontent. Given that the majority of Italians are devout Catholics, the Prime Minister used the power of religion to convince his citizens that his dictatorship was justified and endorsed by the Pope. However, he was not religious in any way and as a young man he had gone as far as accusing priests of causing more harm to humanity than the tuberculosis virus.[10] Far from working with the Church, Mussolini placed the Pope under severe pressure to support his ideology. Feigning cooperation with the Church was a purely political strategy.

It is not known to what extent Italians were aware of Mussolini's hatred of religion – his first publication was an article entitled 'God does not exist'. Nevertheless, he knew that Italians accepted, for the most part without question, the Pope's leadership. By making sure that the Pope was under his influence, he assumed control over most of the population.

The fusion of religion and politics worked wonders for Mussolini's propaganda machine. From as early as 1926, it became commonplace for his supporters to refer to him as *il Duce* (the Leader). He indoctrinated the population further to ensure that his image and that of Christ were merged into one. At the same time, his support from within the Church was also growing. By the early 1930s, his power over the Pope was complete and the Church began to collaborate with the Fascists. This meant that religious groups, such as the Catholic Action groups, who had previously been doing work among communities under the Church's supervision, now had to do the Fascists' bidding. Instead of continuing with their work of Christianising the population, the Catholic Action groups now acted as informants for the Fascist Police, letting them know of civilian transgressions against the State.[11]

When Adolf Hitler came to power in 1933 in Germany, he also imposed a Fascist regime on the nation. Today his style of National Socialist Fascism is mostly remembered for the horrors of the Holocaust. Anyone who did not fit into Hitler's idea of the ideal human being, or who opposed his ideas, was ruthlessly disposed of. In this way, millions of Jews, Roma and Sinti, homosexuals and political dissidents met their end in forced labour or extermination camps. The brutal race laws against the Jews can be traced back to Italy, where Catholic publications warned against Jewish domination. As the Nazi influence grew in Italy, Jews there began to feel increasingly oppressed. By the 1930s, the situation had become so bad in Italy that Mussolini's Jewish mistress of 19 years fled to Paris and then Argentina.[12]

In the southern hemisphere, South Africa had also experienced its share of turbulence in the first decades of the 20th century. At the turn of the century, the two Boer republics of Transvaal and Orange Free State had lost their battle for independence against the British Empire. By 1910, the two British colonies of Natal and the Cape merged with the two Afrikaner republics to form the Union of South Africa. However, it would take more than political unification to unite the population entirely.

The First World War broke out in 1914, with wounds from the South African War still festering among Afrikaners. When the Union government decided to support Britain in the war, a rebellious group of Afrikaners rose up, angry that their government was siding with their former enemy. The Afrikaner Rebellion of 1914, and its suppression, caused further divisions among the people of the Union.

By the time the First World War ended in 1918, the world had lost its innocence. In Europe, political leaders and great parts of the populations of Italy, Germany and Spain began to seek order from chaos in Fascism. South Africa, although far removed from the events in Europe, also saw a growing rise in Fascism among parts of the population.

In 1938, on the eve of the Second World War, many Afrikaners celebrated the exodus of Boer trekkers from the Cape Colony a century before, in 1838, with the symbolic Great Trek. With this, they reaffirmed their wish for an independent Afrikaner state. In the wake of this nationalistic outpouring the *Ossewabrandwag* (Oxwagon Sentinel) emerged.[13] It insisted on being a cultural movement, although in due course it would also start a paramilitary wing called the *Stormjaers* (Storm Troops). The

Ossewabrandwag had pro-Nazi leanings, and in many ways it stood for similar ideals as Mussolini and Hitler.

Smuts was acutely aware of the rise of Fascism and he must have realised that if war broke out in Europe, his men would be fighting a physical war on the battlefront while he would have to fight a propaganda war on the home front.

With the start of the Second World War in 1939, it was touch and go for Smuts, since Parliament was not overly enthusiastic about the prospect of the country participating in the war. Presented with a choice, however, ministers favoured Smuts, if only with a majority of 13. Still, it was enough for South Africa, at that time a British Dominion, to offer its support for Britain's war effort on the side of the Allies. However, Smuts wanted to avoid a repetition of the Afrikaner Rebellion of 1914, when former Boer generals had campaigned against the country's participation in the First World War on the side of Britain. Unlike in 1914, though, this time the government called for volunteers to fight.

Despite Smuts's careful approach to war, he had many critics, among them the previous prime minister, JBM Hertzog, the *Ossewabrandwag* and later clandestine militant organisations such as the *Stormjaers* and the *Terreurgroep* (Terror Group). The paramilitary groups embarked on acts of sabotage, hoping that doing so would dissuade Smuts from taking the country to war and young men from volunteering. The campaign started with a bang when home-made bombs were used to blow up pylons in January 1942. This was followed by an anti-climactic crusade of cutting telephone wires and disrupting the electricity supply.[14] In some cases, fights between Smuts men and *Ossewabrandwag* members broke out on the streets.

While the Fascist leaders in Italy and Germany pressed their populations into submission, the South African government was more lenient in how it handled opposition in the 1930s and early 1940s, at least towards the two white races of the country.

In contrast to members of the *Ossewabrandwag*, many young men, mostly English-speaking, were eager to join the Union Defence Force (UDF) to 'do their bit' in the war. Some were after adventure while others were pressed into signing up after a few beers with friends. Despite many Afrikaners' misgivings about fighting on the side of the British, many of them also signed up as they felt pressured by economic hardship.[15]

The opposition parties and the *Ossewabrandwag* continued their resistance to Smuts's war effort for the duration of the war. In 1943, for instance, Smuts was forced to put off a trip to London because the political situation on the home front required his full attention. In January 1943, he wrote as follows to Winston Churchill about the coming election in South Africa and the precarious situation he found himself in:

> As you know, my government is a coalition of three parties, united only on the issue of carrying on the war and my leadership is perhaps the only bond keeping the Parliamentary majority together ... Parties now in Government coalition may not be in agreement on other policies than the war and may fight for their own platforms and interests and divide our vote. The Opposition sections, although much divided amongst themselves, will almost certainly all combine against me on the war issue and my own party strength is not such that I can take any risks. Main planks of Opposition are neutrality, republicanism and separation from the Commonwealth ... A decisive defeat for the Opposition policies would go far to stabilise the future of South Africa and its relations to Empire.[16]

While the Smuts government fought against Fascism beyond its borders, Fascists also lived within them. Despite these complexities, a large number of volunteers joined the UDF to fight, first in East and North Africa, and later in Italy.

Despite the political divides, the economy was doing relatively well, with especially gold production putting the country on a profitable path. In 1941, for instance, South Africa reached a peak in gold production of 450 tonnes.[17] International investments, mainly from Britain and the United States, and also mergers between local and international companies, led to the establishment of large mining and industrial companies such as Anglo-American[18] and African Explosives and Chemical Industries (AECI) in the years before the Second World War.

An added benefit was that South Africa was geographically far removed from the theatres of war and did not suffer damage from any battles in its territory, bombing raids and the like.[19] With the Union of South Africa being such a young country, the nation was still in its infancy and its citizens were still a long way from viewing everyone who lived within its borders as a single nation. Racial and social unity were unthinkable concepts. It is no surprise, then, that when Smuts brought the country into the war, some of its citizens began their own fight for freedom on the home front.

Once Mussolini declared war against the Allies, it meant that Italy's African colonies were also drawn into the war. The UDF was deployed to fight the Italian forces first in East Africa and after that the Germans and the Italians in North Africa. It was there that thousands upon thousands of Italian men, soldiers and colonial administrators were captured.

The Italian POWs were sent from East and North Africa to different Commonwealth countries and British Dominions. Smuts was enthusiastic about receiving the POWs: for him this was an opportunity to show that, despite its divisions and the plotting by the *Ossewabrandwag*, South Africa was in fact a loyal supporter of the British war effort. Because Smuts also knew that the POWs would be a useful source of cheap labour, he offered to take far more of them than the country was able to accommodate at that time. In Smuts's mind, the POWs would replace the UDF volunteers for the duration of the war and in this way the economy of the country could remain on track until peace returned. Smuts also believed his willingness to take in so many POWs would be seen as an act of loyalty to the British Empire. He was eager to show that there was more to South Africa than the divisions between those in support of, and those opposed to, the country's participation in the war.

No doubt, in taking on the POWs, Smuts had a long-term plan but he failed to consider a number of practical matters. First, the thousands of POWs had to eat every day, they needed suitable places to live and sleep and they required medical attention, to say nothing of their desire to communicate with their families back in Italy. Complicating matters somewhat was the fact that the Union had to provide these needs in such a way as to satisfy the inspectors who represented the International Committee of the Red Cross (ICRC), whose task it was to ensure that the stipulations of the Geneva Convention were met.

Secondly, the divisions in South African society were difficult enough to manage, but add thousands of Italian POWs to the mix, most of whom had grown up in a Fascist dictatorship, and the stage was set for further tensions to develop. Did Smuts and his cabinet plan for the possible threat to the Union if Fascist POWs met like-minded farmers when they were sent out to help with harvesting? How sure were they that the guards who looked after the POWs were not Fascists themselves and would not help their captives to escape?

The popular thinking at the time was that the Italians were 'docile' and their habit of surrendering in large numbers did nothing to contradict this belief. Because of this, the authorities in the Union were perhaps a touch too lenient when the first Italian POWs arrived in March 1941. By the time the first POWs began their return journeys to Italy after the war, the military authorities were displaying a very different attitude towards them – the result of many blunders, mishaps and a string of disenchantments that are described in this book.

More than 70 years after the war, most South Africans and Italians seem to recall only positive tales about the POWs' time in the Union. According to some, POWs and UDF guards formed friendships as the captives settled down happily in their prison camps. Those who were sent out to work on farms to help with the harvesting or to clear farmland of prickly pears and other unwanted plants apparently did so with a spring in their step. According to these accounts, when meeting Union citizens, the POWs were always on their best behaviour and presented themselves as gentlemen who wanted only the best for their captor hosts. These happy stories are found in memoirs and in the anecdotes shared by war veterans and civilians after the war. Yet they capture only a part of the story. The nostalgia in these memories tends to show a longing for a romantic past – which is not entirely true.

The archives reveal another side to the story. Thanks to the evidence found in war-time documents, I was able to bridge the gap between these nostalgic recollections and the actual historical events. It is the historian's duty to follow the evidence and, in this case, it tells of many unhappy POWs who lived in terrible conditions at the Zonderwater camp; of conflict between guards and POWs. It also tells of prisoners who were desperate to escape, some running away from the authorities, others towards the love they had found in farmhouses across the country. Illegal socialising – and more – between POWs and local women occurred at a regular rate, mostly by mutual consent.

While many of the long-suppressed Italians experienced their first taste of individual freedom in the Union, others found it impossible to free themselves from the constraints of years of Fascist indoctrination. These men believed it was their duty to convince the South Africans that Fascism was the best ideology to follow and to this end they embarked on a mission to convert everyone they came into contact with. Using ingenious propaganda methods, they even enlisted the help of eager locals.

On the other hand, those POWs who embraced their new-found individuality outside a Fascist regime were met with anger and, in some instances, knife-wielding fellow POWs who refused to forsake Fascism. Many simply wanted to make the most of what this freedom could offer and, as a result, the Zonderwater camp saw daily escapes, with many POWs being aided and abetted by South African guards.

The true story of the Italian POWs in South Africa is a combination of the well-behaved, helpful and reliable wartime prisoners and the ruthless, inept, angry and often sad captives. Within this range, the physical evidence of their time in this country can be found. Their contributions to the harvesting schemes were enormous, as was their work on road-building projects, the most well-known of which is the Du Toit's Kloof Pass in what is today the Western Cape Province. Others brought their craftsmanship and created handsome buildings and striking artworks and showcased their musical talent.

Hundreds of POWs first learned to read and write while in the Union. In a sense, all of them were given an opportunity to free themselves of Fascist propaganda and to nurture what was unique to each of them. Some grabbed this opportunity, others did not. Despite often leaving some of the UDF command with their hands in their hair, the prisoners' return to Italy after the war left a void in South African society.

Principal personalities

ON THE ITALIAN SIDE:

Giovanni Palermo, the 'true prisoner' of Zonderwater prisoner-of-war camp
Pietro Scottu (and his dog, **Chippie**), the escapee
Luigi Pederzoli, husband to Barbara and father to Ennio and Emilia
Paolo Ricci, a tailor at Zonderwater
Raffaello Cei, a chef at the Pietermaritzburg camp

ON THE SOUTH AFRICAN SIDE:

Jan Christiaan Smuts, Prime Minister of the Union of South Africa
Brigadier General Leonard (Len) Beyers, Adjutant General of the Union Defence Force
Colonel David de Wet, commandant of Zonderwater from September 1941, when he took over from Colonel G Rennie, to December 1942
Colonel Hendrik F Prinsloo, commandant of Zonderwater from January 1943 to 1947
Professor HH Sonnabend, Director of Welfare at Zonderwater
Lieutenant (later Captain) JA Ball, Welfare officer at Zonderwater
Lieutenant Colonel L Blumberg, Head of Medical Services at Zonderwater

1

Young Fascists in Italy's African colonies

Benito Mussolini liked to show off his body, especially in propaganda photographs. After all, as a Fascist dictator who wanted to create the ideal man, he had to set an example. Photographs of the bare-chested Mussolini were supposed to inspire Italian men and fill Italian women with awe. These photographs showed the population the type of man their leader required them to be; the athletic and virile hero who works hard and who looks obediently to Mussolini, *il Duce*, for leadership.

While Mussolini was certainly ambitious and his propaganda campaign was consistent and focused, he did not manage to convince all men of fighting age. Living in Fascist Italy was difficult, food was scarce, and everyone worked hard for very little. These were the circumstances in the 1920s and the 1930s in which Italian children grew up in. Among the millions of boys growing up in Italy during this time were five who, at some time or another during the Second World War, would end up in prisoner-of-war (POW) camps in the Union of South Africa. It is their stories that we follow in these pages.

Giovanni Palermo

The first of them, Giovanni Palermo, lived his life according to Fascist principles. The textbook *Book and Musket, Perfect Fascist*, taught children everything they needed to know about being good citizens in a Fascist country. The title of the book was also used as a propaganda slogan, 'book' referring to Fascist education and 'musket' implying war. It dominated Giovanni's existence and hinted at the undertone of militarism that was so prevalent during Mussolini's dictatorship. A sergeant in the 116th Regiment of the Marmarica Division, Giovanni identified with the Arditi Unit, whose members were known as 'the daring ones' during the First World War. Never surrendering his faith in Mussolini, Giovanni became one of the so-called true prisoners who rejected any form of cooperation with the 'English', which for him included everyone in the Union Defence Force (UDF).

PIETRO SCOTTU

In stark contrast, Pietro Scottu had no emotional attachments to Mussolini. Growing up in the coastal city of Genoa in the north-west of the country, he became self-reliant at a very early age. His father died even before he was born and with only a rudimentary education, Pietro began contributing to his family's income. Ever the optimist, he regarded 'such [working] experience the best type of school for learning how to cope with the various situations one may find oneself involved in life'.[1] When his conscription papers arrived, Pietro was assigned to the driving school, a skill that would become very useful a few years later. Pietro began his service in Asmara, the capital of Eritrea, at that time an important centre of Italy's East African Empire.

The views of other Italian conscripts were moderate in comparison to those of Giovanni and Pietro. Childhood experiences shaped their view of the world, despite Mussolini's best efforts to capture their minds.

LUIGI PEDERZOLI

Luigi Pederzoli's childhood was marked by tragedy and hardship. Born on 30 June 1914 in Gattatico, near Parma, Luigi's formative years were characterised by the devastation of the First World War. At the end of the war, he lost his mother and newborn brother to the 1918 Spanish Flu epidemic. Luigi also became ill, but he was 'lucky' by not becoming one of the 410 000 children who lost their lives in Italy.[2] In the difficult times that followed the war, Luigi's family cultivated silkworms, tomatoes and grapes in order to survive.

His father remarried but Luigi rebelled when his stepmother took control of the household and as a result he was sent to a boarding school in Bergamo. By the time he emerged from school he had been saturated with Mussolini's Fascist ideology – the aim of the school system and the military structures being to create young men in the image of a so-called 'Superman', the Fascists' ideal form of masculinity.[3] As a young boy he

Luigi Pederzoli and his fellow soldiers arrive at Port Said, 1936
(Photo courtesy Emilia Pederzoli)

would have had no choice in joining the youth organisations designed to indoctrinate. Although he 'escaped' twice from boarding school, he was conscripted in 1932 shortly after his 18th birthday.

Luigi began his military career with a new AGFA camera and a notebook, because he was determined to write a book about his experiences. He must have been hopeful about the future: not only did military service bring relief from poverty and rejection, but he was also going to see the world. In 1935 he was conscripted into the Colonial Service and decided that he would remain in the service in a permanent capacity once his two compulsory years had come to an end. He stayed on in the Italy's African colonies, was promoted and landed a comfortable office job. By 1936 he was in Mogadishu and in 1938 he married his sweetheart, Barbara, by proxy. She joined him in Ethiopia the following year.

Luigi Pederzoli and his wife Barbara shortly after she joined him in Gimma, Ethiopia (Photo courtesy Emilia Pederzoli)

PAOLO RICCI

When I interviewed him, the soft-spoken and friendly Paolo Ricci tactfully avoided the matter of his personal political affiliations. Born in Savignano on 29 March 1920, his boyhood was a relatively happy one and he recalled his early life under Mussolini's dictatorship as a time that was 'very nice [because] Mussolini did really, really good things'. Here he was referring to state-controlled welfare services, education, work permits and even compulsory attendance at mass rallies. If someone were thought to be disloyal, their prospects would be severely restricted or even halted completely.[4]

At the age of 20, Paolo left home for the first time to join the 26th Regiment Artillery of Rimini. He underwent a mere ten days' training before his regiment was sent to Africa. Years later, as he reflected on his readiness for war, he said, 'you're not prepared for [war] ... anyway, one thing and the other and on top of that we lost the war ... we chased a lot of them, they chased a lot of us, up and down, up and down, you know how the war is ...'.[5]

RAFFAELLO CEI

Raffaello Cei came from Lucca, a town on the north-west coast of Italy. There, every week, a group of men calling themselves the 'flask society' would gather in a café to discuss politics. Raffaello, the son of one of these men, remembered them as a harmless mixed group of blue-collar workers, farmers and artisans who would drink wine and smoke cigars at a table in the café while exchanging opinions as 'moderate democrats'.[6]

Now, of course, Fascism forbade open conversation or any form of dissent, so when they were found out, some members of the 'flask society' were forced to drink castor oil and others were beaten. From that day onwards, Raffaello received his political education through 'hints' from his father, because his mother banned any such discussions. His conscription papers arrived shortly before his 21st birthday and he left his home town of Lucca for the first time in 1941.

After receiving his first army pay, he considered himself a 'soldier in all respects', he says. Raffaello remembers his training in Ferrara as a lonely time. On the one hand, he missed his mother's cooking, especially as he noticed, even at that early stage of the war, that the Italian army was unable to feed its soldiers properly. On the other hand, he was eager for his adventure to begin, especially when he remembered how his mother used to warn him, '"be careful, child, always be careful" ... my parents were afraid. They feared for my life,'[7] he wrote.

Looking back at his training, Raffaello later wrote in his memoirs that he was 'like a child playing at war, completely taken by his toys and weapons that shoot without killing. I hadn't realized that war, the real kind, was looming above my head, and that the entirety of my small world and brief youth were about to be torn apart for good'. He was speaking for many young Italian men in saying they were not really aware of the 'black cloud that loomed over Europe'.[8]

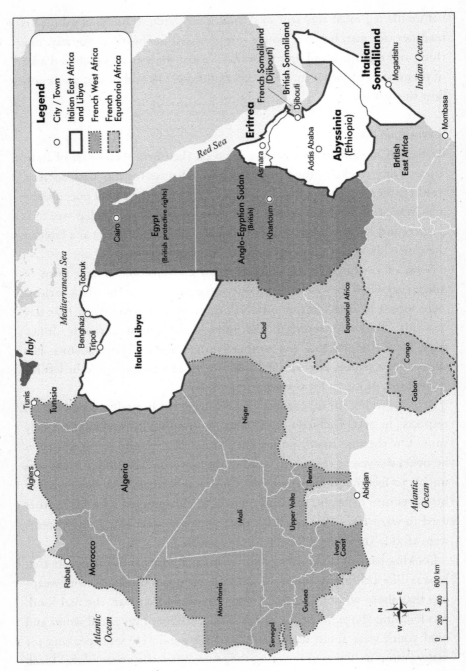

Italian colonies in North Africa

GIOVANNI PALERMO AND PAOLO RICCI (LIBYA)

In 1936 Italian Somaliland, Eritrea and Ethiopia were combined into one country to form Italian East Africa. To the south lay the British colony of Kenya, to Kenya's north-east lay the smaller British Somaliland and to the west was what was then known as Anglo-Egyptian Sudan. On the coast of the Mediterranean Sea lay the Italian colonies of Cyrenaica and Tripolitania that were unified to form Italian Libya: this Italian territory shared a border with the British-controlled Egypt.

With the colonies of countries on opposite sides of the war bordering each other, the stage was set for Africa to be drawn into the Second World War. Yet when Hitler invaded Poland in 1939 and Britain declared war, Mussolini hesitated. It was nothing new for him to first wait and see which way the wind blew. Already in 1937, an author described him as a 'formidable combination of turncoat, ruffian, and a man of genius in modern history'.[9] By 1940 German forces had achieved significant victories and when France fell to the Nazis, Mussolini was finally convinced that he should join the war on Hitler's side.

Secretly, Smuts must have been relieved to have had the extra time Mussolini's hesitation had given him. In 1939 the UDF was small and not prepared for any great battles. When Mussolini declared war on the Allies, he also dragged his African colonies into the conflict. The British and Commonwealth forces responded by sending divisions to those colonies that bordered on the Italian Empire in Africa. Since UDF volunteers had taken an oath to fight anywhere in Africa, the 1st South Africa Division joined the British Middle East Command under Field Marshal Archibald Wavell to participate in the East African Campaign. To the north, the Western Desert Campaign also began in June 1940, but it would be some time before the UDF would send a division to this theatre of war.

In the meantime, combined British forces launched Operation Compass with the objective of defeating the Italian 10th Army in Libya. The committed Fascist Giovanni Palermo and the soft-spoken Paolo Ricci were both in the 10th Army. Although he would never admit it, Giovanni met his match against the British and Australian troops at the Battle of Bardia in Libya in January 1941. This battle was part of Operation Compass and was the first British military operation of the Western

7

A POW's artistic depiction of his battlefield experience
(Photo courtesy NMMH)

Desert campaign. Under the command of Lieutenant General Annibale Bergonzoli, the Italians numbered more than 40 000 against the 16 000 men in the Allied force, yet the Australians achieved their first significant victory of the war here.

Giovanni fought with a sense of purpose and commitment and if it was up to him, he would have defeated the entire Allied force single-handedly. In his memoirs, he described his comrades-in-arms as being 'full of ardour, of frank feelings and absolute self-denial, leading up to extreme sacrifice' during the battle. According to him, the Italian forces fought like 'a single, majestic block, ever more formidable, able to stop the movements of the overwhelming enemy, made up by hundreds of people'.[10]

Giovanni was fighting not only for survival, but also to preserve Italy's honour. His descriptions of the Battle of Bardia were probably coloured by years of Fascist propaganda as he could see nothing but acts of bravery on the Italian side. He described scenes of great heroism, of men on foot attacking tanks and of his commanding officer, with a severe head wound, jumping on an oncoming tank, his 'face dripping with blood, and with new enthusiasm and impetus, towards the top, onto the turret officer (the latter also worthy of admiration for the face-to-face gun duel, but perhaps it was just the effect of an abundance of alcohol) and annihilates him, screaming: "Die!" and then, lifeless, he exclaims: "VIVA L'ITALIA!"[11]

Unfortunately, Giovanni was captured on the first day of the three-day battle and was left with the traumatic memory of three friends having died next to him. The first days of his captivity were equally harrowing. An Australian serviceman searched his pockets for explosives, and then led him to a bomb crater where he spent the next two days with fellow captives. Around them, however, the battle continued, and it was not long before a shell hit their makeshift holding pen. It was packed with prisoners by then, and Giovanni remembered the harrowing scene: 'legs, arms, heads, blood and brains were coiled up into a great mass of flesh'.[12]

Instinctively, those who could run from this scene did so, but the Australian guards thought they were attempting a mass escape and opened fire. During this chaos, Giovanni witnessed an act of kindness when an Italian officer asked, deliriously, how the battle was progressing. An Australian serviceman, somewhat bewildered at the man's tenacity, replied 'Well!'

In 1940, Paolo Ricci's regiment had some successes against the French in Tunisia, but when they were transferred to Tobruk in Libya they again met the Australians, who, according to Paolo, were ugly people, remnants from prisons, and almost always drunk.[13] It was here that his luck ran out.

Heavy fighting at Sollum on the north-eastern border between Egypt and Libya was followed by the Italians' retreat to Bardia, which they soon lost to the Australians in early 1941. Back in Tobruk, the only Italian warship, the *San Gorgio*, was sunk during a brief battle. By now Paolo had been in North Africa for almost a year, but the military experience he had acquired during this time could not reverse his bad luck: he was taken prisoner on 21 January 1941 when Tobruk was captured by the British forces.

This Mediterranean harbour town was of great importance to both the British and the Italians, because whoever controlled it, was able to ship men and materiel to the battle areas. Taking Tobruk in 1941 meant that a further 25 000 Italian prisoners fell into the hands of the British. The Australian forces settled in at Tobruk to ensure it would remain in Allied hands; shortly afterwards, the British Western Desert Force declared Operation Compass a resounding success.

The defeat could not have come at a worse time for Mussolini; he was

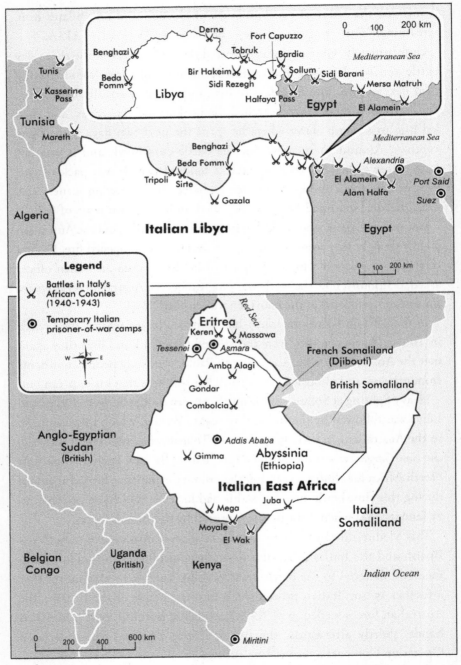

Italian battle sites and temporary Italian prisoner-of-war camps

visiting Hitler when he was informed of the losses. It was at this point that Hitler realised Mussolini's forces needed help in Libya and he dispatched Lieutenant General Erwin Rommel to deal with the British threat.[14] This development made subsequent victories in the region much more difficult to achieve for the Allied forces, who soon began to speak of Rommel as the Desert Fox.

PIETRO SCOTTU (ERITREA)

In the meantime, the UDF were fighting valiantly in East Africa along with British and other Commonwealth forces. They enjoyed one victory after another, struggling with the harsh terrain almost more than with the enemy forces. The South Africans approached the East African Empire from the south, while in the north, British Somaliland came under attack from the Italians. Lying next to the Red Sea, Italian Eritrea was especially important because the British had to maintain control of the Suez Canal.

Just as Operation Compass drew to its conclusion in Libya, and extra Allied troops could be sent to Eritrea, Pietro Scottu's conscription period came to an end. However, the war prevented his return to Italy, so he was stuck in Massawa, an Eritrean naval town. Morale in the Italian army reached a low point when news of the defeat at Tobruk reached Eritrea and when British forces destroyed the aqueduct that had been their only source of water, Pietro's unit surrendered. It was March 1941 and Pietro's time as a master escapee was about to begin.

When Pietro and his friend and 'partner in crime', Guerrea, heard that the British needed transport for the captured Italian materiel, they volunteered their services as drivers with a FIAT 634 and a 'liberated' Ceirano 50 truck 'that still had a splash of librification (sic) system and an external hand brake such as that of a horse carriage'.[15] Cunningly, they placed themselves in the middle of the long convoy, which allowed them to sneak away without the guards at the front or the back noticing their escape.

They made a dash for a local Italian doctor who had a concession of land for cultivation purposes. The two escapees offloaded most of their supplies, no doubt bringing much needed relief to the family. In an effort to secure their fortunes, Pietro and Guerrea sold the Fiat to an Arab businessman for 34 000 lire, which they 'obviously' split between themselves.[16] That night the two escapees slept in the middle of a prickly pear plantation to avoid being attacked by the local Shiftà population, whom they suspected were being 'armed and exploited by the British to prove that the Italians were no longer in the local population's favour'.

When the doctor's son-in-law suddenly disappeared, the two escapees thought they were endangering the doctor's family and so they decided to surrender themselves to the British at Fort Baldissera. Shortly afterwards Pietro and his friend were separated. Pietro was sent to the Tessenei transit camp, where he noted with disgust that there were 'no luxuries whatsoever!!' In fact, they were provided with raw food and left to their own devices.

LUIGI PEDERZOLI (ETHIOPIA)

In Ethiopia, Luigi Pederzoli, who had joined the Colonial Service, had settled into a happy life with his wife, Barbara, who had since given birth to their son, Ennio. Luigi was a member of the 70th Battalion, 1st Company, and his days consisted of planning new towns in the Galla-Sidamo District of Ethiopia.

However, the Italian Empire was crumbling around them and on 21 June 1941 Luigi, along with other officials in the Colonial Office, were ordered to surrender to the British forces. They followed orders, apparently without any resistance. They were now POWs, although they were never fighting soldiers. Luigi and his compatriots were taken to a camp in Addis Ababa, while the wives and children were left to fend for themselves. POWs were not allowed to have cameras, so Luigi's AGFA camera was confiscated and all that remains of his African adventures are the photographs he took before his capture. Once he became a POW, he became an avid diarist, but when his diary was also confiscated, his letters to Barbara are the only record of his captivity.[17]

RAFFAELLO CEI (LIBYA)

For Raffaello Cei, surrender did not come without a drawn-out fight in the deserts of Libya. He was a driver in the 5th Battalion of the *Reggimento Artiglieria Celere*. At first their days were marked by marching from point to point, which was intended to teach all of them 'to keep their aches and moods to themselves, so as not to anger their superiors and their mates.

So, I learnt the lesson'.[18]

By April 1941, Rommel and his panzers had joined the desert conflict. With the Australians occupying Tobruk, a long siege began as the two sides wrestled for control of the harbour. Rommel was ordered to take Tobruk so that they could launch an attack on Egypt from this coastal city, while the Allies wanted to use Tobruk as a base between Malta and Egypt.[19]

Raffaello's regiment arrived in Tobruk on 11 April. Feeling optimistic, he believed

> the German army had come to our rescue with the Afrika Korps. In early March 1941, some German Fifth Division military departments arrived. Our regiment was ready to resume its mission. The wait seemed endless. We had witnessed the sad retreat of the survivors of General Graziani's army and now, with renewed optimism, we watched the German allies' reinforcements parading with the most modern arms. This was good news.[20]

In the days that followed, Raffaello's unit was moved towards Sollum, where, despite most of them not having enough to eat, they experienced victory in battle. From there, they went to Halfaya Pass, where they had time to recover 'their strength in the illusion of having already seen the worst of the war and having overcome it'.[21] He could not have known that Halfaya Pass would soon become known as Hellfire Pass.

Raffaello recalled it was 15 November when the 'hostilities picked up again in full swing. But this time we weren't taken on in the way everyone expected. The English preferred to bypass the obstacle. They played their cards well and we were surrounded ...'[22]

They were also cut off from food and water supplies and the best the Axis forces could do was to drop provisions from the air.[23] For Raffaello, this was a 'godsend raining down from the sky', but one which they could only access at night, as persistent shelling during the day forced them to take shelter in caves. In December their situation deteriorated when the 1st South Africa Police occupied a position from where they could fire on a water source, Point 207.[24] To survive, they drank rusty radiator water and ate worm-invested biscuits.

Raffaello Cei at Tobruk harbour a few months before being taken prisoner at Halfaya Pass (Photo courtesy Zonderwater Block Association)

Throughout the siege, the Italians continued to defend the Halfaya Pass as best they could. However, when Fig Tree Wells, the main water supply, fell into Allied hands and Sollum's defeat prevented any thoroughfare to the coast, the Italian commander finally decided to surrender.[25] It was 17 January 1942 and Major General IP de Villiers, commander of the 2nd South Africa Division, accepted the surrender.[26]

Raffaello recalled that when the siege began in November, they were ordered to 'resist another fifteen minutes'.[27] Those minutes turned into a siege of 59 days.

The British forces had their share of defeats in Libya, too, especially at Sidi Rezegh in November 1941 and at Tobruk in mid-1942 when 33 000 Allied soldiers were captured. Shortly afterwards, the battles at El Alamein signified a turning point and the Allies turned to Tunisia where the war in Africa eventually came to an end in May 1943.

The hundreds and thousands of Italian POWs were sent to temporary camps. For many, these camps brought different kinds of hellish experience. On the long march towards Sollum, it was Giovanni Palermo who claimed that 'it was our spirits that moved our bodies'.[28] The camp at

Sollum did not bring the much-longed-for respite, however, since they found no water there. They arrived at Alexandria a few days later and then moved on to a camp at the Suez, where Giovanni saw lice 'dancing the tarantella' (a Neapolitan folk dance).[29]

In most transit camps, unhygienic conditions and a lack of medical care caused many deaths among the prisoners. Pietro Scottu estimated that 300 POWs died of dysentery, tapeworm and scurvy in his camp. On top of that, the water was so dirty that it had to be strained through the cloth of their uniforms.

Suspicious of every single one of his captors, Giovanni believed that, by not feeding their captives properly, they were playing with their lives without incrimination.[30] This caused him to put himself and others in danger. On one occasion, he and two others climbed the fence that surrounded the food store. Sneaking back into the main camp, they had a narrow escape as a suspicious guard fired two rounds in their direction. Fortunately, no harm came to anyone, but the three hungry men found that the bone they had risked life and limb for was bare.

On another occasion, they dodged the march towards the work area and hid at the far end of the camp. They were spotted by guards and after an entire morning's chase, one of the shirkers was found and beaten 'as a serious lesson'.[31] Giovanni recalled that the unfortunate man had been hiding under a tent, but that his captors 'with great vengeance and an unequalled wrath' sought him out and punished him. Soon after these days of hell, Giovanni boarded a ship and started his journey to South Africa.[32]

Paolo was also sent to Alexandria and then on to Suez. He described this time as terrible, saying they 'were treated worse than animals, not to mention that food [was] scarce and it stank terribly'.[33] Fortunately for him, it was only five months before he found himself on a ship bound for the greener pastures of Durban.

With the war needs taking priority over captives, Paolo found himself first at Fort Baldissera in Asmara, Eritrea, then at Tessenei, a market town in western Eritrea. From there he was sent to Zeidab in Sudan before being moved to Miritini in Kenya, where he stayed until July 1943.

Luigi went on a similarly dreadful journey. With Barbara and little Ennio left behind in Ethiopia at Gimma, he endured a long and tiring time in captivity during which he was moved from Addis Ababa to three different Kenyan cities. After that he was taken to a camp in neighbouring Uganda before being returned to Kenya once more, where he remained stuck until February 1944. There he survived on zebra meat and stale biscuits, leaving the biscuits for the night, because, as he said, in the dark he could not see the mould.

In the meantime, Barbara and other Italian wives who had been left behind had to survive as best they could. The women barricaded themselves, the children and their servants in houses which they thought would withstand attacks from the outside. They all hoped the men would return soon to save them, but as their food began to run out they realised the war was going to carry on for much longer than they had anticipated. When the British took them to tented camps near Dire Diwa, things went from bad to worse and many women were forced to give their food rations to their children as there was not enough to feed everyone.

In desperation, Barbara left Ennio with a friend, escaped from the camp and went looking for something to eat in the town. She returned with a bottle of milk she had stolen off a windowsill. She was reprimanded by the camp command, but that did not dampen her sense of relief when she was at last able to give some milk to her son. It is not known how Barbara and Ennio eventually made it back to Italy, but according to family lore, Ennio was nine months old when they entered the camp, and he was two years old when he arrived in Italy with his mother.

The POW Information Bureau dealt only with prisoners, and had no information on 'evacuees', so very little is known about these Italian women and children who endured such hardships in Africa.[34] Early in 1943, it became known that the International Committee of the Red Cross (ICRC) had a list of 9 000 names of evacuees who had been sent from Ethiopia to Kenya, Uganda, Tanganyika Territory and Southern Rhodesia. At a point it became necessary to evacuate Italian civilians from East Africa so that refugees from Europe could be accommodated there.[35]

General Sir Archibald Wavell, Commander of the Middle East, and British Prime Minister, Winston Churchill, did not see eye to eye on the strategy that would bring victory in North Africa. However, both of them agreed that defending Egypt against the Axis forces was a priority because control of the Middle East depended on control of the Mediterranean. Most of the manpower and materiel were therefore focussed on North Africa, which meant that POWs in Kenyan camps were out of sight and out of mind.

In most instances, POWs were a low priority, but those in North Africa were a nuisance because there were so many of them and they held back operations on the battlefields. Unlike the POWs in Kenya, the POWs in the deserts of North Africa had to be moved to permanent camps at a faster pace. Those in Kenya found themselves on a territory where the battles had been completed and, as such, they were left where they were until the military authorities could spare a moment to focus on them.

The mild-mannered Raffaello Cei described his captors as 'patient [and] peaceful' and he tried very hard not to irritate anyone. After his surrender at Halfaya Pass, his first journey as a POW ended in Alexandria in Egypt. There he was not put off by lice disinfection because he believed 'if you present yourself clean and tidy you have more chances of being treated well, so I fixed myself up like a dandy'.[36] Two days later, he was on his way to Ismailia on the Nile River and there he and his fellow POWs were fed rice, lentils, tea and an occasional spoonful of jam. At times they were also given pieces of boiled camel with an egg and a chunk of bread.

Things changed for the better when a British soldier asked about his culinary skills. Standing next to Raffaello at that moment was his friend Bosi, a chef by trade. 'Let me go to the kitchen,' Bosi whispered; 'I guarantee you won't regret it'.[37] Raffaello agreed and 'every night when leaving the kitchen, this Bosi would put some pieces of boiled meat in the pockets of his overcoat, then, when he got to a scarcely lit area, he would nod in signal for me to go and fetch it'.[38]

Raffaello ate his stolen gifts in secret because it was 'survival at all costs. It was the only, terrible law that made us all equal,' he wrote in his memoirs.[39] Food nevertheless remained in short supply, but Raffaello gave his captors the benefit of the doubt, mistakenly believing that an abundance of food would harm their emaciated bodies and 'so, although we didn't understand it then, the English were right to distribute [food] parsimoniously'.[40]

When they were taken further south to Suez, Raffaello became philosophical about his captivity. And when he spotted women boarding a ship, he became poetic. He reflected on how the 'Suez sun cast a dazzling brilliance upon the blue water, and the scent of those unknown girls inebriated us and made us forget where we were and why'.[41] He later added, 'That's how man is; for a seagull's wing will brush against his head, and he will imagine he is free'.[42]

When they saw a number of women boarding a ship, Raffaello could only speculate about who they were or where they were going, thinking there was 'no point in asking [about their fate] and whether they'd make it back home to Italy. Nobody knew the answer. We all began to wave handkerchiefs from the deck and some shed a tear'.[43]

Raffaello did not know it at that moment, but the same could be said of the thousands of POWs who would soon be making their way towards South Africa.

2

Early days at Zonderwater camp

When Giovanni and his fellow Italian POWs sailed from Suez in 1941, they had no idea where they were being taken by the Allied authorities. It was a very 'slow and terrible voyage, one that took us towards infinity and the unknown or perhaps even the end of the earth',[1] he wrote.

But his apprehension dissolved when he laid eyes on the coastline and the city of Durban. For him, it was

> a marvellous city: the gulf, skyscrapers and greenery; green, green, green everywhere. We deceived ourselves a little by closing our eyes and imagining we'd arrived at our unique, beautiful and charming Naples and felt relieved for a while; instead, it was Durban, a city in the Southern Hemisphere. The closer we got, the better we could see the spectacle of the city: a European city, and this apparition, after many, many months of sand, desert and fences and a few African cities, seemed even more beautiful.[2]

Setting foot on land was no doubt a relief to him. His voyage included burying a man at sea, Giovanni being tasked with tying iron bars to the dead man's legs before sewing up the bag in which his body was placed.

In fact, he was so happy to be back on land that, when he saw the green lawns where they were made to wait after disembarking, he began – to the astonishment of his friends – to roll around on the grass, shouting 'Lord! ... Thank you! ... Mother! ... your Giovanni will not die ... because this place is comfortable ...'

And when he arrived in South Africa a year later, Raffaello also felt his hopes rise when he saw Durban. For him the dryness and dust of the desert seemed æons away and Natal appeared to have been blessed by God in contrast.

While Giovanni remembered the 'slop' they were given to eat while at sea, Raffaello was put in charge of the kitchen storeroom and as a result his friends and their mess tins were never again to see such 'abundance'.

Paolo was less fortunate: when he was also shipped off in 1941, he found himself in a dark and stinking cargo hold. According to him, the same boat had carried Australian soldiers to Egypt before the POWs embarked on their southerly journey. Many years later, he still remembered that their blankets were full of lice, about which he wrote: 'you've got no idea, they were full, full and full and from the Australians they came to the Italians'.[3]

In the dark, every sound made him jump with fright and so when a loud metallic rattle woke them, his shouts of 'A torpedo! A torpedo!' caused everyone to scramble in panic. Luckily, it was only the anchor chains knocking against the side of the ship when it docked in a harbour to take on supplies. Following this nerve-wracking journey, it was no wonder, then, that when Durban appeared on the horizon, it seemed like paradise.

Just like Giovanni, Paolo did not know where in the world he was when the ship docked. They and Raffaello were among the first to reach South Africa in 1941; they were also among the last to leave after the war.

Packed with captives, the dark hold of a ship was a place where imaginations could easily run wild out of sheer fear. Uncertainty and speculation caused POWs to jump at every strange noise. But their fear of torpedoes was real, as the POWs on the HMS *Nova Scotia* were to experience in 1942. The ship, which was carrying UDF troops on their way home, had picked up Italian internees and POWs at Massawa, Eritrea, where Pietro had been stationed before his capture.

Near St Lucia on the coast of Natal, a German U-boat spotted the *Nova Scotia*, took aim and fired three torpedoes. The ship sank within ten minutes. Despite the German commander's discovering that he had targeted a boat carrying both UDF troops and German allies in the form of Italians, he simply continued on his way because German ships were not allowed to rescue Allied troops. He did, however, contact Lourenço Marques, from where a ship was sent on a rescue mission. According to survivors, men struggling to stay afloat in those warm subtropical waters were attacked by sharks, dozens of them being taken in this way.[4] One of these victims, Sammy Levine, was known as the clown of his unit. His pet monkey, which he had acquired in Kenya, was seen holding on to Sammy's shoulders as the two tried to swim away. Neither survived.

Of the 765 Italians on the *Nova Scotia*, only 115 survived. Of the South Africans, 184 soldiers drowned. In 1945, the Red Cross sent a list of names to the Department of Defence indicating both those who had perished and the survivors. The names of the next-of-kin were obtained from survivors and, as far as possible, all the Italian families were informed about those POWs who had died. Since most of the survivors were rescued by a Portuguese vessel, they were taken to Lourenço Marques.[5]

After they set foot on South African soil, the initial elation of the POWs quickly evaporated when they were taken for delousing and a rudimentary medical inspection. They were then packed into trains which, according to Paolo, had just been used to transport livestock. 'You can imagine the trip ... !' he exclaimed. The men were being transported to the inland transit camp at Pietermaritzburg.

For Giovanni, however, the South African landscape was a sentimental reminder of his beloved Italy and as they travelled to the camp he stayed glued to the windows of their coach the entire day, and also that night, admiring what seemed to him to be the new paradise on earth. Other POWs, he noted, were not that impressed and some would curse that bounty, shouting 'Look! Look! All these pleasures and gifts of God! And we starve?' Not without justification: during their two days on the train, he recalled, they were given only a tin of beef, some bread and water.[6]

Giovanni and Paolo arrived in South Africa in 1941, Raffaello in 1942, Pietro in 1943 and Luigi in 1944. By 1943, Italian war prisoners were commonplace in the Union; and while some South Africans did not mind their being in the country, others objected.

More sinisterly, anti-war groups such as the *Ossewabrandwag* saw in them an opportunity for collaboration to overthrow the Smuts government, or at least to disrupt the war effort. When Pietro arrived in Durban in 1943, he was bemused by some of these extremists he encountered. As his group made their way to the disinfestation station, some locals greeted them with the 'thumbs up' sign. The sign was most probably intended to welcome the Italians and be a tentative first attempt at befriending

The Zonderwater station (Photo courtesy NMMH)

like-minded kinsmen. But what the South Africans didn't realise was that it was an offensive sign in parts of Italy.

Pietro could see the humour in the confusion, but many of his fellow POWs responded with the umbrella gesture, which was immediately copied by the South Africans, perhaps thinking that that was a corresponding 'hello'. About this Piero wrote: 'I will leave you to imagine the reaction of our soldiers'.[7] The gesturing continued until the Italians were out of sight. Years later, Pietro came to the conclusion that those locals who had showed the thumbs-up sign were 'surely Boers – at the time they were with the Axis'.[8] Unfortunately for the military authorities, some of these 'Boers' were UDF members who had not taken the service oath to serve in Africa, so they were deployed to guard the Italians at permanent prison camps, the main one being Zonderwater near Pretoria.[9]

Set on a desolate piece of land next to a UDF training camp, Zonderwater was initially nothing more than a collection of tents with poor hygiene facilities and inadequate security. In contrast, by the end of the war, Zonderwater consisted of 14 blocks, each of which could accommodate 8 000 men. Each block was divided into four camps of about 2 000 men each – a far cry from what it had been when it opened in 1941.

Giovanni and Paolo arrived at Zonderwater in 1941. Giovanni was

Prisoners waiting their turn at the delousing station at Zonderwater
(Photo courtesy www.zonderwater.com/it)

pleased because, for him – a committed Fascist and a lifelong loyal supporter of Mussolini – captivity was something he had had to endure because, without experiencing suffering, he could not be a 'true prisoner'. Unlike other POWs, he thought

> the air was good, water abundant [and] food was decent compared to that received at our previous arrangement [in the desert] and consisted of: first course, almost always wholegrain maize (the kind one feeds to pigs), a little bit of main course, not much bread as usual, and some fruit, as well as five cigarettes a day. The list of victuals was poor, but we thought it very good.[10]

Perhaps Giovanni found out only later that the name Zonderwater means 'without water' in Dutch. Unlike the green fields and moderate climate of Durban – or of Italy, for that matter – the local climate was more extreme, with minimum and maximum daily temperatures differing by as much as 10 to 15 degrees.[11]

As soon as Giovanni arrived, he realised he would 'die of boredom, nostalgia and stasis', and for this reason 'they started to do things, because

The officers' camp at Zonderwater was very similar to the POW camp during 1941 and 1942 (Photo courtesy ICRC)

Tents and blankets await occupants during the early days at Zonderwater (Photo courtesy www.zonderwater.com/it)

Prisoners taking in their new surroundings. The prisoner in the foreground is dressed in an outfit provided by the camp authorities (Photo courtesy www.zonderwater.com/it)

life is movement'. He also created profiles of the Fascist leaders at the entrance to the tent using clay and a bit of cement.[12] In the early months at Zonderwater there were no organised sport or recreational activities, but at least one 'lover of the theatre' set up a makeshift stage on which to entertain the men with the occasional farce. Giovanni and others painted the backdrop for the play onto empty corn bags with their beard brushes, using lime and coloured earth.

Paolo's views on Zonderwater were perhaps more accurate in describing their everyday reality. According to him, they arrived there

> with only the rags we had on! Once we arrived at the camp, they gave us blankets and some personal clothing. We slept on the floor, under a cone-shaped tent for eight people. It was total confusion without any form of organisation and a total want of everything, especially clothing. Even the food was scarce, and it tasted terrible; almost always we got cooked wheat.[13]

The truth of the matter was that those in command at Zonderwater had no idea what had hit them. The original plan was for the camp to hold 24 000 men, but just a month after Paolo's arrival in the Union, Smuts agreed to accommodate an additional 15 000 POWs at Zonderwater, pushing the total number up to 60 000. A further 40 000 would eventually bring the total to what Smuts actually had in mind.

To complicate matters, there were pro-Smuts (and therefore pro-war) and anti-war men among the guards. Furthermore, with race relations being a sticking point, the coloured Cape Corps guards among the 'European' staff presented another headache. To make matters worse, despite the number of POWs continuing to increase, staff numbers remained the same.

Smuts's bold idea was to replace with Italian POWs that section of the workforce represented by the black South Africans who were by then serving in the war. Therefore, before the first POW had even set foot in the Union, Smuts had approached the National Roads Board to start planning for Italian prisoners to work on road-building projects.[14] The Italians would also help to bring in the harvests, in this way keeping the local economy going and expanding the infrastructure.

To sell Smuts's idea to the public, pro-government newspapers wrote about the advantages it held. As early as February 1941, the *Cape Times* reported on the usefulness of Italian labour, explaining that

> work on national road schemes has been somewhat curtailed since the outbreak of the war as many members of road staffs have gone on active service and others 3are employed on certain essential works which the Road Board is carrying out for the Department of Defence.[15]

With road- and rail-building projects a priority, the General Manager of the South African Railways and Harbours (SAR&H) met with Brigadier General Leonard (Len) Beyers, Adjutant General of the UDF, in October 1941 to discuss the use of Italian POW labour. For the management of the SAR&H, the aim of the meeting was to make sure that they would benefit from using POW labour. To this end, they came armed with a report on the use of Italian labour in East Africa.

The author of this report, Sergeant GJA Lindenberg, the Assistant Chief Mechanical Engineer in East Africa, was positive, emphasising that 'it is worth our while to make use of the services of Italian Prisoners of War in our workshops and running sheds and, if we pay them good wages, they will react and deliver the goods'.[16] To emphasise his point, Lindenberg warned that POWs should be paid only for work that had been completed, because

> as soon as they had been fattened up and had a few schillings to spend on little additional luxuries, they slacked off, and they were only giving about 4 hours' work a day.[17]

On the matter of the Geneva Convention,[18] which prohibited the use of POWs for any work connected to the war effort, Lindenberg confirmed that the Italians were 'naturally averse to performing any duties connected with the production of munitions'. Yet it seemed that the authorities in East Africa were less concerned about the Convention, since the report also stated that some, even, have signified their willingness to work on armoured cars and others were actually employed in Nairobi on repairing wireless sets (military) and on gun optics and other instruments [and] other duties directly connected with the war effort.[19]

In his experience, it was also 'better to employ the older men than the younger ones, who are mostly ardent Fascists ... as they are still of the opinion that Germany will win the war'.[20]

The report played a significant role in convincing everyone at the meeting (between the General Manager of the SAR&H and Brigadier General Beyers of the UDF) that the employment of Italian labour would be a practicable measure. Since Beyers was also responsible for the personnel policies of the UDF, he emphasised that it would be to the country's benefit if they 'endeavour to weed out the Fascist element'. He believed that at least 75 per cent of all the prisoners would be willing to work. And while he did not foresee any trouble being caused by the Italians, he felt that most of the difficulties, if any, would arise from outside as anti-war propagandists might have wanted to 'get at them'. Here he was referring to the likes of the *Ossewabrandwag*, the *Stormjaers* and the *Terreurgroep*.

The General Manager of the SAR&H was eager to take on cheap Italian labour, while Beyers was under pressure to put Smuts's plan into practice. For its part, the UDF needed more volunteers to serve in North Africa and they would have to be replaced by POW labourers. On the other hand, Beyers predicted that local artisans – especially those who belonged to trade unions – would object to Italians taking their jobs. The General Manager, however, was prepared for such an objection and quickly reassured everyone that most of their trade union members had already applied to be released from their employment for active service in Africa.

Beyers – no doubt with the ongoing recruitment drives in mind – accepted this reassurance, especially when he was told that 'if a [labour] union can show that a prisoner is keeping any man out of employment, we will be prepared to consider its representations'.[21] It was therefore up to the unions to prove that prisoners were depriving South African citizens of work opportunities. No doubt the General Manager saw increased profits in the SAR&H's future. With each delegate at the meeting looking

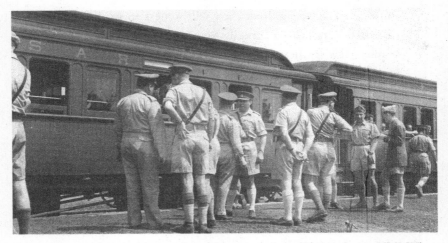

Prisoners on their way to outside employment projects (Photo courtesy NMMH)

after his own interests, they all forgot about the 'propagandists' who were waiting to target the POWs with their subversive messages.

The outcome of the meeting was that POWs would be employed on the construction of roads, railways, camps, depot stores and other similar projects. To keep things simple, it was also decided that only those POWs who volunteered would be sent on outside employment (OE) assignments. Each group of workers would have a leader who would be responsible for giving instructions and orders. In addition, they were required to maintain a high standard of discipline and any insubordination, disobedience or slackness would be dealt with promptly and drastically.

While on outside employment, POWs would continue to be subjected to the same disciplinary measures as those in camp and they would not be allowed to visit towns on their days off. If a POW did not perform adequately, he would be returned to the camp. To ease problems with communication, 'the better class of POW' would be taught English so that they could act as interpreters.[22] It is not known how the authorities planned to identify such 'better class' individuals, but they did register all POWs before they were sent on outside employment, perhaps thinking they could tell Fascists from non-Fascists simply by their looks. With thousands of POWs arriving at Zonderwater, though, registering them all became problematic for the small number of UDF staff employed there.

Anything to keep the prisoners occupied (Photo courtesy NMMH)

Giovanni witnessed the number of prisoners multiplying daily, and as they poured in it quickly became clear that the camp facilities were inadequate and the number of staff far too few to cope with the influx. Overcrowding, poor hygiene and too little food led to tensions rising among both prisoners and staff.

In these circumstances, the prisoners were moved from one block to the next as space was made for new arrivals. Recreational activities were a low priority and the prisoners had to find ways of entertaining themselves. Although some found suitable distractions in sport, singing and theatre, they had to endure many idle hours every day, from 06:00 through to 22:00. High levels of boredom led to frustration and soon trouble started to brew.

Giovanni found that writing gave him an outlet for his thoughts and so he began to 'write, write, and write nonstop' on anything he could lay his hands on: toilet paper, packaging paper, cement sacks, jam-jar labels, etc. He wrote that he set about 'alternating philosophical research with great and dynamic physical movement'. Already a staunch Fascist, his writing served to entrench his beliefs in this way of life and, as time went by, he began to see himself as a man on a mission, his writing beginning to 'suggest the proper and exemplary [Fascist] behaviour to the weakest individuals before our master detainers'.[23] The 'weakest' were, of course, those who were less loyal to Mussolini.

For most prisoners, Giovanni's high and uncompromising standard was largely unobtainable; for others, it was unwanted. Nevertheless, he and his friends formed an 'Academy', for which Giovanni drew the emblem: a snake coiled around a pen with laurel branches. Apparently, the Academy began to serve as a centre of improvement, where many young men could learn to read and write while also getting a political and Fascist education. For Giovanni this was a wonderful way in which he could hand out 'spontaneous and passionate counselling or opinion' that served all of the teachers and their students 'as we educated ourselves through teaching and deepened our knowledge'.[24]

While the overall camp management was the responsibility of the camp commander, Colonel David de Wet, he was also forced to handle nearly all of the petty administrative duties as there were very few support staff. Thousands of POWs had to eat every day; they had to live and sleep in decent accommodation; and their regular efforts to escape also had to be prevented. Consequently, De Wet had his work cut out for him, not least because he had to maintain a standard that had been set by an external authority – the Geneva Convention of 1929.

All the countries that were signatories to the Geneva Convention were obliged to hold prisoners according to defined standards set for accommodation, diet, medical care, clothing and religious and intellectual needs – as laid down by the Red Cross. Although South Africa was not a signatory to the Convention, Britain was, and the Smuts government felt it only right that, as a Dominion, South Africa should apply the same standards.

Another good reason to adhere to the Convention was the treatment of UDF servicemen who had been captured by Axis forces. They were considered 'British' and consequently they were treated according to the rules of the Convention.[25] As a result, if South Africa were to treat the Italian POWs badly, then the Italian authorities could very well do the same to the UDF POWs in Italy – something the Union government could not countenance.

But retaliation against South African POWs was not the only concern: more importantly, South Africa's international reputation was also a key consideration for Smuts. Again, it was up to Beyers as Adjutant General to make things happen: Zonderwater simply had to adhere to the regulations of the Geneva Convention. In other words, the living standards had to meet a set standard, which they did not at the time of Giovanni's incarceration. The camp also had to be orderly and secure, which it was also not.

Beyers and the camp command were not in a position to take any risks, though. If anything were to go wrong, they would have to report it to the Red Cross and to Switzerland and Brazil, the two [neutral] Protecting Powers. Given that Beyers was ultimately responsible for South Africa's adherence to the Geneva Convention, any wrongdoing would be an embarrassment. However, as a British Dominion at the time, South Africa could also expect a stern reprimand from the British War Office should the standards required by the Convention not be met.

In effect, then, Smuts had put Beyers in control of the country's reputation. There was no way that Beyers could disappoint the prime minister, because he knew that Smuts would not want to let Winston Churchill down. The two prime ministers' decades-long friendship had begun during the South African War, when they met as adversaries, Smuts interrogating a bedraggled Churchill shortly after his becoming a POW in Boer hands. Later, the two men worked closely together during the First World War, when Smuts joined the Imperial War Cabinet, and they also came to rely on each other for the duration of the Second World War.

The Young Men's Christian Association's (YMCA) War Prisoners' Aid, another international organisation, was also involved in making imprisonment easier to bear, even if it was not on the same scale as that of the Red Cross. Their aim was to help POWs maintain 'a proper balance during their captivity and to prepare for a fuller and better life on their return to Italy'.[26]

Unlike the Red Cross, however, the YMCA representatives did not have the unreserved trust of the military authorities. Their activities were also limited to relief from sickness, boredom and distress. The YMCA could provide extra equipment for recreational activities, medical supplies, occupational training, braille, books and so on, but it was not allowed to interfere with the work of the Red Cross. Furthermore, only Red Cross delegates could act as middlemen between POWs and the camp command, especially when POWs had complaints about their living conditions or treatment. In addition, YMCA men were not allowed to provide any equipment to the camp, although they were supposed to pay over money to the Red Cross, which would then purchase whatever was needed. While the War Office in London made it clear that they encouraged YMCA representatives to supply aid to the POWs, the Intelligence sections first had to determine whether their donations met the security requirements.

This meant that all books had to be censored to prevent prisoners gaining access to propaganda material. No radios were allowed because war news could affect morale or stoke protests. Games and sports equipment had to be inspected for hidden maps of escape routes. The British War Office felt that a representative who was not 'entirely trustworthy' was likely to encourage clandestine activities and confusion among the POWs. Because the Red Cross was an aid organisation and the so-called guardian of international humanitarian law and therefore of the Geneva Convention, its representatives were trusted by most countries that held prisoners during the war.[27]

To be on the safe side, the South Africans thought it best not to allow any YMCA members to have any contact with POWs as the camp at Zonderwater was too large to control such meetings. By mid-1942, for instance, Zonderwater held 60 000 POWs, while none of the camps in England held more than 1 500.[28] It was only in 1945, when the POW numbers had dropped significantly at Zonderwater, that a representative of the YMCA was allowed to visit the camp.[29]

In the meantime, the POWs did not make things easy for the camp command. In 1941, for instance, the Quartermaster General, who was in charge of construction at Zonderwater, complained that POWs deliberately destroyed the roofs and screens of the camp toilets. He made a veiled threat that no further building work would take place unless the camp commandant could ensure that no further vandalism would take place.[30]

At that time, only the food and hygiene facilities were up to standard. POWs were still sleeping in tents, as did hordes of lice, and the Consul-General of Brazil presented the inmates' complaints to the authorities.[31]

Strictly speaking, tents were supposed to be a temporary arrangement for POW camps and De Wet knew that the Geneva Convention would not approve of their prolonged use. He was desperate to save the Union from an embarrassing situation and therefore ordered that the POWs build their own huts for accommodation.

However, De Wet could only do so much. While he ordered all prisoners to shave their beards and all of them were sent for another delousing treatment, to build permanent huts he would need building materials and the approval of his military superiors. Apparently, Smuts did not take the Geneva Convention seriously and remarked to one of the members of the National Roads Board that the POWs were lucky to have tents in the first place.[32]

While the Zonderwater staff worked double time, the POWs were utterly bored. But it was not long before they began to take matters into their own hands. They began stealing everything and anything that could help them stay busy, including picks, shovels, hammers, paint brushes and chisels. Using these tools and materials, the men made curios, which they then sold to visitors to the camp. Many of the camp guards apparently helped the POWs to sell these 'gifts', something which the camp command did not view kindly. Everyone on the camp staff knew that this practice was not permitted and, accordingly, the POWs received a vague threat of 'disciplinary action'. Meanwhile, the Director of Works at the camp remained unhappy about his work being held back by ill-discipline among the POWs and informed De Wet that the engineering staff were unable to cope with the situation. However, De Wet apparently did not have 'the necessary staff to prevent the thieving from taking place'.[33]

In the meantime, the POWs decided to expand the boring menu by bartering with guards for foodstuff. Unfortunately, language differences sometimes got in the way and, as tempers flared, stones instead of food were thrown over the fences. As a remedial measure, new orders were then announced: POWs were forbidden to talk to guards; and if they came within two yards of the fence, they would 'render themselves liable to be fired on'.[34] The camp command was hopeful that this would also prevent POWs from trying to escape.

The Smuts government may have been irritated or humiliated by the complaints about Zonderwater, but it was not the last time that the POWs would show the authorities up as being incompetent.

All the countries that held Italian POWs viewed them as a source of labour. Being closer to the battlefronts and feeling the effects of the war to a greater degree, Britain also experienced a serious labour shortage and so, to fill this gap, they informed the military authorities that their needs should come first. However, these requests irritated the military authorities in South Africa because it became their responsibility to identify and select POWs with the specific skills Britain was asking for. With the enormous workload brought about by the constant arrival of more prisoners from African battlefields, the Zonderwater command had no time to select and send Italians to Britain.

A standoff ensued. The War Office in London pointed out that South Africa was a Dominion of the British Empire and that it was perhaps getting too big for its boots.[35] The matter was resolved only when Smuts laid out the facts. The Dominions were autonomous communities in the Empire and all Dominions had equal rights, but they were all subordinate to Britain.[36] Smuts was adamant that good relations had to be maintained with Britain, perhaps because he knew that the country's contribution to the war was small compared to those of other Dominions and also that Britian did not look kindly on the anti-war faction among its citizens.

The exchanges of prisoners then went ahead and in January 1942, for instance, 19 000 prisoners arrived at Zonderwater from the Middle East, but at the same time 21 000 POWs were selected to be sent to Britain to work. For some reason, the selection process did not always go smoothly and so when 2 000 Italians landed on British shores early in 1942, the British authorities found that they had none of the skills they had asked for. They wanted Italian prisoners qualified in specific trades, but when their skills were checked, it was found that the nominal rolls sent from the Union did not 'in any way tally with the information obtained'.[37]

Although the South African High Commissioner admitted that the POWs may have deliberately 'hoodwinked their interrogators' back in the Union, the blunder caused additional work for the British because they had to conduct trade tests before the prisoners could be put to work, wasting valuable time.[38] Adding to the embarrassment for the Union, it emerged that when the POWs arrived in Durban to board their ship to London, they were found to be in possession of potentially dangerous weapons such as hammers, carpenter's saws, razors and knives.

The irritated London authorities sent a stern warning to Beyers to ensure this did not happen again.[39] At Zonderwater, the camp command was starting to realise that they may have had the wrong idea about their Italian captives. They were shrewd opportunists and this had nothing to do with what had happened or had not happened on the battlefield, or even how quickly or how many Italians surrendered.

When Raffaello Cei, who was stationed in Libya and had surrendered at Sollum, arrived in the Union in April 1942, the situation had improved slightly, at least at the Pietermaritzburg POW camp. By this time, it had been transformed into a permanent camp and he would remain there until he was repatriated after the war. As he recalled:

> There were six barracks or cages, as they called them, equipped with showers, toilets, kitchens ... Cage 4 was the most organized. It had prisoners selected accurately according to their specialization: musicians, cobblers, gardeners, bricklayers, even famous soccer players. Number 5 and 6 housed passing prisoners. When arrivals came – sometimes up to 8 000 people arrived – Cage number 4 was alerted for welcoming.[40]

Again, luck was on Raffaello's side. He met a fellow POW who hailed from Montecatini, his parents' home town. On discovering this shared heritage, the man saw to it that Raffaello was moved 'to the kitchen of [cage] number 5. Clearly my fate was to be in the kitchen'.

For three months, prisoners arrived at Pietermaritzburg, were registered there and then sent on to Zonderwater. It was during this time that Raffaello put in every effort to make a good impression. Working in the camp butchery, he and a friend did their

> best and tried to be friendly to everyone, especially those that most needed it, because in the face of hunger and suffering, all men are

equal. Luckily for us, we had to guard a well-equipped pantry that was not so difficult to draw from.

In contrast, Giovanni in Zonderwater believed that to be a 'true prisoner' one had to suffer. However, he remembered 1942 as his best year of captivity. Believing that the war was going in the Italians' favour, he felt that 'the English began to treat us better: perhaps they feared what was to come'.[41] But he was wrong: the slight improvements at Zonderwater in 1942 were the result of the negative Red Cross reports that haunted De Wet.

Because the prison authorities were not yet able to provide sporting equipment, books or other means of recreation, it was up to the prisoners to keep themselves busy. Some of the more creative-minded inmates began to fashion trinkets out of whatever they could lay their hands on, including a miniature train and a submarine fashioned from jam jars and a violin made of matches. The prisoners also felt the need to showcase their emotional state and so a canvas emerged depicting 'the prisoner's prayer', as did many embroidered works that had the Madonna or an angel as their favourite theme.

As Christmas 1942 edged closer, Giovanni and others in his block started to prepare a nativity scene, and Giovanni was asked to create the baby Jesus:

> I duly, quickly and Christianly tried to perform the task; I found some clay, and managed to mould the sweet Babe, colouring him with some earthen tints. He was very simple and roughly made, but he really represented humility and poverty ... He was warmly placed on top of a bit of hay, in a clay grotto, and Saint Joseph and the Madonna, as well as the ox and the donkey, were all represented by cardboard figurines.
>
> It was a prisoners' nativity scene, of the most simple, but in it was transfigured all the feeling and soul of the prisoners that, suffering to infinity, purified themselves and ascended in spirit to the bluest and purest skies ... it seemed as though he were speaking and comforting us, saying: 'O, my dear children! ... I am closer to you, because you are suffering and in suffering there is redemption and purity'.[42]

3

CHEAP LABOUR: POWs FOR HIRE

SINCE THE ITALIAN POWs were a great, readily available source of labour, the Union government identified a number of work schemes they could be employed on throughout the country. Accordingly, satellite camps for outside employment were established for POWs working on harvesting schemes and on public works such as road-building and forestry.

In October 1942, the first POWs were sent to the outside employment camp at Worcester. The largest camp apart from Zonderwater, it was able to hold 3 000 POWs. From there, most POWs would be sent out to work in the vicinity.[1]

With so many POWs applying for outside work, Beyers reminded the camp authorities that restrictions applied to the use of POW labour – for example, they were limited to urban areas, to work other than in agriculture and in proximity to the coast. The reason for this was that it was thought that POWs may attempt to escape from one of the harbours in the coastal cities, so they were not allowed to do any work in Cape Town, Hopefield, Simonstown, Wynberg, Bellville, Port Elizabeth, East London, Durban and Somerset West.[2] Yet, when circumstances demanded it, POWs were placed at other districts that also posed the risk of escape. One instance was the camp at George, where POWs were placed to work on road and forestry projects.

The Italian POWs could also be hired by members of the public, most of them being engaged on private farms, where they worked on all manner of projects. However, when the press announced in July 1942 that 'Italian War Prisoners may now be hired', it was made clear that 'no guarantee will be given that they will be able to do any particular kind of work'.[3] It was up to each employer to make sure that the prisoners were clothed and fed, had suitable accommodation and did not escape from the place where they worked. The employers had to pay a deposit of £9 for each prisoner's

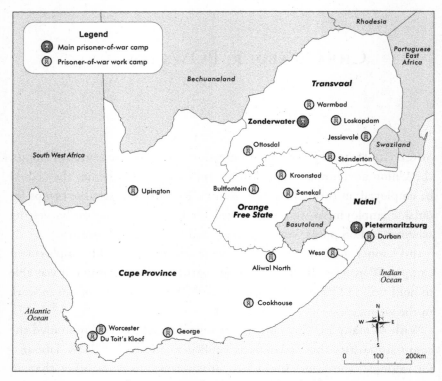

Italian prisoner-of-war camps in South Africa

clothing and equipment and all the prisoners had to be escorted from the camp to the farm where they would work. The POWs were to be paid six shillings per week, but half of the money had to be paid directly to the camp authorities.

An additional set of rules was sent to each employer, not so much to control the POWs but to inform the public of the rules that had to be followed when Italians were employed. Because Smuts was acutely aware of the anti-war faction in the country, he wanted to make sure that POWs with Fascist ideas would not end up working for civilians who held similar views.

In this regard, Smuts and the Zonderwater command espoused different approaches: Smuts wanted to make sure that employers were politically sound, while De Wet, and later his successor, thought it more practical to scrutinise prisoners for subversive tendencies before sending them out to work. In the end, though, Smuts and the Zonderwater command tried a

A farmer collecting his Italian prisoner employees from a camp
(Photo courtesy www.zonderwater.com/it)

variety of different methods. Smuts got his way in that civilian employers were warned that any person who knowingly assisted or attempted to assist any prisoner of war to escape or to attempt to escape from any place of detention would be charged. These 'places' were defined as POW camps and places of outside employment, that is, farms, road-building camps, forestry camps and so on. The convoluted legal jargon used to inform the public probably contributed to the rules being ignored or misunderstood, with very few South Africans realising that they could be arrested if caught.[4]

On the other hand, the Zonderwater command followed the advice of the Red Cross inspector, who suggested that a vetting system for POWs be implemented. Each prisoner who wanted to work outside the camp had to sign a declaration of cooperation. This declaration, the camp command believed, would separate the Fascists from the non-Fascists. Those who refused to sign it were not allowed out of the camp and became known as 'non-cooperators' or simply as 'Fascists'. To simplify matters, it was also decided to create so-called Fascist Blocks for those who refused to sign the declaration. But while separation at first seemed like the easy answer, in the early years of Zonderwater the camp command had no appreciation of the complex nuances of the situation.

The outside employment scheme had hardly begun when newspapers were asked to print an article to remind employers that POWs were not 'allowed to visit places of public entertainment', as some employers regarded their Italian workers as having the same rights and freedoms as the locals. On the other hand, others considered the Italians to be enemies and so the writer of the same article felt moved to point out that POWs were 'entitled to go their way free of molestation by any person'.[5]

Although outside employment often meant an increased rate of pay, it did not necessarily mean better living conditions. For instance, at Du Toit's Kloof in the Western Cape, where the Italians helped to build a pass, the problems were similar to those experienced at Zonderwater in the early days. There were too few toilets and huts and those that were erected leaked. Many tents were rotten and there was no canteen or sick bay. Almost a year after it had been established, the camp at Du Toit's Kloof still did not conform to the regulations of the Geneva Convention. However, regardless of the efforts to improve living conditions, outside factors also played a role: for instance, in May 1944 there was a severe potato shortage and the POWs and staff complained that they did not get enough nourishment.[6] Complaints about rancid butter were also raised, and upon investigation it was found that the storage facilities were below standard, causing the food to rot.

The work camp at George experienced similar problems. For instance, POWs there could not shower or flush toilets because the reservoir had dried up. And regardless of the lack of water, the National Roads Board asked for more POWs to be sent to George. However, by June 1943 it was decided to withdraw the men until improvements could be made. The POW camp authorities at Zonderwater admitted that the Geneva Convention was being violated, but it was the humanitarian aspect that troubled them most. Justifiably, it was thought that a 'POW cannot be expected to work willingly under existing conditions and therefore it probably is not economical for the National Roads to employ them at all under present conditions'.[7]

While the POWs had to make do with leaking tents, no water for ablutions, washing their clothes in nearby streams and holding on to tents for hours to keep them from blowing away in strong winds, the staff at these camps also lived in equally poor conditions. At George, eight of the camp staff members slept in the detention barracks and at Du Toit's Kloof some of the staff lived in small iron huts and had to build a kitchen at their own expense as the authorities did not provide one in time.[8] It seems that the National Roads Board was responsible for the building and maintenance of the camp, but that it was inspected by staff from the Zonderwater camp. Ultimately, the well-being of the POWs was the responsibility of the UDF because they had both to report to the Red Cross and to comply with the Geneva Convention.

At Cookhouse, where POWs worked on prickly pear eradication, things were different. In November 1943, an inspection showed that the camp was in good condition overall; it even had a school for POWs and had received books from Zonderwater. This was quite remarkable, since this camp was initially supposed to be temporary.

As the number of outside camps increased, POWs came into contact with civilians more regularly. However, in some areas of the country, the local communities felt especially belligerent about having the Italians in their towns and a propaganda campaign was launched to prevent public resistance to the work schemes. In April 1942, the *Cape Times* published an article that characterised the captives as innocent young boys and as victims of a cruel Fascist dictatorship. Readers were informed that when they were issued with butter on their arrival in South Africa, they were bewildered as to its use. And regarding political ideas, the article mentioned that the Italians had 'no enthusiasm for the war' and that the so-called friendship between Italy and Germany was the result of an 'imposed' alliance in 1935. The widespread support for Fascism in Italy was put down to the fact that the population had no choice in the matter, quoting a prisoner as saying, 'we are all Fascists in Italy; if not, we starve'.[9]

With this kind of reporting in the press, the idea of the Italian POW as an easily controlled and non-aggressive worker was strengthened among potential South African employers. To emphasise the point, the article pointed out that the POWs 'realise that they are among friends ... they are keen and anxious to work'.[10]

In reality, though, not all of the POWs were keen to work because the opportunity to do so came with personal doubts and political complications. Many of them believed that if they worked or cooperated with their captors in any way, they were betraying Mussolini and Italy. As time went by, the camp command could not have predicted the trouble that the seemingly simple solution of giving POWs the choice to sign the declaration would create.

Back in Pietermaritzburg, Raffaello continued to work in the camp kitchen. He specialised in 'roasts, lamb chops, stews, meatballs and cold plates', but he was especially fond of the 'fruit and custard, phyllo pastries with chocolate or rice boiled with milk and sugar, all things that we didn't eat at home in Italy'. He was proud of his work, but also realistic, admitting about the UDF staff that they 'certainly didn't have five-star menus, but to judge by how much they ate, the South Africans seemed pretty satisfied'.[11] He was paid for his work and must have signed the declaration of cooperation. However, the fact that the head chef 'was an avid supporter of the *Duce*' shows that the declaration was not wholly effective in separating the Fascists from the non-Fascists.

Since many POWs merely signed the declaration because they were bored and wanted to get out of the camp, it became something of a pseudo escape mechanism. It also meant that they did not always have the skills they claimed to have. One unlucky employer – General Kenneth van der Spuy – soon experienced this first hand.

Van der Spuy was the military attaché for the UDF in London and when he returned in 1941, ready to retire, he bought *Old Nectar*, a farm near Stellenbosch. But then he was called to Pretoria for further service and his wife, Una – the gardening legend and writer – was left behind with a new home, two sons and a barren piece of land where there should have been a garden. The solution was to ask for skilled POWs from the camp at Zonderwater.[12] In May 1942, Van der Spuy asked for a chef, a qualified nurseryman, a florist, an experienced farmer and a general handyman. It was up to Zonderwater to send the POWs with the right skills, yet because there was too little time to test their skills, the POWs could get away with inventing qualifications if they wanted to get out of the camp.[13] The POWs were warned that 'any misrepresentation made as to their knowledge or ability in any specific trade, or any particular subject' would render them liable to disciplinary action.[14]

As must have been the case here and with many other POWs on outside employment, language got in the way of comprehension. When I interviewed Una in 2010, she recalled that 'The POWs spoke no English and I spoke no Italian. So the first Italian word I learned was *letame*, which means manure. Because obviously we needed manure to fertilise the garden'.[15]

Only one month later, things started to go wrong. Four of the five POWs were returned to Zonderwater as they were unsuitable. The fifth man, Borraro, had to be hospitalised. When the magistrate of Stellenbosch was told of the need to hospitalise a POW in his district, it emerged that he had no idea the men were employed in the area. Beyers apologised to the magistrate, saying that 'failure to do so is due to the fact that full details of the [outside employment] scheme had not been finally decided upon'.[16]

Meanwhile, a new batch of POWs at *Old Nectar* did not fare much better. On 1 August, the POW supervisor at the farm, a Mrs Richards, wrote to De Wet complaining about two of the men. In her opinion, they had been

> feigning ill continuously, simulating fainting and so on … their behaviour in general has been neurotic and creates a bad feeling amongst them all. Two of the other three POW told Dr de Villiers, who came out to interpret for me, that they considered their behaviour disgusting and inferred that they were practising homosexuality. The other three prisoners all thought that these two should not be allowed to remain here.
>
> I received a telephone call from the local Roman Catholic priest who said they had been to him and threatened to run away if they were not returned to Sonderwater (sic) immediately. [The priest] described their behaviour as hysterical. Bellantuoni on the same day told the priest that he would run away unless returned, pleaded with me not to return him. They have not been guilty of insubordination and I did hope to keep them for the remaining month …[17]

Two days after Mrs Richards' letter was received, the military police escorted the POWs back to Zonderwater. When they arrived, the two

POWs, Bellanthoni and Battista, who were accused of feigning illness and 'practising homosexuality', made extraordinary claims in a written statement. Apparently, the two POWs became friends with a man by the name of Molinari, who lived in Stellenbosch. Molinari produced papers that he had been released from an internment camp for suspected Axis cooperators or informers. He also claimed that he had hidden an escaped POW in his house and had even arranged for the escapee to go to Johannesburg.

Later, Bellanthoni and Battista were approached by someone who introduced himself as Frans Malherbe. At the very least, Malherbe was opposed to the country's war participation, but it is also likely that he was a member of the *Ossewabrandwag* who was trying to befriend or influence the two POWs. He claimed to have been to Italy to attend 'conferences relating to the Fascist Party' and invited Bellanthoni and Battista to his house, where he showed them an Italian book with the phrase 'Mussolini is always right' printed on the first page. The two men also claimed that De Villiers, who acted as interpreter to the farm manager, befriended them and claimed that he, De Villiers, had attended Rome University, owned a doll dressed in the uniform of an Italian Cub (an Italian Fascist Youth Movement) and regularly listened to Italian music and patriotic Fascist songs.[18]

De Wet reported these claims to Beyers as 'confidential and secret', referring to 'subversive influences ... endeavouring to contact Prisoners of War employed on outside employment'.[19] Two days before Christmas, Beyers informed Van der Spuy of these claims, asking that the matter remain 'strictly confidential and ... not to be divulged to any other person'.[20]

By this time Van der Spuy had evidently had enough of dealing with staff matters at *Old Nectar* and he got the Defence Headquarters to manage things for him. In August 1942, they asked De Wet to select a qualified bricklayer for *Old Nectar* as the previous one 'sent him had never laid any bricks. Kindly ensure that he is provided with as good a bricklayer as the camp can supply'.[21] De Wet had no choice but to send yet another man, but this time he would have had to be selected based on both his actual skills and his political ideology.

At this point a third aspect of outside employment became apparent: some POWs became involved in amorous relationships with local women.

At the end of 1942, Van der Spuy told the authorities that one of his POW labourers had 'gone to houses of coloureds in the vicinity [of Stellenbosch] although frequently warned of the penalties attaching thereto'. In the same letter, and perhaps in response to information on the Fascist activities, Van der Spuy told Beyers that he was 'satisfied that the strictest supervision is being exercised by Mrs Richards over the POWs under her control and I will further discuss this matter on my return to Pretoria'.[22]

Early in January 1943, Gualini Guerino was sent back to Zonderwater because he was not the cook he claimed to be. Van der Spuy added that Guerino was 'a slovenly and dirty worker'.[23] Upon his return to Zonderwater, the alleged culinary imposter was interrogated. Apparently, he was sent to the farm as a gardener, but when two workers left, he was asked to take their place in the kitchen. Incompetent and reluctant, he eventually performed general domestic work.

Mrs Richards had a short temper and when Guerino one day pointed out to her that it was 'unjust' to speak to him in such a rude manner as she did, even if he was a POW, she hit him on the head with a frying pan. Guerino wanted to report the matter to the police, but she 'came out with a revolver and ordered him into the house'. Offended and angry, he was soon back in the garden, but she found him and locked him in the bathroom 'from 17:00 hrs until 07:00 hrs the next day'.[24] It would seem that Guerino's complaints were justified, especially when another report came to light stating that Mrs Richards had slapped a POW in the face.[25]

By October 1943, complaints about Mrs Richards become enough of a concern that the commandant of the nearest work camp at Worcester, Major RS Miller, sent an inspector to investigate the living conditions on the farm. The inspector was told that 'the action to be taken is a matter for your own discretion'. In general, the report was positive, but the inspector noted that 'several reports from POWs indicate that the manager [Mrs Richards] treats them well as a rule but is very quick-tempered and has on several occasions struck a POW. They do not make the complaint in the presence of the manageress'.[26] So the inspection did not make life better for the POWs and it is unlikely that a visit from a military inspector would have motivated Mrs Richards to change her ways.

Writing about the early days at *Old Nectar* many years later, Una

POW labourers left their mark in the Jonkershoek mountains near Stellenbosch
(Photo courtesy of Helène Smit)

described the POWs as 'crafty' and always having a reason for not helping. However, she noted that the youngest of the lot, Aurelio Gatti, was different. According to Una, he remained at the farm until the end of the war and returned to the Cape as an immigrant a few years later. Relieved of his gardening duties, he could now focus on his passion, making ice-cream. It was not long before Gatti's became a successful business.[27]

Even when the problems at *Old Nectar* seemed to have been partially resolved, Stellenbosch remained a thorn in the side of the military authorities. In May 1943, the camp commandant at Worcester informed Beyers that he had been to Stellenbosch to investigate reports of irregularities committed by POWs in the town and district. He noted that the public of Stellenbosch were divided over the POWs, with some being strong supporters of the war effort and others not. He went on to report that many civilians in Stellenbosch wanted stricter control of the POWs, who were wandering through the town 'at too late an hour'. Other civilians, apparently, were known to treat POWs as 'honoured guests and invite them to cinemas, tea rooms and on one occasion it is alleged three POWs were taken to a party at a Student's Hostel patronised by students of both sexes'.[28]

Van der Spuy was not the only high-ranking member of the UDF who made use of POW labour. General Sir Pierre van Ryneveld, Chief of the General Staff, employed eight POWs, one of whom was a pig and poultry expert. There is evidence that the camp command at Zonderwater gave instructions that the Van Rynevelds – who had a farm, *Spitzkop*, at Bronkhorstspruit – be provided with beds for the POWs in their employ. This was not in line with regulations, as employers were supposed to be responsible for the POWs' accommodation.

Van Ryneveld became slightly irritated by the fact that the military authorities apparently did not treat his wife's requests for POW clothing with urgency. In April 1945, he wrote to Beyers:

> My wife wrote to Sonderwater a fortnight ago regarding basic pay and new clothing for Italian Prisoners of War employed at *Spitzkop*, requesting that these be forwarded to OC Spitzkop Camp, SAEC for distribution. Nothing has arrived. Please ascertain cause for inordinate delay.

When the reply came from Zonderwater, it emerged that Lady van Ryneveld had apparently not paid the account for the clothing, which must have caused at least one red face. Nevertheless, the Zonderwater authorities proceeded to send the parcel of clothing that same day.[29] Van Ryneveld was not happy and he wrote angrily that he had the receipt for a payment that was made. The reply he received was an explanation of accounts paid and a note that 'your debit balance is now £1.0.9. This amount has been long outstanding and I must insist that you forward me your cheque within 10 days from date'.[30]

Another case where a UDF officer insisted on special treatment involved Lieutenant Colonel L Blumberg, the medical director of Zonderwater camp. One day a large number of POWs were waiting at the Pretoria station for a hospital train to pass through when the investigating officer at Zonderwater noticed three prisoners who were not wearing their POW uniforms. This was against regulations and pointed to a possible attempt to escape. When asked for their permit to be out of the camp, the three POWs presented a 'composite' permit, something which the officer found strange and against what was usually allowed.

When Blumberg appeared on the platform, he informed the officer that he was exempted from the usual provisions concerning POWs on outside employment. The officer then requested the camp command to 'be furnished with a list of persons who are in possession of this type of exemption … to facilitate our duties'.[31]

By 1945, when this incident took place, there had been several attempts by POWs to escape from Zonderwater or while on outside employment. The camp command also knew that some of their guards, who did not support the war effort, could not be trusted; yet exceptions were apparently made when enforcing rules and regulations.

It was not only POWs who were returned to Zonderwater if their work was thought to be below standard. In June 1943, three UDF staff members at the work camp at Du Toit's Kloof were sent back because one was of little use, while another was thought to be of weak character and unreliable and the last was reported to be quite useless. Given the poor living conditions of the staff at this camp, these staff members may have acted deliberately.[32] It is not known what the Zonderwater camp was supposed to have done with these three men.

Those POWs who were sent back to Zonderwater, and any prisoner who was considered, for whatever reason, to be unsuitable for work outside the camp, most often ended up in one of the Fascist Blocks. Regardless of whether they were Fascists or not, POWs who were thought to be troublesome workers had to be separated from those who were more reliable. In the Fascist Blocks they shared accommodation and living space with individuals such as Giovanni Palermo who were committed Fascists. In this way, the authorities tried to simplify the arrangements at Zonderwater, but in reality they forced people with different political ideologies together and that held the potential for future conflict among the prisoners.

Fortunately, during the first year or two, the majority of the POWs in the camp were mostly concerned with making life more comfortable for themselves as their living conditions still did not match those set out by the Geneva Convention.

4

TROUBLE BREWS AT ZONDERWATER

DURING THE COURSE of 1941 and 1942, POWs continued to arrive at Zonderwater at an alarming pace. With some coming in from the battlefronts in North Africa in great numbers and others leaving Zonderwater for outside employment, maintaining control over them was almost impossible. As early as the end of 1941, De Wet's staff were unable to keep track of the inmates, but they realised that often the numbers of those going out did not add up to the numbers returning.

A report on the matter revealed the chaotic state of affairs: it stated that handling the situation would be

> extremely difficult [as] prisoners are coming in at all hours, frequently overcrowding the camp and a reliable roll call is at times an impossibility. When the camps are normal an additional roll call will be enforced.[1]

A few months later, the camp was still more or less a building site, yet Beyers estimated that it could accommodate 79 000 men. The guards and the administrative staff were stunned, though: perhaps they had been hoping that those in control would consider their difficult situation. Some of the anxious young guards probably sensed that if the masses of Italians were to be swept up in a frenzy of discontent, they could be overpowered in minutes.

Zonderwater resembled a small city, albeit one where most of the inhabitants lived in tents. The majority of the residents were Italian prisoners of war and the staff were made up of white, black and coloured guards. Given the race laws at the time, only white soldiers were allowed to carry arms and black guards were issued with assegais and the like. Since most of the young white soldiers were sent to fight, the Zonderwater command was left with older white men who were not always up to the job. Ultimately, most of the guards were taken from the ranks of the Cape Corps and by 1942 they outnumbered their black and white compatriots.[2]

This mixture of nationalities, races and social classes often led to trouble. While most of the interactions between the POWs and the staff were good-natured, there were inevitably exceptions. For example, the Zonderwater command issued an order when they noted that POWs 'persist[ed] in annoying guards and sentries by the throwing of stones and articles of a similar nature'.[3] The POWs were ordered not to talk to or barter with guards through the fences. Anyone who ignored these orders was 'liable to be fired on'.[4]

Some altercations turned out to be deadly, though. In March 1942, Averando Falcinelli was shot by a nervous guard. According to Falcinelli's friends, they were simply strolling along the fence, about 10 metres (11 yards) from the perimeter fence, when Falcinelli was shot in the back. The POWs maintained that the guard gave no warning, but the guard who had fired the shot stated that the POWs had been sitting right against the fence and that he had shouted to them to move away. When they did not comply, he fired a shot slightly to the right, with the search lights blinding his vision.

According to the investigator, blood was found not 10 yards from the fence, but 8 feet from it. The fence had also been tampered with, as some of the barbed wire strands had been removed. De Wet informed Beyers that the police had investigated the matter and that they had concluded that the POW was shot in the course of duty.[5] No further action was taken against the guard.

A few weeks later, a similar incident occurred when Serrao Antonio Francesco was shot and killed. This time, the South African Red Cross asked for details of the death as they had to inform the families of the POWs about deaths and illnesses. Their enquiry exposed the confusion that prevailed among the Zonderwater command in criminal investigations of this kind.[6] Beyers' office informed the Red Cross that an investigation by the civil authorities was underway. In fact, if the death of a POW was caused by a guard, a military court of inquiry had to investigate, not the civil police. If a POW was killed by a civilian while he was working outside the camp, then it had to be investigated by the civil authorities.[7] In Francesco's case, the camp command soon realised that if his death became public, it could cause great embarrassment and reprisals against South African POWs being held in Italy at that time.[8]

To make matters worse, the legal advisor of the UDF said that Francesco's death indicated possible culpable homicide. The Secretary of Defence, AEM Jansen, intervened to fix matters. Following an inquest, they concluded that the death of the POW was 'justifiable homicide [and that] the Attorney General of the Transvaal Province has directed that no further action be taken in regard of this prisoner's death'.[9]

De Wet, however, was not let off the hook and he was told that

> the verdict was only obtained with the greatest difficulty and it is necessary that you instruct all sentries and guards to refrain from any indiscriminate shooting and that they exercise all necessary caution before resorting to the use of arms.[10]

In practice, these orders made little difference when guards did not understand them, were nervous or were simply frustrated. In some cases, however, it is possible that interference with evidence caused even more harm. In August 1942, Angelo Macchiaroli was shot as he sat chatting to two friends near a perimeter fence. A POW in a tent nearby heard the commotion and went out to see what was happening. Two Cape Corps guards were standing near Angelo, explaining that he was shot because he was too close to the fence. When a UDF officer came to inspect the matter, he found the man lying three yards from the perimeter fence, which was within the space where the prisoners were allowed to be.

The guard, Private Wally Bloem, who fired the shot, testified that prisoners had been laughing at his warnings to them to step away from the fence. In desperation, he put a cartridge in his gun, but as he closed the bolt, a shot went off. His intention was not to shoot or kill, yet Bloem was found guilty of gross negligence and a lack of discipline. His testimony was also called into question and it was found that 'the evidence of the POW witnesses seems more acceptable than that of the two Witnesses,

Pte Wally Bloem and Pte David Muller'.[11] Bloem's case was brought before a criminal court, where he was found guilty and sentenced to three months' hard labour or £10.

Beyers felt this sentence was too lenient and he warned judicial officers to deal more firmly in cases such as this. In response, the Secretary for Justice gave Beyers a stern warning not to interfere with the work of the judicial system.[12] Because such cases had to be reported to the Protecting Powers (Switzerland and Brazil), who in turn would share it with the Italian government, the British High Commissioner advised Beyers to limit correspondence to vague statements such as 'the accused had been found guilty and punished'.[13] However, the Union government thought it wise to provide full details to the Protecting Powers, not only because the courts were open to the public and by implication to the Protecting Powers, but they also believed that withholding details would be 'against the spirit if not the letter of the [reciprocal] Agreement entered into between the Government of the Union of South Africa and the Italian Government'.[14]

During De Wet's time as camp commandant shootings were uncommon, but a number of POWs died at the hands of guards after he left in December 1942. For example, early in 1943, Private Barend Schoeman killed a prisoner and wounded two others. Apparently, Celestino Faraone and his friends had thrown stones at Schoeman, annoying him to the point where he fired shots. The Italians were 23 yards away from the fence, so the chances are slim that these men were trying to escape.[15]

As with the previous case, the sentence was thought to be too lenient; Schoeman was sentenced to seven days' imprisonment with hard labour. Because the case went through the criminal court and was therefore open to the public, the authorities also had to report it to the Red Cross. They kept their report brief, writing only the following: 'No 142891 FARAONE, Celestino. Zonderwater Camp. Killed by a shot from the rifle of a coloured guard. The guard was held for trial, and having been found guilty of intentional murder, was sentenced to only 7 days' imprisonment with hard labour'.[16]

It was no surprise that the Italian government wanted more details, but when their request reached the British POW office, the authorities could not trace the report and had to ask the UDF for details. In an attempt to pacify the British and the Italians, Beyers replied as follows:

> The accused was held in custody during a period of six months while awaiting trial and sentence, and as no bail was found, he spent that period in prison. That fact, as well as the conflict of evidence and consequent doubt as to the true circumstances of the case, no doubt weighed with the Magistrate when passing sentence.[17]

Shortly after this, the UDF authorities received a claim for compensation from the victim's dependants. The matter was 'deferred until the termination of the formal state of war' between Italy and the Union of South Africa.[18]

By April 1944, Colonel Hendrik F Prinsloo (commandant of Zonderwater from January 1942 to 1947) had formed the opinion that the high number of escapes was due to the inmates' 'contempt' for the guards. He wrote that

> complaints have been made of taunts and insults to which the sentries have been subjected ... apart from the humiliation which these Coloured soldiers are compelled to endure, it is strongly recommended that authority be given for the issue to all sentries of from three to five rounds of live ammunition ...[19]

It was only by November that the camp report stated that 'the Cape Corps Guards are now issued with ammunition, and although they are not 100% efficient, they do their best'.[20] It was also at about this time that Beyers decided that all similar matters would be dealt with by a court martial. Because the records of courts martial were closed to the public, this meant there would be no need to report details to the Red Cross. Beyers believed that 'if such course is necessary for the administration of Justice', inquiries involving POWs and guards would be dealt with by military courts.[21]

More than 200 Italian POWs are buried at Zonderwater – 254, to be exact.[22]

Unlike the unlucky prisoners who were shot by guards, most of the deaths occurred as a result of illness, accidents and even lightning strikes.

With most of the POWs following the Roman Catholic faith, most burials were overseen by priests from among the POW community. Later in the war, the prisoners built chapels in Zonderwater to allow them to worship indoors. According to Captain Ball, a welfare officer, there were 23 POW chaplains, a number that would have been just about sufficient for the Zonderwater prisoners.

However, those POWs who were engaged in outside employment mostly had to do without any form of spiritual guidance. When it became clear that the Worcester camp would be established, for instance, the Prefect Apostolic wrote to the Secretary of Defence asking for priests from Zonderwater to be sent to the area. At the time there was only one Catholic priest in the district and he would not have been able to work among the prisoners, especially not once they were distributed to farms in smaller groups.[23]

The complexity of the matter was made clear in the reply the Prefect Apostolic received from the Secretary of Defence. Apparently, a number of priests from Zonderwater had already been dispatched to five outside work camps. To fill the remaining gaps, local priests were asked to visit work camps, but they were unwilling to do so. The reasons for their refusal were never stated, but some of the difficulty seemed to have arisen from the costs involved in such visits and who would or would not pay for the priests' visits. The Secretary of Defence did not see the expense as war-related and therefore believed that the Church was responsible for getting priests to their flocks.[24]

But the Apostolic Delegate was not happy; he reminded the Smuts government that the situation was partly caused by the fact that the government had not granted permits to Catholic priests to enter the country before the war began. Secondly, many South African priests of Italian origin were being held in internment camps as they were seen as a possible threat to the Union's war effort. Thirdly, the UDF employed 'a very high number of full time and part time Chaplains',[25] making them unavailable to the POWs.

By way of offering a solution, the Apostolic Delegate suggested that

Colonel Prinsloo escorts the Apostolic Delegate on his visit to Zonderwater
(Photo courtesy NMMH)

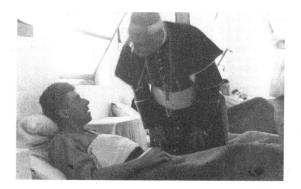

A visit from the Apostolic Delegate (Photo courtesy NMMH)

A temporary chapel at Zonderwater (Photo courtesy ICRC)

some of the priests at Koffiefontein, one of the main internment camps, be sent to the work camps in need of religious services. Shrewdly, he also included a veiled warning:

> In regard to the whole matter, I feel that it is first of all necessary to know whether the International Geneva Convention in regards to prisoners of war, has laid down any rule or regulations in regard to their religious needs. Unfortunately, I am not in possession of a copy of the Convention, but I make bold to say that each Government has a responsibility in this matter.[26]

It is highly unlikely that the Apostolic Delegate was unaware of Chapter 4, Article 16 of the Geneva Convention, which states that POWs should be allowed to practise their religion and that those POWs who are clergy should be allowed to minister to their fellow prisoners. The Apostolic Delegate took a keen interest in the welfare of the prisoners and visited Zonderwater on more than one occasion. His mention of the Geneva Convention also came at an uncomfortable time for the Zonderwater camp command, because they were in the process of adjusting to large numbers of prisoners and realised that they were unable to comply with many of the Convention's regulations at that time.

However, the authorities were not so concerned about the religious needs of the prisoners that they would consider setting free interned priests. They simply could not allow individuals with anti-war sentiments at Koffiefontein, or any of the other internment camps, to influence the Italians in the work camps. It is probably for this reason that the suggestion was made to release interned Catholic priests in Kenya to serve in South Africa. However, the priests in Kenya would also have been interned for their suspected anti-war sentiments, which meant that this suggestion was rejected outright by the Secretary of Defence. He also stressed that

> the number of Italian POW Priests together with the available Roman Catholic Priests throughout the Union should suffice for the Religious needs of both the Italian Prisoners of War in camp, and those employed on outside labour detachments.[27]

The Apostolic Delegate inspecting the building of the
Zonderwater chapel (Photo courtesy NMMH)

The only permanent chapel at Zonderwater.
Today it is a museum (Photo courtesy www.zonderwater.com/it)

With that, the matter was closed.

In the meantime, Giovanni was settling in well at Zonderwater. With self-made Fascist sculptures decorating the entrance to his tent, he and his friends felt rejuvenated; and

> with our energy and strength back, we moved to sport; this was perhaps the most necessary activity for life to begin once more, and with good humour, laughter, jokes.[28]

As he recalled, they received sporting equipment from 'good compatriots residing in South Africa'. A level piece of ground became their football field and three teams – Juventus, Sorci Verdi and Andrea Doria – played against each other regularly. For Giovanni:

> After more than a year of stasis and many sufferings and shenanigans of all kinds, playing and venting with a ball was a fantastic thing. More so for the fans, as only during sport was gesticulating, shouting and complete relaxation allowed [sport was] the only thing capable of making us forget our state as prisoners, lifting our spirits and giving us light-heartedness ...
>
> We all started the tournament in euphoric conditions, among a multitude of fans: with shouts, howls, clapping and whistles happening all at the same time, but in the name of sport. The brave Juventus, truly worthy of its great name and made up by very young individuals, managed to win the championship, though by a hair's breadth. Satisfied with our success, we immediately wore the craved, symbolic badge of victory that had been sewn artistically for us by a fan.[29]

Apparently, the players and the fans were so passionate about the games that fights erupted between opposing sides both on and off the pitch. To avoid a full-blown riot, the camp authorities suspended the games from time to time 'to avoid violent and grave consequences', to use Giovanni's words.[30] There is no doubt that the members of Giovanni's team shared

A game of football being played at Zonderwater
(Photo courtesy www.zonderwater.com/it)

an enormous sense of camaraderie and pride; 1942 was certainly an improvement over the previous year, at least for him. But then again, he did see himself as

> a true prisoner [and] the more intense and the greater the sacrifices, the greater and more elevated the satisfaction derived after having overcome them and victoriously reaching the finish line.[31]

As he had no plans to cooperate with the 'English', he focused on setting himself up as a man of influence in Zonderwater with his philosophical writings. Giovanni recalled that, as the camp expanded, they were moved to new blocks and it seems that each time they had to start from scratch to find ways to entertain themselves. Reading was a popular way to pass the time, but in the early days at Zonderwater there was no library. The prisoners found a way around this by starting their own book exchange. However, to participate, each man had to have a book to start with. Giovanni recalled how one bookless prisoner decided simply to write his own books:

We of the 4th Block were transferred indefinitely to the 7th. There, we recommenced our usual prisoner activities: building sports fields, a theatre to lift the spirits, a library with an exchange system for use of the books, where if you gave one in, you could take one out. In this regard the dear, cultured, and valorous Captain D'Errico must be mentioned, a talented professor who, possessing no books and therefore unable to participate in the library exchange, wrote, in a very short period of time, some very pleasurable 'African Storyboards'. These, full of expression, truth, art, and an incomparable vivaciousness, were accepted to count as a book.[32]

Outside employment remained a difficult system to manage. But with 2 000 POWs working from the Worcester camp on the Montagu and Du Toit's Kloof passes, countless others on farms and 10 193 men working on camp construction and vegetable gardening, things were slowly improving at Zonderwater.

Still, the conditions at Zonderwater remained very basic and still did not meet the standards of the Geneva Convention.[33] After another inspection, the Red Cross pointed out that camp command should make an effort to 'segregate ardent politically minded prisoners from the remainder'.[34] However, the inspector did not propose any reliable methods that De Wet and his staff could use to root out Fascists from among the general POW population of almost 80 000.

In May 1942, Colonel Brett, the War Office POW liaison officer, inspected Zonderwater on behalf of the Red Cross. He was not entirely satisfied and blamed the low morale among the POWs and the staff on poor living conditions. With very little to keep them busy, the prisoners became bored, giving them time to think of – and carry out – troublesome plans. Brett suggested that the POWs should be employed as much as possible on work schemes within the camp. A vegetable garden, for instance, would keep them busy while providing food, which would also make the camp more economical to manage.[35] By making these vegetables available to outside communities, the authorities also saw an opportunity to improve relationships between the Italians and sceptical South Africans.

Brett also expressed his unhappiness with the staff, who were clearly

A tense affair: camp inspection at Zonderwater (Photo courtesy NMMH)

unable to control the prisoners. But as the administrative load and security matters piled up on De Wet's desk, so did the pressure on his staff. In addition, the Afrikaans- and English-speaking guards found it difficult to communicate with the Italians and many of those same personnel also seemed to have been unaware of the requirements of the Geneva Convention.

For instance, while newspapers were strictly forbidden in the camp, the authorities found out that UDF troops at the nearby training camp were supplying POWs with unauthorised reading matter, giving them access to war news, which is not ideal in a POW camp. To stop this, the height of the fences had to be increased. Fences between the different camp sections also needed improvement to prevent undesirable POWs from roaming around freely among the others. As it was, there was a shortage of barbed wire in the Union and the fences remained largely unchanged, as did the security challenges.[36]

Brett's next inspection came a mere five months after his first visit, and with no evident improvements he lay the blame on the camp's management. It was acknowledged that the Union, being the 'largest holder of enemy prisoners of war, by some thousands'[37] was at that time falling far behind other holding countries regarding the treatment of

POWs. Brett was especially dissatisfied with the fact that the bulk of the work fell on 'one or two comparatively junior staff officers'.[38] He suggested that a directorate should be established that would be responsible to Beyers and that 'no man in the world ... can hold himself responsible for the direction of prisoners of war, especially with the numbers involved in this country'.[39]

Brett also made sure Beyers knew that 'the reason for the equitable treatment of prisoners of war is to ensure that our men in enemy hands are given reciprocal consideration'.[40] In another report, Brett was less diplomatic and stated that the 'defects to be found are principally due to over-centralisation, lack of direction [from camp commandant], and ignorance of junior officers'.[41]

These criticisms were perhaps aimed at Smuts himself, because it was he who wanted the POWs in a central holding area from where they could be sent out on labour projects across the country. But Smuts must have taken note, because he acknowledged the necessity for huts after Brett's inspection and ordered Beyers to take direct control of the replacement of tents with huts; he also relieved the UDF Quartermaster General of his direct responsibilities at the camp.[42]

Before these new plans could be implemented, though, matters reached boiling point in November and December 1942, when riots broke out among both the POWs and the camp guards. On 24 November, the prisoners in Block 10, a Fascist Block, began fighting among one another when 22 of them volunteered for outside employment. The fight could have been instigated by men such as Giovanni who believed that anyone who cooperated with the enemy was a traitor to Italy.

By the time that reinforcements arrived at the block, the non-commissioned officer (NCO) had managed to remove 18 of the 22 volunteers, or 'traitors', according to some. To restore order, the Italian trumpeter was ordered to sound the 'General Assembly'. As the larger group of POWs stood on parade, the 22 volunteers were told to collect their belongings. While this was going on, the guards stood watch over those who had been assembled.

But there were still only 2 armed guards for every 2 000 POWs and it was not long before they began to break rank. One group of POWs formed, in the words of the group commander, a 'sort of Indignation Meeting'.[43]

South African staff at Zonderwater with Italian auxiliary personnel
(Photo courtesy www.zonderwater.com/it)

Another group sang patriotic Italian songs with the aim of getting the others to jump into action – which most of them, fortunately, did not.

The trouble was actually fomented by an Italian NCO. The Zonderwater command had been using Italian *carabinieri* (Italian Military Police) to maintain discipline among the POWs, mostly because of the shortage of South African UDF staff. The problem was that it was not always possible to determine for sure what the political views of these *carabinieri* were. *Carabiniere* Tavoni was one such a man. He accompanied two of the volunteers to their tents to collect their clothing, but when they were out of sight, 'he assaulted them by striking them in their faces with his clenched fist and prevented them getting their private effects'.[44] Tavoni was clearly one of those Fascists who did not approve of POWs working for the enemy. Others shared his views and another complaint was laid against two company commanders who had attacked some of the 22 volunteers.

In another instance, the Cape Corps guards took to rioting when they heard that they would receive their pay only on 1 January 1943, while the white personnel would receive their salaries a day earlier, on 31 December 1942. Ten minutes before midnight on 31 December, a fire alarm sounded.

A short while later, 100 men were dispatched with ammunition to take control of the situation. Apparently, De Wet had ordered them to guard government property, but by that time the kitchen and the mess room were already on fire. While this was going on, shots were fired and it was soon established that the Cape Corps men were armed with .303 rifles and .38 revolvers. By 06:00, the kitchen was completely destroyed.

When the officer in charge inspected the damage, he found

> the whole camp was a mass of broken beer bottles, some could still be used as weapons, we found approximately 20 details going through the burnt out rubble, the remainder of the camp was quiet ... saw the remains of 3 carbines and one .303 rifle, which must have been burnt. Commenced at the top row of tents asking if any body was hurt and keeping a lookout for arms. Found one carbine ... and removed Service Rifles and 5 Carbines also bayonets ... Captain Carfax helped to pacify the men, most of them appeared to be drunk and very excitable. Two details were inciting the others, one was arrested by me later.[45]

At one point during the night, the reinforcements tried to establish order by chasing 30 to 40 of the Cape Corps men out of the block. Most of them were 'intoxicated' and tried to resist, while their friends fired on the officers. Once the Cape Corps men were out, they were met by the Zonderwater command and, as they were still clearly hostile, De Wet

> personally hit several of them who resisted his authority. At the same time other Cape Corps details emerging from their Camp gate to assist their comrades, were driven back by these officers in spite of rifle shots and a heavy barrage of stones, bricks and other missiles thrown from within the Cape Corps camp ... Col de Wet ordered his Officers to 'man-handle' the rioters and although all Officers carried revolvers, no shots were fired.[46]

Two of the Cape Corps men died during the riot and six of the white officers and fifteen other ranks were admitted to hospital.[47] While all of this was going on, most of the POWs in the nearby blocks took cover and did not get involved in the rioting. Some POWs, however, helped the camp command to restore order.[48]

De Wet hardly had time to catch his breath when ominous messages such as 'be ready for the signal', 'it is happening tonight' and 'the word will be given later' were heard between Cape Corps guard posts. A day after the riot, the Cape Corps guards were busy planning their retaliation.

De Wet again asked for reinforcements, specifically for armoured fighting vehicles (AFVs), but was told they were not an option. He was also told that no reinforcements would be sent unless something actually happened, so the staff at Zonderwater had to hold themselves 'in readiness for any emergency'.[49] De Wet was worried that another riot could break out at any moment and informed Colonel Pilkington-Jordan, the Military Police Commander in Pretoria, that this time it was 'likely to be even more serious', because it was not the result of drunkenness among the Cape Corps, but a planned riot.[50]

By nine o'clock that evening the situation had changed to such an extent that the AFVs were made available, but only on the outside of the camp. Within an hour, the AFVs were on the roads outside the camps and blocks where the unrest was brewing and within sight of the conspirators. At this point, De Wet was able to report that he had no further cause for anxiety, as a deterrent – the presence of a single AFV – 'was superior to that of 50 armed men'.[51]

'For the sake of brevity', De Wet's report did not include detailed descriptions of the 'ugly and brutal assaults' by the Cape Corps members on white officers and non-commissioned officers, most of whom were at that time still in hospital.[52] De Wet and Smuts both thanked those POWs who had helped to re-establish order; and Smuts, who had previously not concerned himself with the Geneva Convention, now quickly reported the matter to them. After all, trying to keep news of a riot under wraps was impossible and would cause embarrassment if the press got hold of the story.[53]

Afterwards, De Wet was at pains to point out that the main duty of the Cape Corps was to guard POWs and that if they could not be trusted, the POWs might take advantage of the situation. De Wet, who tended to expect the worst to happen in a situation, warned his superiors that 'without an adequate number of alert and reliable sentries the mass escape of 65 000 POWs with disastrous results, could hardly be prevented'.[54]

After the military authorities had had time to think about what had happened, they blamed De Wet for 'the lack of administrative ability' and said that he had 'failed to control and utilise his staff properly'.[55]

De Wet's fate was sealed, and arrangements for his replacement were soon underway. In his place would come a new camp commander, Colonel Hendrik F Prinsloo. By this time, Prinsloo was already in service at Zonderwater as Assistant Camp Commander, but now greater responsibilities lay ahead for him. Smuts remembered Prinsloo's father, the hero of the Battle of Spioen Kop.[56] Possibly hoping that the apple had not fallen far from the tree, he summoned the son of this war hero to his office. According to Captain Ball, the conversation went something like this:

> Smuts: I have a job of international importance for you to do. The honour of South Africa is on the line, our name is being dragged through the mud regarding prisoner-of-war relations. Now it is time for us to take our name out of the mud to build it up to keep it high for the future. Hennie, my feeling is that you are the man for the job.
>
> Prinsloo: Oubaas, I will do my best, as long as you don't tie my hands.[57]

During the First World War Prinsloo had fought in the German South-West Africa Campaign and he later served in France, for which he received the *Croix de Guerre*.[58] In fact, he was on his way back to the battlefields as Commanding Officer of the Regiment Botha in November 1941 when he was transferred to the Prisoner-of-War Battalion and began his service at Zonderwater. In December 1942, he was promoted to Assistant Camp Commander and then to Commander in January 1943.

The end of 1942, was also a moment of truth for Raffaello. Since his capture he had not had any news from home, but towards the end of the year the first letters finally started to arrive in Pietermaritzburg.

His emotions were a mixture of joy and sadness as he tried to deal with unrelenting homesickness. The sadness did not leave him and he expressed his emotions in his memoirs, writing: 'I kept holding them and looking at each line not one but one hundred times, smiling and crying like a child'.[59] Yet the news from home was incomplete, and he soon realised that his mother was not telling him the full story:

> It didn't take long for me to notice the absence of my father's signature. I knew his calligraphy well, and couldn't accept the notion that he would renounce his duty as head of the family by not writing himself. In the letters, my mother made few references to him, and all of them ended with a general 'lots of kisses from mom and dad', which began to make me suspicious … at night I couldn't sleep at the thought that something terrible had happened to my father, because deep in my heart I was certain it had.
>
> I'd left home as a young man certain that nothing and no one could hurt me and there I was, in some forgotten hole on the other side of the world, alone and a prisoner. I regretted not having hugged my father tighter when I'd left home, and now something told me I'd never see him again on this earth. That thought poisoned my existence, and suddenly one day I felt with crystal clarity that my suspicions were correct and that my father no longer existed. Naturally, nobody told me how things really were at home in Italy.
>
> So the concerns about my mother and sister compounded the grief of my father's death, which I knew was certain. The thought of my two women alone and defenceless in the war, now without help and support, filled my heart with anguish. How would they survive without a man in the house? My sister was only nineteen and knew nothing about life. Dark thoughts never left me, not even when I looked busy with something else. Every day my wish to go home was greater.[60]

The following year was a time of great change at Zonderwater. For the prisoners, 1943 brought both hope and despair, and concern for their families in Italy, as the war wrought enormous hardship and turmoil back home.

5

AN 'EPIDEMIC OF ESCAPING'

No MATTER HOW brave they were, or pretended to be, the POWs were bound to become homesick. As far as they knew, they were stuck in the Union for an indefinite period, and for many the prospect of being incarcerated indefinitely was unbearable. This sense of hopelessness made many POWs react rashly – many of them finding it surprisingly easy to escape, even without much planning.

The escapes began as soon as the first prisoners arrived in the Union: some jumped from the train even before they reached Zonderwater, while others simply walked out of the camp after arriving. Escaping became a trend that would continue until well after the war came to an end in 1945, making Zonderwater the POW camp from which the greatest number of POWs escaped during the Second World War.

Many of the men escaped without thinking about what they would do once they were outside. Others were simply adventurous and did not want to subject themselves to captivity or to confined spaces for any longer than necessary. Another group of escapees were so committed to Mussolini that they believed they could return to Italy to take up the fight again. The fact that Italy was thousands of miles away and practically unreachable for an escaped prisoner did not stop them, though. And although this does not say much about geography education in Italy before the war, it speaks volumes about the inmates' determination and the kind of men the UDF authorities were dealing with, even if this group was in the minority.

Vito Tunzi and Oronzo Triggiani were two of the Italian prisoners who were overcome by a desire for freedom and adventure. They were among the first to escape, jumping from the train before it arrived at Zonderwater. Upon arrival at the camp, the POWs were counted and the absence of Vito and Oronzo was noted. The man in charge of the POWs on the train – an Italian non-commissioned officer – explained 'through the interpreter that he missed these two prisoners at 05:00 that morning and he thought they may have been in the lavatory'.[1] A UDF guard testified that the escort of 30 guards per train was not enough to keep a close eye on all the POWs during the journey.

Vito and Oronzo were eventually recaptured at Dannhauser, about 360 kilometres south-east of Zonderwater, close to the railway line between Durban and Pretoria. For each escape, a court of inquiry was convened and, in this case, the investigation concluded that 'no one was directly or indirectly to blame for the escape ... that the occurrence was not due to negligence or irregularity or lack of discipline on the part of any person'.[2] This became the standard conclusion for almost all the investigations into POW escapes as the camp command seemed unwilling to lay the blame on the camp guards or the prisoners.

In some instances, POWs did not even wait for the train journey to begin before they made a dash for freedom. On the night of 22 and 23 August 1941, for example, a few POWs escaped from the Clairwood Camp in Durban. They did not remain free for long, though, and when the matter was investigated, it was recommended that the camp security needed improving and that the POWs would have to enter the camp by the same gate from where they exited.

A change in the way in which roll call was conducted was another recommendation. Before the escape, roll call was held only once a day; but after the escape, it was suggested that roll call should take place twice a day. However, the brigadier of the Natal Command replied that a second roll call at 17:30 would be

> extremely difficult [as] prisoners are coming in at all hours, frequently overcrowding the camp and a reliable roll call is at times an impossibility. When the camps are normal an additional roll call will be enforced.[3]

Three years later, the security measures at most camps, including roll call, were still inefficient. This made Sergeant Luigi Irace's escape seem effortless. He escaped from the detention barracks in the Pietermaritzburg camp where he was being held as punishment for an earlier attempt to escape from the mental hospital. He escaped on 12 May 1944, 'on the spur of the moment due to [his] mental state'. According to Irace, a heavy storm allowed him to kick out two pieces of wood from the cell without anyone hearing, enabling him to get out. It emerged that his plan was to go to Mozambique because it was a 'neutral zone ... he heard there are people there [he] could get assistance from'.[4] As a Portuguese territory, Mozambique was neutral in the war and a number of POWs tried to reach its borders to find a way from there back to Italy. Not surprisingly, the court of inquiry found that security at the camp needed to be tightened.[5]

Zonderwater camp commandant De Wet knew from the start that the situation was more complex than simply preventing escapes from taking place. Because some of the UDF staff also supported Mussolini's political ideas, De Wet realised that some guards might sympathise with the POWs or, at the very least, turn a blind eye during their escape. On the other hand, the staff numbers were so low that they struggled to maintain discipline and order among the prisoners. With inadequate staff and with the camp still being constructed, De Wet was forced to think of other ways to keep the prisoners within the bounds of the camp. By allowing POWs to write to him about their frustrations, he believed, he could keep them sufficiently docile. To his mind:

> It seems to be quite a good principle to allow the prisoners to give vent in words or writing of any grievances from which they may feel they are suffering. I rather welcome this privilege being retained by the prisoners as it can be the means of bringing to my notice points of genuine misunderstanding which may exist. My reasons for asking for details of complaints are that a number of more or less frivolous complaints of a general nature has been reaching me which, through lack of such details it was quite impossible to investigate ... in some cases investigations are made in regard to complaints received and such complaints are never carelessly thrown aside.[6]

De Wet was putting his trust in the prisoners, but at this early stage of their captivity, there was no sign that they would reciprocate. While building relationships of trust is an admirable approach, De Wet made the mistake of thinking of the POWs in a stereotypical way. Among the Allied troops, especially the South Africans and the Australians, there was an impression that the Italians were an unworthy enemy.

This assumption was largely based on the relatively effortless way in which the Italian colonies in East Africa were overrun. For instance, the first battle involving the UDF forces at El Wak in 1940 could be described as an anti-climax because the Italians hardly put up any resistance. Then the Battle of Bardia the following year gave rise to the myth of the brave Australian soldiers who fought against the cowardly and weak Italians – who surrendered at the first sign of danger.[7] The idea that the Italians were easily defeated and docile in their acceptance of their fate became popular among the Allies, and in South Africa the military authorities never suspected that the Italian POWs would give them any trouble while they were imprisoned at Zonderwater or placed out to work on farms and public works. They were wrong, of course: the Italians were as diverse in their thoughts and actions as any of the other nations that participated in the war. Those who chose to view Italians through a stereotypical lens were in for a shock.

De Wet soon received a rude awakening. He did not consider that with 60 000 prisoners there would be almost 60 000 ways in which they would respond to his strategy to keep them in line. With the lack of control over the prisoners at Zonderwater and with incomplete lists of names, the language barrier and too few staff, escape was not a matter of *if* or *how*, but *when*. Most escapes were easy enough, especially during the early years when Zonderwater was little more than a chaotic collection of tents. In one instance, three POWs 'made the exit from the main gate by jumping on a Troop Carrier'.[8] No one questioned them as the truck left the camp.

With no security measures in place there, the camp hospital also became a favourite escape route. There escapees were 'facilitated by darkness, lack of lighting and beats that took sentries "round the corner"', allowing the POWs to escape with ease.[9] It eventually dawned on the camp authorities that the Italians needed a greater deterrent than giving 'vent in words or

Getting ready to escape? (Photo courtesy NMMH)

The Zonderwater hospital: an infirmary, an escape route
and a meeting place (Photo courtesy ICRC)

writing of any grievances',[10] and so it was decided that all those escapees who were recaptured would be assigned to the Fascist Block in Zonderwater. Once there, they would be treated the same as those committed Mussolini supporters who had refused to sign the declaration of cooperation and who were not allowed to go on outside employment projects.

At Zonderwater the implications of throwing men of different political ideologies together in a segregated part of the camp were not immediately

Hugh Spargo, the Zonderwater hospital administrator
(Photo courtesy Mark Shaw)

comprehended. There was no love lost between the cooperators and the non-cooperators, and as conflict between the groups increased, it was no wonder that many tried to escape from that part of the camp. It was not long before the guards discovered the entrance to an escape tunnel leading from the Fascist non-cooperators' block to the outside of the camp. De Wet guessed that the escapees must have had help from outsiders, possibly members of the *Ossewabrandwag* or other South Africans who did not agree with Smuts's participation in the war.

De Wet duly ordered a search of the perimeter of the camp.[11] In writing up his findings, his frustration was clear as he bemoaned the lack of adequate lighting around the camp. He also believed that 'if the concrete hutment scheme is sanctioned, a great many of our difficulties with regard to Security, Escapes, Hygiene, etc will be solved'.[12] At this time the number of escapes must have been much higher than what De Wet or anyone else was aware of. In an attempt to put an end to the 'epidemic of escaping', the prisoners were told that they would be shot if they tried to escape.[13]

It was shortly after this desperate threat that small POW labour parties started working on projects on the outskirts of the camp. Predictably, the prisoners saw this arrangement as yet another way to gain their freedom. It was as if the threats from the camp command had no effect whatsoever. Many of the daily reports repeated what had become a worn-out truth that 'time and time again it was shown that a lesser number of POWs were brought back in the afternoon and this fact was not reported'.[14]

The reality was that the efforts to stop – or at least limit – escapes were hopeless. With too few men to guard the camp and too few administrative staff to control the exits and entries of the labour parties, De Wet's hands were tied. The Italians were running amok as he watched on helplessly. But he would not give up. This time, he devised a cunning two-pronged plan where he would not only rely on trust between the POWs and the staff, but also make the POWs responsible for discipline and order. Although any outsider might have thought it a mad plan, this strategy had some success and continued to be used by the UDF authorities until the war came to an end. Disciplinary officers were selected from among the prisoners, usually men from the Italian Military Police known as the *carabinieri*. Italian medical orderlies were also used for this purpose.[15] The hope was that the POWs would take greater heed when they received orders from their own.

Again, not all of the *carabinieri* could be trusted; some had their own motives for taking on the role of camp police. One such orderly was Prisciano Martucci, who arrived at Zonderwater in 1941 and soon afterwards was sent to Pongola on outside employment.[16] By the following year, he had had enough of the dreary work routine and he escaped in November 1942. When he was recaptured, he was sent to Zonderwater, where he was sentenced to 28 days in the detention barracks. Two months later, Martucci escaped again, and this time he was able to remain on the run until 11 April 1944, when he was captured in Vryheid. The Police Commissioner of the Natal Division informed the court of inquiry that Martucci was captured as a result of 'information gained from the Superintendent of the Pongolo irrigation scheme'.[17] It is not known where Martucci spent his time during his period of liberty.

The camp at Pietermaritzburg had a similar outside employment scheme, but Raffaello recalled that before being accepted [for work] one had to speak to the farmer, always with the assistance of the [camp] office staff. One wasn't always accepted. The farmer had a keen eye. Every month these prisoners would come back to camp to visit their friends, get a change of clothes, and take care of other small matters. They always brought something for their friends that had stayed behind. There was one boy that came every month with thirty guinea fowls that, he claimed, he hunted using only a stick. Many had risqué stories to tell that made more than a few long to try the countryside experience.[18]

Smuts was able to see the Italians only as a source of cheap labour and he seemingly remained unsympathetic to De Wet's plight. There was also evidence that the POWs were 'fraternising' with members of the public, something that was frowned upon by some, enjoyed by others, but was nevertheless against the law.[19] It was just as well, then, that De Wet received some help from sources outside the military sphere.

Clara Urquhart was the head of the South African Red Cross Society. In an effort to help with the loads of administrative work and to help prevent escapes, she suggested that each POW be issued with an identity disk that would indicate his permanent POW number. In her view, a disk would

avoid a great deal of confusion which arises owing to the fact that these men are given a Prisoner-of-War number in [the Middle East] and seem either to forget it or lose it by the time they reach the Union.[20]

The number system was already being used in Europe and the United States. In South Africa, it was argued, it could help reduce the confusion created by misunderstandings between Italian-speaking POWs and Afrikaans-speaking guards. More often than not, however, the Italians would swap their surnames and names around, a tactic that confused the South Africans no end. Those with plans to escape could, of course, discard a disk as easily as they could forget a number. In this regard, Clara Urquhart had good intentions, and the Red Cross played a very important role regarding the POWs, but the plan to issue personalised disks to thousands of prisoners was as impractical as it was cumbersome.

Escape was often a matter of seizing an opportunity when it presented itself, and at Zonderwater it happened often. It is astounding that, with so many POWs breaking out of the camp, the authorities remained surprisingly lax at times.

Certainly, picnics outside the camp presented an obvious opportunity to escape, yet the Zonderwater authorities allowed POWs to go on such outings. Salvatore Mellilo took advantage of this when, according to him, he fell asleep during one such outing. He claimed he was confused when he woke up, that it was dark and that an approaching thunderstorm caused him to walk away from the camp.

When he was recaptured three days later, he was not at all embarrassed or upset, saying that he had wanted to 'enjoy a few days' liberty'.[21] At the inquiry, the guards all confirmed that a count was made when they arrived at the picnic spot and that another count was made when they returned. According to them, the 'in' and 'out' counts were correct; however, the next morning someone realised that Mellilo had not slept in his bed. Most guards claimed that it would have been almost impossible for anyone to escape from the line on the way back to Zonderwater as there were guards both in the front and at the back of the party. In this case, however, the report of 'all present' was made by the Italian Company Commander.[22]

The inquiry found that the escape was made possible by

a miss count [sic] ... too much reliance was placed on the Italian Company Commanders, but this is inavoidable in so far as the officer in charge was concerned, owing to the lack of UDF staff.[23]

It further concluded that 'POW Mellilo Salvatore had premediated (sic) his escape and the Picnic site lends itself to assisting anybody wanting to hide'.[24] Mellilo made his escape long after De Wet had been replaced by a new camp commander, which shows that the inability to prevent escapes was not solely to be blamed on him.

At the Kroonstad camp, where POWs were accommodated before going out on harvesting work, Aldo Cella escaped with ease in 1944, even though he was captured a month later and transferred back to Zonderwater. When the authorities investigated, they naturally asked about the security measures at Kroonstad. The camp commandant wrote to Beyers that

> it is well-known that this is an open camp and in the absence of sufficient UDF personnel to perform sentry duty around the camp day and night, it is possible for any POW to make his escape between the daily count from one morning to the next.[25]

This happened two years after the recommendation was made that roll call should take place twice a day, yet at Kroonstad it had not been put in place.

Opportunistic escapes were one thing, but in some cases overly sympathetic or ill-advised guards caused many headaches for the camp commanders. Some even helped POWs to realise their artistic ambitions, as was the case with Gregorio Fiasconaro. Gregorio started a theatre company in the Pietermaritzburg camp, but as his shows became increasingly popular, a UDF sergeant, who also enjoyed music, took him for auditions to perform in a show at a local Durban radio station. These outings were usually followed by a hearty lunch at the sergeant's home. It seems the sergeant was a talent scout of sorts, as Gregorio achieved fame after the war when he became professor and the first director of the University of Cape Town's Opera School.[26]

After two POWs escaped from a train at the Matroosberg station on their way back to Zonderwater from outside employment, the Worcester camp commandant wrote in his report that the two had managed to escape 'because of the reluctance of the sentries to fire on them. Their manner of escape requires further investigation'.[27] Perhaps the sentries did not know when they were allowed to shoot at escapees; perhaps they were scared or they were simply unsure whether it was an actual escape; but it could also have been that they were sympathetic towards the POWs' plight.

The civilian population could not always be trusted to adhere to the rules and regulations regarding the POWs. By the time it had become commonplace for the POWs to work on farms and road-building projects, the authorities knew that they would have to control civilians as much as the POWs. For this reason, War Measure 49 of 1942 was adopted. It stipulated that those on outside employment were allowed to leave their place of work only if they had a written permit from the employer; but evidently some employers ignored this regulation as they did not regard POWs moving among the public as a threat to security.[28]

However, not all POWs were fortunate enough to be placed with such open-minded employers. Many escaped from farms because they felt they were being treated unfairly. For them, returning to Zonderwater seemed like a better option. However, once there, they faced being consigned to a Fascist Block regardless of their political beliefs, since they would have been seen as unreliable workers.

Some POWs were so desperate to get away from hardline Fascists in the camp that they even ignored the risk that they could be shot should they try to escape. In 1943, three POWs escaped from Zonderwater because they wanted to avoid being sent to a block where they believed they would have to face Fascist POWs. When the first of the three was recaptured, he said that he 'couldn't worry' if the guard fired at him while he was running away. When asked why he had tried to escape, Eolo Rosati answered that he wanted to be recaptured so that he 'would have to face the Colonel', because he wanted to plead with him not to send him to Block 12 in the Zonderwater camp, which he thought was a Fascist Block. [29]

The second escapee, Guiseppi Mario Lizzio, also escaped because he was afraid of Block 12. Lizzio was sent back to Zonderwater from outside employment in George after contracting a venereal disease – in his words, due to 'a mistake I made'. He also declared that he was a 'sailor and have got nothing at all to do with the Fascists ... I most definitely do not want to go to that Block ... I want to work, not to loaf'.[30]

However, these three escapees were under a false impression. Block 12 was not a block for political prisoners and was opened solely for the purpose of housing POWs who had proved themselves unfit for outside employment 'owing to misbehaviour or misdemeanour, or gross breaches of discipline within different Blocks such as non-political agitators'.[31] In short, Block 12 was merely used to segregate so-called 'unreliable' prisoners from the others.[32] Rosati and Lizzio were now deemed unfit for outside work and would spend the rest of the war in Block 12.

By now, the perception of the 'docile' Italian must have started to lose credibility among the camp command. Furthermore, POWs could not always be believed when they gave statements during the courts of inquiry.

This is exemplified by the case of Mario Birbibo and Proietti Ferdinando, who escaped from Zonderwater in December 1943 by hiding in a lorry, after which they were given a lift by an 'unknown European'. Once they arrived in Pretoria, each went their own way. Birbibo was arrested in Johannesburg, where he seemed to wander around aimlessly. When questioned, he explained that

> I have been a prisoner of war for three years and two months. I have never heard from my relatives. My brain became so muddled that I could not think of the consequences if I am caught after escaping. It was an easy matter to escape from the Zonderwater camp. Anybody could get into a lorry and leave the camp with it when it goes out. The temptation could not be resisted.[33]

The problem was that, at the time, Birbibo was in jail because he had been arrested for theft, which meant the military authorities were unlikely to believe his story of being homesick.

When Ferdinando was recaptured, he declared that they had escaped by climbing through a hole in the camp fence, from where Ferdinando had tried to go to Pietermaritzburg because he 'wanted to purchase certain articles'.[34]

In October 1945, Birbibo escaped again from outside the Supreme Court, but he was recaptured a day later. In his statement, Transport Corporal Henning said Birbibo was being transferred from the Supreme Court to Zonderwater when the POW escaped from the transport van and mingled with the crowd at the station, causing the guard to lose sight of him.[35]

On *Kilfinan Farm* near Sandown in Johannesburg, a Mrs Forsyth-Thompson was in charge since her husband worked for the Department of Mines and was frequently away from home. She managed the 26 acres, where she farmed with poultry and other livestock with the help of a few Italian POWs. Arturo Pizzie escaped from the farm on 10 October 1943.[36] During the investigation, Forsyth-Thompson admitted to the police that she threatened her workers with a revolver, but this is where the similarities between her statement and Pizzie's statement ended.

In a letter to the Zonderwater camp authorities, Forsyth-Thompson expressed her belief that Pizzie had access to a large sum of money and that he received help from a certain 'Giglio' at Barclays Bank in town. In her view, Pizzie had been planning his escape for a long time. He managed to get hold of civilian clothes, which he wore when he escaped. According to her, Pizzie also told others that 'when important things have to be done, they must be done alone', implying that he was about to escape. She added that Fontana, another POW in her employ, was definitely not 'hiding anything' about the escape and she believed that Fontana was 'open and honest, and has confided a lot of his troubles in me'.[37]

Forsyth-Thompson did not mention anything about Pizzie's allegation that she 'made immoral suggestions' which were 'against my reputation', and which 'made things very difficult for me'.[38]

POWs were escaping for almost as many reasons as there were POWs, yet many chose to remain where they were, hoping for repatriation, which was the legal way to return home. In the Pietermaritzburg camp, for instance, Raffaello never saw escape as an option; for him, it was too big a risk:

The prospect of escape was basically non-existent. Where would we have gone and by what means? We were miles from home, in an unknown continent filled with dangers, real ones. Nobody, not even the most rebellious among us, could imagine escaping our English jailors. [To Raffaello's surprise] the enemy, who'd been portrayed as cruel and evil [revealed] not only a human side but also a welcoming and sensitive one ... the fact that our enemy treated us with such kindness made us reconsider everything we'd been taught and created serious confusion. It would have made anyone lose their mind![39]

So instead of finding ways to escape, Raffaello and his fellow prisoners focused on creating entertainment for themselves and in this way they made camp life more tolerable and interesting. Despite the occasional joyful event or interesting endeavour, Raffaello still hoped to return home sooner rather than later: 'What we were really all waiting for was repatriation. But the months went by and we were still in that unknown land in Africa'.[40]

It must have been at about this time, mid to late 1943, that Pietro Scottu began his journey towards South Africa. Following his daring but failed first attempt in 1941 to escape from a British convoy with a stolen Fiat truck, he was taken to Zeidab in Sudan, where he had endured 'the worst stay during his entire imprisonment'. It was in this camp where the POWs had to filter water through their clothes to make it more or less safe to drink. He was immensely relieved when they boarded a ship, as Sudan held memories of men dying from dysentery as they struggled towards the toilet areas. For many years after the war, Pietro remained mystified about the fact that he had never read anything about the circumstances in those Sudanese prison camps. 'How can one hide or ignore such events?' he asked.[41]

When he heard that he would be going to South Africa, he became hopeful. By this time the news of Zonderwater as a relatively well-maintained POW camp had reached prisoners further north in Africa. After a short stop in Mombasa, the journey south by ship continued, albeit accompanied by such violent windstorms that they caused the ship to 'roll and pitch [and] at dinner only two of us showed up! It really is true that in the worst times in life, funny things happen'.[42]

Colonial administrator Luigi Pederzoli, who was still stuck in Kenya, was surviving on zebra meat and mouldy biscuits. He kept his hopes up by writing optimistically to his wife, Barbara. He reminded her of the idyllic days they shared when she arrived in Africa; and if she had any doubts about her beauty, Luigi constantly reassured her. His letters focused on the future, on being free again and on making plans. He left out the terrible things he had to endure daily, since he did not want Barbara to worry about him. Luigi did not know if any of his letters found their way to Barbara, but perhaps he continued to write them because he knew that his words meant as much to him as they did to her. He was trying to protect Barbara from his reality, but he was also raising his own morale in doing so.[43]

6

PRINSLOO TO THE RESCUE

COLONEL HENDRIK PRINSLOO took control of Zonderwater on 13 January 1943. In the long run, most of the POWs would see the change of leadership at Zonderwater as a turning point, since that was when their prisoner experience began to improve. In the short term, however, there was a lot of work to be done.

If Prinsloo had had an inbox on his desk, the document on top would have been the report compiled in 1942 by Colonel Brett, the War Office POW liaison officer, after his inspection of Zonderwater camp. Reading like a 'to-do' list, the report highlighted everything that was wrong at Zonderwater; and if Prinsloo could not fix it, he and the Smuts government would have some explaining to do before the Geneva Convention. Fortunately, the report also recommended that more staff be appointed, so Prinsloo was able to delegate some tasks, unlike his predecessor, Colonel de Wet, who had had to carry the burden of the camp management almost entirely on his own. With a new administrative hierarchy in place, it was hoped that maintaining control over the POWs, and also over the staff, would become easier and that things would begin to improve at Zonderwater.

Prinsloo's philosophy was to 'combine discipline with kindness and under-standing'. He also knew that cultural differences and language barriers would be difficult to overcome and that is why he was willing to, as he said, 'take into account the peculiarities of the Italian character'.[1] Over time, Prinsloo's management style started to inspire both his officers and the Italians. For those veterans who lived to see old age, Prinsloo remained a hero.

After the war, Captain JA Ball, one of the welfare officers at Zonder-water, described Prinsloo's work as that of a 'genius ... in the field of human relations'.[2] Prinsloo's achievements were also acknowledged offi-cially after the war and he, along with Ball and two other officers, received the Order of the Star of Italy from the Italian government. Later, the Pope

Colonel HF Prinsloo, Zonderwater camp commander, 1943–1947
(Photo courtesy NMMH)

Captain John Ball (seated) and his brother Kenneth while on service in Cairo
(Photo courtesy Zonderwater Block Association)

bestowed on Prinsloo the Order of Good Merit.[3]

In 1943, however, Prinsloo was not thinking of any rewards: he had a major mess to clean up and it demanded his undivided attention. Unlike Smuts, Prinsloo was not motivated by outside factors to do his work, but by a real concern for the well-being of the prisoners. Smuts was more concerned about how any negative news about the POWs and their treatment would affect the country's standing in the eyes of the British Empire and whether it could cause Churchill to think the Union was less loyal to the Empire than its other Dominions.

Despite the difficulties Prinsloo faced, he knew that by focusing on the job at hand he would somehow improve conditions; if ultimately it did not turn out well, at least it would offer him hope for the present. Prinsloo's motivation could be ascribed to his personal experience, because he was all too familiar with the hardships of war and the sacrifices it demanded. In the First World War, he had fought in the German South-West African Campaign, but it was the South African War at the turn of the century that really prepared him for his task at Zonderwater.[4]

When he entered Zonderwater, the scene of the rows upon rows of tents would have looked familiar to him. Like many boys who were far too young for war, Prinsloo joined his father on commando to fight against the British forces. During a skirmish with the enemy, the young Prinsloo was taken prisoner because he was carrying arms. Because he was only 12 years old, the British decided not to send him to one of the overseas POW camps, but to let him stay with his mother in the concentration camp at Barberton.[5]

However, this was not an act of kindness, as most of the concentration camps were places where only the strong survived. The Prinsloo family were relatively fortunate, because the superintendent of the Barberton camp, one B Graumann, managed the camp with great efficiency: the tents were lined up in rows and rations were handed out swiftly according to a pigeonhole system devised by the superintendent. Wooden flooring, an unheard-of luxury in other camps, was laid out in most tents. Consequently, the death rate at Barberton was much lower than that at most other camps, where measles, typhus, typhoid, diphtheria and other diseases claimed lives.[6] As if these diseases were not enough, in many camps there was too little food and many inmates simply withered away.[7]

At Barberton, the conditions were better, fewer people died, the camp was kept cleaner and somehow more food was available. Children under 12 were given fresh milk and frozen meat was available to all the inhabitants. Graumann even arranged for a bakery to be set up; a school for the children was established; and employment was arranged for the older men in the camp. Some families were even allowed to live outside the camp.

Apparently, when the war ended, the captives left, most of them grateful for the kindness they had experienced. Prinsloo, however, left the camp angry and with a desire for revenge. Although he had survived the concentration camp, his father did not live to see the end of the war: On 7 November 1900, the Carolina Commando was led into an ambush at Witkloof and as his father dismounted from his horse he was shot and killed.[8]

Over time, however, Prinsloo underwent a change of heart. Perhaps he realised that remaining angry would only lead to more conflict. After all, the past could not be changed, but the future could still be shaped. He started to believe that 'honourable peace' carried more weight than war. For him, the leadership of Smuts and Louis Botha was a great example. They had both fought against the British in the South African War, but in 1914 they supported the British Empire during the First World War.

In 1947, on his way back to South Africa from the Geneva POW conference, Prinsloo addressed the 10th Battalion Middlesex Regiment in London. Summarising what he had gained from his war experience, he explained his viewpoint and how he had come

> to grips with [the] reality on the ruins of our wars, realising that only on the foundations of good fellowship, through mutual respect for one another's sentiments, was it possible to form our British Commonwealth of Nations within the broad framework of which we have learned to co-operate, to think and feel alike and to act and sacrifice for the common good of the whole which, in view of the present world conditions, is indeed a fine example for suffering humanity struggling in their ruins towards peace with security to follow [unless we] make way for a new life of unselfish co-operation in a system of sympathy and sacrifice for humanity as a whole – mankind will fail again.[9]

Back in 1943, however, the Geneva Convention followed Prinsloo like a shadow. He had barely found his feet when Brett's inspection was followed by another Red Cross inspection in March of that year. Article 10 of the Convention required that

> Prisoners of war shall be lodged in buildings or huts which afford all possible safeguards as regards hygiene and salubrity. The premises must be entirely free from damp, and adequately heated and lighted.[10]

In 1943, Giovanni and his friends still referred to Zonderwater as *tendopoli* (tent city), while other, less philosophical POWs referred to Zonderwater as *la citta' senza donna* (the city without women).[11] Whatever it was called, the camp was not presentable and things did not look good for Prinsloo or his new staff members.

To begin with, the commandant made a few changes to the standing orders, but these related mostly to security measures, not the living conditions. Furthermore, had the Red Cross inspectors arrived a few weeks later, their report would have been even more damning: heavy rains left the POWs sleeping on muddy ground under leaking tents. As a result, morale declined among both POWs and staff.[12] The accommodation for POWs remained a sticking point throughout 1943 and in December of that year a report noted that most huts were yet to be built and that, of those completed, many were still without beds, windows or roofs.[13]

Prinsloo had the benefit of more staff: by the end of his first year in command, he had 177 officers, 28 warrant officers and 3 401 other ranks to depend upon.[14] In particular, the so-called welfare officers would make a significant difference in the camp. One of the new officers was Captain JA Ball, who had served in the Intelligence Corps in East Africa. He shared Prinsloo's approach regarding the treatment of POWs, his greatest concern being the low morale among them. When caught up in a downward spiral of depressed spirits, servicemen and prisoners alike were likely to become difficult to motivate and manage. In other words, there would be no discipline and things would descend into chaos.

In the case of the UDF soldiers, the dangers of low morale were quickly

Building work in progress at Zonderwater (Photo courtesy www.zonderwater.com/it)

identified during the first campaign in East Africa. To break its negative effects, different forms of propaganda were used. For example, 'selective censorship' of correspondence was one way to control bad news and it was soon discovered that 'a number of men … may be regarded as disaffected, mainly amongst the Afrikaans section of the SA Forces, and the reason for the disaffection is almost entirely attributed to boredom'.[15] As most soldiers know, war entails a lot of waiting around with a few bursts of action in between.

The most popular way to combat boredom was to provide the men with entertainment, including mobile cinemas and a newspaper aimed at the troops.[16] To assist them with their propaganda efforts among the troops, the UDF enlisted the help of Henry Sonnabend, Professor of Sociology at the University of the Witwatersrand. Sonnabend was regarded as an 'expert propagandist' and along with Advocate G Saron, he took on the task of improving troop morale.[17] Sonnabend was also involved in the work of the Union Unity Fund, which worked alongside the Union Unity Truth Service. Their aim was to promote the ideals of the Smuts government and its participation in the war, and to offer alternative views to the Nazi and Afrikaner Nationalist propaganda that was threatening the security in the country. Saron also focused on a propaganda education

Laundry day at Zonderwater (Photo courtesy www.zonderwater.com/it)

programme, lecturing on Nazism and fifth column activities. The goal was not only to lift morale but also to limit subversive elements among the troops so that they could be dealt with before their negativity spread among the other comrades.[18]

Because so many POWs sat around idle in the camp, exactly the same propaganda methods were used on them. Discipline and security were among the two most important issues to be dealt with by a propaganda campaign among the captives. Prinsloo had to find a way to convince the POWs that they liked the camp and that they actually wanted to stay there until the end of the war. He reckoned that if the prisoners had nothing to complain about, they would not feel the need to escape. In turn, the camp guards would have a lighter load when maintaining discipline and security would not be such a perilous issue.

Any improvements would obviously cost a lot of money and during the war money was, of course, a scarce commodity. Yet Prinsloo had a solution to this problem. The canteen at Zonderwater generated a profit and this money was used in the camp for projects of all kinds. By the end of July 1944, more than a year after Prinsloo had taken over at Zonderwater, the 'welfare fund' showed a credit of £21,691.13.1, of which £18,150.7.1 was used for projects that improved the living conditions in the camp.

Prinsloo's welfare ambitions seemed endless – he had even planned on sending money to the POWs' relatives in Italy. He was very disappointed that the canteen did not generate enough money for this scheme, although it was probably a blessing in disguise because at that stage Italy was still an enemy state and it would not have made Prinsloo very popular among Smuts supporters if they had heard about the scheme.[19] In addition, the Geneva Convention stipulated that all profits from a camp canteen had to go towards the improvement of living conditions for POWs, so, in line with that stipulation, at Zonderwater most of the money went towards building or fixing barracks. Some money was also kept aside for Christmas celebrations and to improve conditions in the outside employment camps.

Despite the profitable endeavours at Zonderwater, money alone could not fix all the ills, so Sonnabend was brought in to do the less obvious welfare work required in the camp. It seemed that he was the right man for the job, because he saw himself as

> an unrepentant optimist. Neither age nor experience has dispelled my belief in the unmined treasures of human nature. I have had many disappointments and I have buried many illusions, but I still believe that man *can* be good and reasonable, life beautiful and society just.[20]

When he agreed to help, a relieved Prinsloo gave him the title of Director of Welfare, probably because 'Principal Propagandist' would have sounded somewhat suspect. Some have described Sonnabend's work at Zonderwater as 'cultural–educational experiments', while Sonnabend himself has been described as a specialist in 'psychological warfare'.[21] Nevertheless, his 'experiments' resulted in significant benefits for the POWs, including a literacy project, theatre productions and other forms of entertainment and education.

In his memoirs, Sonnabend described his work among the POWs as essential because, according to him:

> Barbed wire psychosis infected many of the 70 000 men of
> Zonderwater ... After a few months the prisoner hates his captors,
> his guards, his comrades and the whole world that seems to have
> conspired to keep him behind barbed wire. His constant irritation
> creates a state of morbid pride.[22]

Sonnabend worked at the camp for three years, during which time he tried
to make the POWs' time in this country more meaningful, while at the
same time making it easier for the camp command to maintain discipline
and control. Not all of the camp staff agreed with his methods, though.
Some viewed him as being too lenient and thought that his lenience
would lead to ill-discipline and more escapes among POWs. However,
Sonnabend's idea was to 'foster self-help and promote self-confidence'.[23]
He believed in what he was doing and he

> assured my opponents that South Africa would one day take pride
> in what happened at Zonderwater. In the course of one year, welfare
> activities had grown from a delicate sapling into a widely spreading
> tree deeply rooted in the life of the camp'.[24]

His methods have indeed stood the test of time and, many years later, the
legacy of Zonderwater remains devoid of any criticism in the public memory.

Since there was so much to do at Zonderwater, Prinsloo did not have the
time to see to the many complaints he received from farmers and other
outside employers who were unhappy with the Italians who worked for
them. He tried to solve this problem by placing greater responsibility on
the shoulders of the outside employers. In theory, this meant that every
single letter of complaint would not land on his desk but would instead
be resolved between the employer and the POW.

By the first half of 1943, about 4 000 POWs were working on farms
across the country, with the demand for Italian labourers increasing
almost daily. According to a UDF report, in '90% of cases both farmers
and POW [were] satisfied'[25] with the arrangements, but, of course,
there were exceptions. Prinsloo made it clear that employers, especially

farmers, could not hold the military authorities responsible if the POWs were found to be unsuitable for specific work.[26] In some cases, farmers asked for prisoners with specific skills but were saddled with men who knew nothing about the work they were supposed to be able to do. Not all the Italians knew about farming methods and many farmers had to train the POWs or send them back to Zonderwater, taking the risk of irritating the military authorities to the point where they refused to send them more workers.

At least Prinsloo was now free to focus on urgent matters at Zonderwater, but it was not long before the newspapers began to pick up on stories about dissatisfied farmers. Even worse, the press played on the fears of many civilians and published articles about how dangerous the POWs could be if they abandoned their work and roamed free because they did not get along with their employers. In the same month that Prinsloo took over from De Wet, for instance, the *Rand Daily Mail* reported on POW workers in the Stellenbosch district, warning that

> Many farmers in the fruit-growing areas of the Western Cape are perturbed ... They declare that the lack of proper control over the movements of prisoners is endangering the security of the State as prisoners are spreading subversive Fascist propaganda among the coloured population. [Farmers] added, however, that the [agricultural employment] scheme found favour among poor white and *Ossewa Brandwag* farming communities and among those Nationalist farmers who sympathised with the Axis.[27]

A few days later, the government responded to counter the criticism in the press of their use of POWs as a labour force. A follow-up article in the *Rand Daily Mail* made it clear that POWs were not criminals but soldiers who had 'temporarily lost their freedom'. At that time there were many South African soldiers being held captive in Italy and the article pointed out that the South Africans were also enjoying 'some freedom in Italy', just as the Italian POWs were in South Africa.[28]

The farmers were blamed for the lack of control over POWs and the article pointed out that the military authorities were perturbed by the farmers' inability to exercise power over their workers. Farmers were, according to the article, responsible for the POWs and if the POWs wanted to leave their farm for some reason, the farmer was supposed to accompany them. In contrast, the Nationalist Party Chief Whip, Paul Sauer, also seized the opportunity to defend farmers who supported the nationalists and the *Ossewabrandwag*. The article stated that

> Mr Sauer refuted the suggestion that certain farmers with pro-Axis or anti-war sympathies were employing Italian prisoners of war for the purpose of giving them back their liberty. Mr Sauer said that farmers to-day were suffering from a shortage of native labour as a result of the war, and added that even the most philosophic minded anti-war sympathizer was not likely to waste good money and labour to afford Italian prisoners a little extra liberty.[29]

With this, Prinsloo now had the reassurance from the anti-war faction that they would not misuse POW labourers and he could leave them, for the most part, to control the prisoners in their employ. In the end, therefore, things came down to trust and pride, especially for the nationalists, as Sauer had made a promise in the press on their behalf. So, just as De Wet had to rely on Italian company commanders and *carabinieri* to help with discipline and security, Prinsloo now relied on farmers and other employers to take responsibility for the POWs in their care.

But the difficulties at Zonderwater and the way the authorities in London controlled the use of POWs clearly annoyed the UDF brass hats, even if they remained tactfully diplomatic. London often insisted, at short notice, that South Africa take in more POWs, only to demand a few months later that they send back a few thousand POWs to Britain to work.

While Smuts wanted POWs for labour projects in the Union, it seemed that neither he nor his imperial masters fully understood the difficulty involved in arranging suitable accommodation for a continuous inflow of POWs. Early in 1943, Smuts at last confronted the British, but it was unclear how successful he was in bringing about a change. In April of that year, the British High Commissioner at least apologised to Smuts for any misunderstanding about the previous arrangements for the probable reduction of the number of prisoners held in the Union, since they, for their part, had attempted to give the Union authorities the longest possible notice.[30]

In the same letter, the commissioner thanked Smuts for his willingness to take in 2 000 German POWs even though Smuts had made it clear from the start that he was not willing to take in any.[31] One reason was that if news about the German POWs had leaked out, the *Ossewabrandwag* or any of the other anti-war groups could have used the situation to cause a stir, or possibly even foment an uprising, among the many pro-German and anti-Smuts South Africans. Although this group of Germans was 'in transit', most probably to Canada or the United States, it was still a great risk for Smuts to take them in, but he had little choice. When the Germans arrived, there were also 1 650 'French Coloured' internees with them, but the plan was to have these men interned on Madagascar.[32]

Four months later, Smuts decided against accepting any more German POWs. His telegram to the High Commissioner in London stated that

> due to internal political considerations [South Africa] will not, repeat not, be able to accept German prisoners of war. [We] will be happy, however, to accommodate Italian prisoners of war up to overall figure of 100 000 as already indicated.[33]

Could it be that the British authorities were trying to manipulate Smuts? In justifying his refusal not to take any further German prisoners, though, Smuts agreed to accept many more Italians than could be accommodated in the Union.

While Smuts and his British counterparts negotiated numbers, Prinsloo was left to deal with the day-to-day challenges of commanding a large POW camp. He took over from De Wet when the relations among staff were at their worst following the Christmas riots of 1942. However, Prinsloo was undeterred and he continued to work towards improving conditions at Zonderwater for both the POWs and the staff.

7

WELL-BEING THROUGH ART,
MUSIC AND EDUCATION

FOR THE POWs at Zonderwater camp, improving their immediate needs remained their greatest concern. By 1943, Paolo Ricci, who was captured when Tobruk fell early in 1941, had been a prisoner at Zonderwater for more than two years. He had also not yet gone on outside employment because at that stage he was not ready to sign the declaration of cooperation. This meant that he was at the camp to witness all the changes brought about by Colonel Prinsloo.

The changes were profound, and many years after the war Paolo described Prinsloo as the 'POW redeemer'. He specifically remembered how they had each received 'clothing comprising ... two suits, two shirts, and all the toiletries necessary for hygienic purposes. Thereafter he had showers, kitchens and hospitals built. In short, all the amenities necessary for a normal life'.[1]

Although Prinsloo's improvements made a great impression on Paolo, he and others had managed to improve their situation even before Prinsloo was appointed camp commandant. As the POWs began to settle into camp life, makeshift theatres popped up in most blocks. Operas, tragedies and comedies were performed, all of which were arranged and managed by the POWs themselves. A total of 21 theatres were established in Zonderwater, with an estimated 1 000 participants.

Paolo was pragmatic. He knew that becoming involved in theatrical productions would make for a better experience, regardless of who the camp commander was. In his view:

> There was something of everything; singers, actors, musicians, and slowly, but surely, the camp evolved into a little city. I was among the most fortunate, and since I was a tailor, they gave me a job in

the theatre. My job was to create women's costumes for the actors. They gave me a tent all to myself, with a sewing machine, a table, and all the materials necessary to work.[2]

His friend, a carpenter, built a bed for Paolo, and from then on he never slept on the ground again.[3]

Creative arts was also an important pastime for those in the Pietermaritzburg camp. And when they decided to establish a theatre, Raffaello remembered that 'a feverish search for screenplays, costumes and scenic designs thus began. The art lab worked like a gem and those who could sew, cut, paint and draw did their best'.[4] Everyone became involved, even those 'without particular talents'. For Raffaello, who was fast becoming an accomplished chef in the Pietermaritzburg camp kitchen, the project 'made us feel useful as men and not the useless remnants of war that many thought themselves to be'.[5]

Later, as prisoners started to benefit from Prinsloo's work to improve the conditions at Zonderwater, it became easier to create elaborate stage decorations. Props became more realistic and less imaginary. Once in their costumes, the actors and 'actresses' had their stage make-up done and had wigs fitted before performing in productions such as *Cin-Ci-La*, *La Cena Delle Beffe* and *il Cardinale*. On occasion, the theatre attracted large audiences, including the Zonderwater staff. The prisoners in Block 1 were particularly ambitious and invited Smuts to their performance of *Cyrano de Bergerac*. (It is not known whether Smuts attended the show.)[6]

Another pastime that required no encouragement from the camp authorities was different kinds of musical performance, but especially singing. During the difficult early days of the camp, men simply sang to each other as their voices could reach across the fences that separated the different prison blocks. Music reminded the POWs that they were more than prisoners: they were Italian.

The sense of pride in who they were motivated many to create a pleasing living environment, transforming the camp into a city of sorts. The camp command encouraged this trend because it helped them in their efforts to establish better order among the POWs. As time went on, audiences grew to include UDF staff, many of whom were to hear Italian ballads for the

The Teatro Roma at Zonderwater. A guard tower is visible in the background
(Photo courtesy www.zonderwater.com/it)

Hair and make-up were important to render all the characters believable in this
theatrical production (Photo courtesy NMMH)

A dramatic scene from an opera (Photo courtesy NMMH)

Two prisoners performing in one of the many camp theatres
(Photo courtesy NMMH)

first time. Soon, singing schools sprang up, each with its own instructors.

The prisoners at Pietermaritzburg also sang to entertain each other to relieve their boredom and depression. While Pietermaritzburg was still a transit camp, new choir or orchestra members arrived at regular intervals. Raffaello remembered

> A musical band had also been formed, and it slowly grew in numbers as fresh prisoners transited through the camp. There was even a violinist from the Eiar orchestra [*Orchestra Sinfonica dell'Eiar*] at one point, a true professional that gave the band new life. There were many opportunities to perform. There were plays and concerts that we took on with an effort as big as our desire to confirm our dignity and that of the country we'd come from.[7]

Raffaello took great pleasure in scouring the local newspapers for reviews of the camp orchestra's performances. He recalled one occasion when a newspaper commented on the orchestra's performance at the town's theatre. Apparently, it was a 'splendid programme' that the citizens of Pietermaritzburg had 'rarely' experienced in their city hall.

Later, as musical instruments became more easily available, orchestras and bands became common. Soon music presented new opportunities for the prisoners. At Zonderwater, it seems, the art of music-making became contagious and UDF staff also wanted to become involved in this creative outlet. Inspired by the prisoners' musical skills, the staff started also to explore ways of expanding their musical horizons. The prisoners were quick to take advantage of this – making musical instruments and selling them to guards became a lucrative pastime. Taking advantage of their guards' lack of musical knowledge, the Italians convinced them that their hand-made instruments, especially violins, were the products of master craftsmen. Of course, this was not the case, and one POW described his improvised violin as sounding 'like a cat in love'.[8]

The wood for the instruments came from any number of benches, chairs or beds, while the strings came from animals that had the misfortune to be in the vicinity of the camp. As late as January 1946, a senior administrative officer wrote furiously that

The audience at a special theatrical performance at Zonderwater. Colonel Prinsloo is seated in the front row (Photo courtesy NMMH)

reports have been received that tails of UDF mules and horses grazing in the Prohibited Area have been deprived of their hair. It is thought that this hair may be used for the manufacture of violin bows, shaving brushes, etc. Disciplinary action will be taken in respect of any POW found interfering with Government animals, and continuance of this nuisance of which complaint is made will result in a curtailment of the privilege [of the extended freedom scheme] presently enjoyed by POWs.[9]

Music certainly helped the Italians cope with camp life, but the excitement surrounding their music-making also seemed to make some of them forget that they were prisoners. At the Pietermaritzburg camp, one orchestra had big dreams, but not the necessary instruments. They needed 'six violins, three saxophones, two clarinets, one flute and one double bass in E Flat'. To solve this problem, the bandmaster, one Amorelli, wrote to a friend at Zonderwater, instructing him to gather the required musicians and join them on a tour of the country. Amorelli made it clear that it was not only the POWs who would benefit from the music, but that the orchestra evoked real enthusiasm amongst the English officers, our officers, and the men, in the Blocks who have spontaneously in the last few days subscribed to the sum of £30 for the orchestra to improve our fare during this period of preparation [for the tour]. I have already been interviewed by the musical critic of the [Rand] 'Daily Mail' in connection with my concert tour of the larger centres and the music we will play, which will be almost entirely Italian … you and your work as a flute player would be precious help to me, but you will understand that no superior Command would be inclined to deprive a group of officers of the pleasure to enjoy the performance of a good violinist of your worth … Insist – and Resist.[10]

But Amorelli had overestimated the good-naturedness of the camp command. When his letter was intercepted by the censors, his plans were firmly rejected.[11] Raising morale was one thing, but the idea of a POW orchestra touring the country crossed the line. In contrast, when the Italians chose to use their musical talents for religious purposes, the military authorities felt more at ease. Each block at Zonderwater was viewed as a Roman Catholic parish, each with its own choir.[12] Just as with the operettas and the mobile cinemas, the choirs 'toured' the Zonderwater Blocks, sharing their music with the rest of the POW population.[13]

It seems as if the beginning of 1943 was a time of improvement at most POW camps, and in Block 4 at Pietermaritzburg, the prisoners, according to Raffaello, initiated the building of a church. Father Conte was the 'main catalyst' for the project and he had the support of two UDF majors at the camp. As the work on the church began, the skill of two stone cutters, Bruno and Spano, made an enormous impression on Raffaello, who also remembered that the building team was never

short of labour. From a quarry nearby the camp heavy rocks were transported to the chosen site by means of a simple cart. There were so many hands pulling, lifting, breaking and mounting, but it was a huge job nonetheless. Father Conte never failed to incite us, reminding everyone that the endeavour we put in would not go to waste. The building of the church took up a year of our life as

The garden at the camp hospital (Photo courtesy ICRC)

prisoners of war, but in the end, when we saw it finished, beautiful and white against the blue African sky, we felt an indescribable pride. The apostolic delegate, Archbishop van Gijlswijk came to inaugurate it with a solemn mass.[14]

Although Raffaello did not actually participate in the building work, he was proud to say that he had brought food to the builders. He firmly believed that the '500 portions of tagliatelle [which] took quite a bit of time and effort' served as comfort food for the workers and, like them, Raffaello 'could take pride in the progress of the construction'.[15]

Idle POWs were put to work in other ways too. By the end of 1944, the 30 morgen (25.7 hectares) camp garden yielded 145 711 pounds (66 093 kilogrammes) of vegetables, some of which were sold to the public, bringing in £992. This improved the menus, and camp diets now included gem squash, turnips, beans, carrots, spinach, beet, tomatoes, green mealies, wheat and rye. About three tons of self-made compost was used daily. The agricultural section of the camp also produced 32 beehives (with swarms) in 1944, along with 160 baskets and 350 brooms. This work was carried out by 208 POWs with 13 UDF staff supervising the projects.[16]

Besides these accomplishments, it was the creative works that left visible evidence of the POWs' presence in the country. Paintings, wooden toys and sculpting occupied the hours of those who needed a break from political talk or those who were true artists and managed somehow to live out their creativity in Zonderwater. Many items were offered to the public at exhibitions organised by the welfare section. Even Giovanni, usually bitterly opposed to anything organised by his captors, recalled an exhibition of POW arts and crafts that left 'all visitors speechless, both civilian and prisoners'.[17]

On the many farms across the country where they worked, artistic POWs also left behind reminders of themselves, from small wooden carvings to larger sculptures. One such artwork was crafted by Edoardo Villa, who was to achieve national and world fame as a sculptor: it depicted the young sons of Captain Ball. Villa, who was born in a village on the outskirts of Bergamo and attended the Andrea Fantoni Art School, was wounded in North Africa during the war and spent some time in an Egyptian hospital.[18] He was shipped to South Africa in 1942, and once he arrived at Zonderwater he was able to reconnect with his interrupted sculptural vocation.[19]

In his memoir, Hi Berman, the South African officer assigned to ensure the smooth functioning of the art schools and theatrical workshops at Zonderwater, offered the following sketch of the prisoner whom he called 'Maestro':

> Edoardo at that time was sculpting a plaster of Paris and in the mode of the great French sculptor, Auguste Rodin. As a consequence, all that he wanted was plaster – and more plaster – and any illustrations of Rodin's work that I could find. One of the highlights of a visit to the studio was to find Edoardo closely examining a head that he was modelling. Suddenly, with one swoop, he completely destroyed the head and then in his customary loud voice shouted, *'Abiamo facciamo uno fok-op!'* – translated as: 'I have made a f**k-up! – and started all over again!'[20]

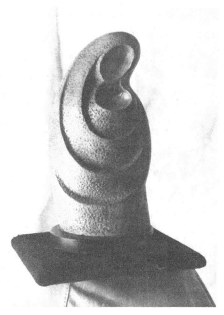

An example of the inmates' artistic expression (Photo courtesy NMMH)

A sculpture by Edoardo Villa depicting Captain Ball's three young sons
(Photo courtesy Zonderwater Block Association)

Among Villa's many works is a bronze statue of Prinsloo, which can now be seen at the Zonderwater Museum.

By all accounts, he also developed a friendship with Sonnabend, the two of them often discussing the meaning of Italy's and Villa's sacrifice in view of Italy's many defeats on the battlefield. Sonnabend admired Villa, saying that

> it was not difficult to detect in the *via dolorosa* of this prisoner of war a growing opposition to detail, a determined drive towards extreme simplification of volume and shape contours. This simplification was not an aim in itself, but a means of coming nearer to ultimate truth, the mystery of life and death, the real meaning of things that matter. By disregarding the ornamental, the superfluous, the prisoner-of-war artist strove to lay bare the essence of reality.[21]

In Pietermaritzburg, the creative and handcraft skills of the prisoners also became well-known among the civilian population. Raffaello recalled that there were

> various laboratories [in the camp]; a goldsmith used silver coins confiscated from the prisoners to create some simple but exquisite crafts. Aluminium from large propellers was used to make necklaces and cigar lighters.[22]

According to Raffaello, a shop in the town centre exhibited all of the POWs' creations. Furthermore:

> In the carpenter's shop they made a piece of furniture for an officer who was so impressed that within a few days much more complex machinery and good quality wood were brought in. So it was that furniture started being made not only for officers but also for civilians. Our hunger for workmanship had spread to the city. This fact made us more proud of ourselves than we usually were, also because the enthusiasm we had when the war started had progressively waned, and many of us suffered from various forms of depression.[23]

A bust of the Duke d'Aosta at the school named after him (Photo courtesy ICRC)

Prisoners attending a class on Mechanical Engineering at the Duke d'Aosta school at Zonderwater (Photo courtesy NMMH)

The HF Prinsloo Vocational Centre at Zonderwater (Photo courtesy NMMH)

Bookbinding at the HF Prinsloo Vocational Centre (Photo courtesy NMMH)

When reflecting on their situation, Raffaello viewed the arts and crafts as an essential aspect of camp life. He often saw how idle men found it difficult to cope with their captivity, while those who participated in entertainment developed their skills or those who worked, as he did, in the kitchen, were able to adapt to the difficulties that came their way. By keeping busy, they could endure the 'distance, suffering and disappointment' of captivity.[24]

In 1944, a third exhibition took place at Zonderwater and with the previous two exhibitions having been so successful, an exhibition hall was added to the growing POW city. In 1944, all the articles that were exhibited – a total of 227 – were sold, bringing in £3,264.15.6 for the benefit of the camp.[25] Among many other objects, Giovanni recalled that he saw a handmade train and a submarine, both constructed from jam jars, a violin made of matches, many statues and a painting entitled *The prisoner's prayer*, which won first prize.[26] In December, civilians attended a special exhibition of articles that were later sent to a POW arts and crafts exhibition in Geneva.[27] Regardless of the sense of pride among POWs and staff, those who attended were strictly controlled to avoid any mishaps that could possibly lead to unwanted socialising between prisoners and civilians.[28]

Other entertainments included a circus in Block 5, attended by an estimated 20 000 men; public lectures; and a literary competition in which 100 men participated. As the number of POWs started to decline in 1944, at least one orchestra was disbanded, leaving the camp with only one band of 60 players and their instruments and four orchestras of about 17 men each.

The improvements to Zonderwater were not only for the benefit of the POWs, though. They were also roped in to erect floodlights around the perimeter of the camp in the hope of improving security measures. A sewerage system and a number of chapels to serve the large Catholic POW community were further new additions to the camp.

For prisoners without skills, the HF Prinsloo Vocational Centre provided educational programmes, while the Duke d'Aosta School focused on literacy. An estimated 9 000 men learned to read and write while they were in captivity.[29] The Zonderwater command believed that the vast school system represented a great experiment in adult mass education. Men of 20, 30 and 40 years of age attend to their studies driven by no compulsion but by a deep desire to learn … There are a great amount of specialised courses and many hundreds flock to the classes in English.[30]

Many POWs preferred the outdoors and so sporting events attracted large crowds. The men participated in athletics, boxing, fencing and all manner of physical activities. More often than not, camp staff also attended; and in an effort to build positive relationships and camaraderie with the prisoners, Prinsloo and other high-ranking camp officers often handed out prizes.

Occupied minds and bodies helped the authorities maintain order, yet if the living conditions remained inadequate, discontent was likely to lead to trouble. By the end of 1943, a report on the progress of building work at Zonderwater indicated that a number of huts were yet to be built and that, of those completed, a number were still without beds.[31] Prinsloo had to get the camp into a better condition, not only for the sake of the POWs, but also for the reputation of the country.

However, building materials and labour were not readily available, so it made perfect sense, from the camp command's point of view, to use POWs for building work in the camp. The men could build their own brick accommodation and, in the process, gain useful artisanal skills that they could take back to Italy.

However, when word got out that POWs were 'employed' in construction jobs, the locals demanded an explanation. They believed Italian POWs were stealing jobs that were rightfully reserved for South Africans. In particular, the South African Trade and Labour Council expressed the view that it did not like the idea of POW labour and questioned the wisdom behind this strategy. Unemployed Union citizens, some of whom also had the option to volunteer for the UDF, were not the only concern, though.

The Labour Council was concerned that the construction industry would come under pressure as the Zonderwater project required a substantial number of bricks – according to them, between 120 000 and 150 000 per day.[32] The building work at Zonderwater also meant that many tools were being used by POWs, creating a scarcity among private construction projects. In essence, the Council believed that the hut-building project

Boxing was popular among POWs and useful to vent frustrations
(Photo courtesy NMMH)

Colonel Prinsloo (right) declares the winner of a boxing match
(Photo courtesy NMMH)

Zonderwater was the only POW camp at which the prisoners could participate in fencing (Photo courtesy NMMH)

Athletes and spectators often enjoyed large sporting events (Photo courtesy NMMH)

was causing the private building industry to stagnate, leaving Union tradesmen workless and without building materials.[33]

When the issue was raised in Parliament, the Minister of Defence made the point that POWs were being used to build their own accommodation blocks and 'for security reasons, civilian labour from outside the camp could not be utilised'.[34] The minister emphasised that local artisans did not have to fear unemployment, as it was government policy that Italian POW artisans would not be used where local artisans were available. Obviously, this was the case only as long as the building work was not in a POW camp.[35]

The befuddlement of the civilian population continued, however. But by February 1944, they had had enough. Local contractors could not continue with projects because there was a shortage of bricks – building materials were being diverted to Zonderwater for the work there. In addition, the use of Italian labour at Zonderwater left local artisans without work. Not only did the Italians do all the work themselves, but they did it at a fraction of the cost. It was no surprise, therefore, that 'the feelings of trade union officials, members, and unemployed men are naturally bitter'.[36] A month later, it was reported that many POWs were employed as building artisans in Pretoria, outside of Zonderwater. It is not known whether the employers searched among South African artisans first before employing the Italians, but the official policy on POW labour was they were to be used by private citizens only in agricultural work.[37]

The relationship between POWs, civilians and UDF authorities remained complicated and delicately balanced throughout the war. But there were no easy solutions because, again, there were as many viewpoints as there were individuals: while some civilians welcomed the POWs for their labour, others welcomed them for political reasons. Many white South Africans saw the Italians as belonging to the white race and did not approve of their being used to perform manual labour, work which at that time was reserved for black South Africans. And at a time when interracial relationships were against the law in the Union, many whites found it very difficult to digest the idea of POWs mixing with local women of colour when such relationships came to light.

It is not known whether Prinsloo was aware of all of these complex political and philosophical matters, but if he was, he would have had little time to think about them. This was because more pressing matters required his attention – not least keeping order among the tens of thousands of POWs at Zonderwater.

Another important matter that had to be attended to was the physical health of the POWs. For this reason, a far less pleasant – at least to the POWs – project was implemented. A rigorous campaign of inoculations and vaccinations, especially against smallpox and typhoid, was started. The chief medical officer, Lieutenant Colonel Blumberg, was very proud of his regime of 'scrupulous cleanliness' in the 1 600-bed hospital and the disinfestation stations that were capable of delousing 1 000 prisoners each day. The high standard of medical treatment and the good diet made the Zonderwater hospital, in Blumberg's modest opinion, 'the best POW hospital in the British Empire'.[38] Another motivation for the prevention of infectious diseases was the proximity of the UDF training camp to the POW camp and the fact that many POWs came into contact with civilians when they were on outside employment. Nobody wanted to get infected by POWs who carried diseases, so the POWs had to be kept clean and healthy.

Hygiene at all the POW camps was of great importance, but especially at Pietermaritzburg and Zonderwater, where new POWs continued to arrive until almost the dying months of the war.

Luigi Pederzoli was one of the last POWs to arrive at Zonderwater, having spent months in the terrible camps of East Africa. Although the conditions were deplorable, nothing could persuade Luigi to sign the declaration of cooperation that would allow him to go work on a project outside the camp.

Luigi was still in Kenya when he decided against becoming a cooperator, but his decision was not without consequences. He wrote to his wife, Barbara, about the harassment, abuse and humiliation those like him suffered at the hands of fellow Italians who had signed the declaration. He was adamant that he would not fight against his 'brothers', which was how he interpreted cooperation with the British. However, he was also careful not to cause concern in his wife, writing that she did not have to worry or think ill of him, as he had not lost his temper or his head.

It was only when he was in his 90s that Luigi confided to his daughter why he had a scar on his forehead. Apparently, a group of cooperators tried to convince him to sign the declaration and when he refused, their words turned into fists. Luigi, as always, remained true to his beliefs.

Many POWs used the matter of the declaration to their own benefit, though. The policy at the time was to transfer all non-cooperators to Zonderwater and so, as letters arrived in East Africa, word began to spread about the excellent conditions in South Africa, especially at Zonderwater. It was also well-known by this time that non-cooperators remained in camp, so many POWs in East Africa claimed to be just that. Their tactic of gaining better living conditions while not doing any hard work was successful for a while, but when the military authorities got wind of this ploy, they immediately stopped the transfer of all 'able-bodied men' to prevent those who were needed for work in Kenya from finding their way to South Africa. For some time, therefore, only those POWs who were 'medically unfit for work but who could stand [a] voyage on troop decks' were taken to South Africa.[39]

As a non-cooperator, Luigi was also set to be shipped to South Africa, but his journey was beset by trouble. According to him, the original plan was that they would be transferred to Zanzibar, which was known among the POWs as the 'Island of Serpents, where certain death awaited them'.[40] The men were transported to the harbour in 'box cars', but when they arrived in Mombasa, the ship was undergoing repairs. The prisoners were taken back to the box cars, where they had to wait two days before they were eventually allowed to embark. A second disaster then struck the unfortunate prisoners as the ship experienced another breakdown just outside the harbour. The men were removed from the hold, but all their possessions were lost at sea. They were now back at the 'zebra meat' camp, waiting for another ship.

When Luigi eventually arrived in South Africa, the system of keeping the non-cooperators in separate blocks was well established. While the cooperators benefited from higher pay, those who chose to remain behind at the camp also gained because they were able to attend the schools set up by Prinsloo at Zonderwater. Luigi arrived in Durban on 23 January 1944, and after the many years of deprivation in the East African POW camps, his luck was about to change at last.

Upon his arrival at Pietermaritzburg, he described the experience with one word: 'Salvation'. After so many months of suffering in the Kenyan camp, Luigi and his fellow prisoners were reduced to a state of 'malnutrition and brutishness'. Fortunately, the South Africans

> immediately made us undress the filthy rags we were wearing, they made us wash and put on new uniforms which we thought were beautiful. We immediately felt better, treated like human beings, almost like a rebirth. South Africa gave us a hope of life.[41]

He eventually arrived at Zonderwater towards the end of 1944. By this time, the camp conditions had improved significantly from the De Wet days and he made the best of his new situation. Although he was placed in a tent, he did not mind. He loved the views around the camp and he was particularly impressed with the food, which he described as 'excellent and plentiful'. For the first time, Luigi could write to Barbara without hiding anything from her. There was no need to make things sound better than they were, and, as he described to her, 'a new captivity has truly begun! ... it is the most beautiful country in all of Africa'![42]

Luigi had probably never been more optimistic in his life and so he grabbed all the opportunities presented by Zonderwater. Almost immediately he took a place at the Duke d'Aosta School and with a sense of great pride he took the Advanced English, German, Spanish and French classes. To preserve his books, he cut up his pyjamas and used the cloth to cover them. He also copied the library textbooks into his exercise books, so that he could study while the camp library was closed.

For his part, Raffaello was more logical about his language lessons. He accepted the fact that he would be a prisoner for some time and so it made sense to him to learn the language of his captors. At Pietermaritzburg, however, it seems that the language lessons were presented in a more informal manner. Early in 1943, he decided to learn English and in the camp library he met a 'professor' who offered to help him with the basics.

> After a while, thanks to my sincere interest in the language, I started to understand something of what the English were saying. It was mostly orders, so it was easy. Sometimes the tone was sufficient to

understand what was being said, but conversing was something else altogether. I needed to learn grammar, and in that way the professor was of great help. Every morning, while running errands in the city, I also had time to look at the local newspapers. Then there were the books in the camp library.[43]

Raffaello's rudimentary English opened new doors for him. He made friends with UDF guards and officers, which made life for him in the camp a lot easier and more enjoyable. But during wartime things change all the time, and soon the events in Europe cast a shadow over Zonderwater, Pietermaritzburg and all the other camps in the country.

8

THE FALL OF MUSSOLINI

FOR GIOVANNI THE events that took place between 25 July and 8 September 1943 were 'perhaps the most tragic blow in the history of Italy'. No doubt he would have wanted to be in his homeland to chase out the 'traitors', but he had no choice but to witness Mussolini's fall from power from the inside of a POW camp on the other side of the world.

As the news reached Zonderwater, Giovanni and his Fascist friends were astonished and they became increasingly angry. Yet they were not speechless: 'It was the end of the world, not of the war: It was July 25th! ... it was September the 8th! ... We all became pale, breathless, unbelieving. It is impossible ... it is English propaganda!' he wrote in his memoirs.[1]

Like Giovanni, Mussolini was uncompromising. As the Allied forces started a devastating bombing campaign on Sicily, he remained unmoved. He had already lost his entire African Empire, and now the American and British commanders decided on a strategy of 'saturation bombing' on Italian soil.[2] As soon as the Allies set foot in Sicily, Mussolini must have known that their next goal would be the mainland of Italy. Yet he could not, or would not, accept what was happening. Now was the time for him to act, to put up a monumental fight to save himself and his country, but he remained aloof or ignorant, or both.

The Italian military authorities were equally deluded and as a result the preparations for a war on their doorstep were second-rate. At this time, though, they still had the German forces on their side. However, the German pilots no longer trusted the Commander-in-Chief of the Luftwaffe, Hermann Göring, and neither did they trust the Italian pilots, who seemed oblivious to the urgency of the situation. Worse still, soon after the bombing began, the German command apparently wrote off Sicily as a lost cause.[3] That left the long-suffering Italian civilian population powerless in the face of an overwhelming Allied attack. To add to their misery, air-raid shelters collapsed as people sought safety from the bombing, causing high death rates.[4]

On 9 and 10 May, Palermo was the first city to be bombed and many of its anti-aircraft defences were destroyed, which made subsequent raids safer for the flight crews when they returned in July. Overall, Palermo was targeted 69 times and other Italian cities started coming under attack at the same time.[5]

With increasing despair, the ministers in Mussolini's cabinet looked on as Sicily and its people bore the brunt of the attacks. Then, at last, they scraped together the courage to take action against the man who was responsible for their hardship. On 25 July 1943, they voted King Victor Emmanuel III back into power. The King had Mussolini arrested on the same day. So began Italy's journey back to freedom. But things would get worse before they got better ...

When Marshal Pietro Badoglio took control of Italy, he began the process of peace negotiations with the Allied forces.[6] In the meantime, on 3 September 1943, British Field Marshal Bernard Montgomery, who achieved fame in the Battle of El Alamein, led the 8th Army in its invasion of the Italian mainland. Five days later, the Italian forces surrendered to the Allies. However, Italy was still crawling with German forces and this meant that a war between the Allies and the Nazis would be fought on Italian soil.

The upshot was that it turned into a monumental disaster – the Italians were caught between two enemies who fought like dogs over a bone that did not belong to either of them. Although Badoglio was able to negotiate an armistice agreement with the Allies, the guns did not fall silent. Mussolini's hard-headedness had convinced many of his followers that he was invincible and so they vowed to continue the fight against the Allies. Others celebrated the end of Fascist rule in Italy and welcomed the Allied forces with open arms.

This conflict among the Italians sowed the seeds for continued fighting. The Fascists supported the German forces, while the Partisans[7] did all they could to help the Allies drive out the enemy. In the cities and small villages, an atmosphere of suspicion reigned: no one could be sure who or what to believe. For the Allied soldiers, the circumstances were just as difficult: How could they trust the Italians now? First, they did not know who was a Fascist and who was not and, secondly, they had been enemies since 1940.

Like Mussolini, Hitler was uncompromising. When an American war correspondent heard about the Italian armistice, he apparently reacted by saying that the Italians 'double-crossed every ally they ever had. Now it's Hitler's turn'.[8] Hitler, however, did not see it this way. For him, conflict was a natural state of being and, in any case, he was not about to lose face. With German troops stationed all over Italy, he believed his forces stood a good chance of defeating the Allies. But first his disgraced friend and ally needed his assistance. It is likely that at this time Hitler thought of Mussolini as nothing but a weakling, yet because the former Italian leader still had followers that could prove useful to him, Hitler had to act.

First, he sent a rescue squad to take Mussolini out of his enforced retirement. Next, he forced Mussolini to accept a new position as head of a puppet regime in the North of Italy, and the former Italian leader had no choice but to follow humiliating orders from his German superior.[9] For a brief moment, Mussolini held new hopes for Fascism in Italy, but as the Partisans began to outnumber those Italians who fought alongside the Germans, it started to dawn on him that perhaps things were not going particularly well. But still he did not throw in the towel.

In the meantime, ordinary Italians knew only war, hunger, disease and misery.[10] Many resorted to cooking dandelions and wild herbs as their harvests burned. In many homes, Italian mothers and wives sat down to write long letters about their hardships. Soon, the news of their daily struggles reached Zonderwater.

With Zonderwater being a microcosm of Italian society, the battle lines were drawn. In Italy the Fascists and the Partisans confronted each other and in Zonderwater the Fascists, or non-cooperators, drew a line in the sand and dared the cooperators to cross it. Some, like Giovanni, dreamed about Mussolini making a comeback, while others, like Raffaello, believed that a free future lay ahead.

In the Pietermaritzburg camp, Raffaello heard about the armistice on the loudspeakers in the dining hall. The news set in motion a great rush to pack, with POWs preparing to leave the Union at short notice. They collected foodstuffs they knew would be scarce in Italy, mostly obtained from Raffaello, who was still working in the camp kitchen. These items were then carefully packed in suitcases that were made by nailing leather straps to wooden crates.

'[M]any of us were convinced that repatriation was imminent,' Raffaello recalled in his memoirs many years later, adding:

> The wish to leave became a true state of restlessness, felt by all the Italian prisoners. After so many years in Africa, there was nobody that didn't want to go back home. We'd left Italy as boys, some very young, and now that the war was over, we suddenly found ourselves aged by pain, disease, nostalgia and various forms of deprivation.[11]

But the prospect of going home was considerably dampened by the knowledge that the war was now being fought in the cities and towns where their families lived. Raffaello complained desperately about the difficulty in getting up-to-date news from Italy – it was sheer hell not knowing what was going on. Hearing about a bombing raid in a specific town would set off an avalanche of letters to Italy and a frantic search for information from all POWs who had family in that town. Yet the post was slow and sometimes replies took months. Often, no news would come as letters were lost in the chaos of war or families had lost their literate letter writers and readers, or worse.

Giovanni seemed less concerned about his family at home and more so about the survival of Fascism. He was not ready to surrender the beliefs he had grown up with. For him, there was no other way that a country, least of all Italy, could function:

> Because a flock without a shepherd, even a chosen flock of good breed, gets dispersed and loses its way; very few will manage to find the good path to lead them back to the sheep pen, to their beloved home and cherished Land.[12]

As the news of the armistice sank in, though, Giovanni became very suspicious. He detected a change in the attitude of the camp command towards the prisoners. The 'English', as Giovanni referred to the UDF camp guards, seemed to grow careless in their control of war news to the camp. He became even more distrustful when the 'English began authorizing the sale of newspapers, a truly surprising thing, because the English do nothing and will never do anything at all without there being some gain for them!'[13]

He did not consider that the newspapers were deliberately made available to them so they could see for themselves that the Allies were gaining the upper hand over the Fascists. According to Giovanni, prisoners were previously prohibited access to news about the outside world. When 'English' newspapers were followed by loudspeakers all over the camp, many prisoners came to the conclusion that 'the war was bending to [the Allies'] advantage'.[14] They were right, but Giovanni was also right to be suspicious of the 'English', because they did not stop using propaganda now that the tide of the war had begun to turn in their favour.

What all the POWs had in common, though, was the desire to return home. Rumours of repatriation began to spread in the Zonderwater Blocks, especially when the POWs heard that the American commander, General Dwight D Eisenhower, had promised that all Italian POWs would be sent home as soon as possible. What the POWs did not hear was that Churchill was not in favour of sending the thousands of POWs back. For Churchill, and most probably for Smuts, the POWs were still far too useful as a labour force.

Eisenhower's mistake was not to distinguish between the different POWs. Only the most recent captives would return to Italy – in other words, those who had been captured in Sicily and Tunisia. POWs in prison camps across the Commonwealth who had been captured earlier in the war would stay where they were until the liberation of Italy was complete.[15] It soon became clear that this information was not clearly communicated to the prisoners or not understood by them all.

By now, also, the UDF authorities had come to realise that many POWs would sign the declaration of cooperation only to start mixing with dubious *Ossewabrandwag* types as soon as they arrived at their outside employment stations. Sending thousands of POWs back to Italy was too risky because, once there, they might switch sides and re-declare their loyalty to Mussolini. Furthermore, there was no way the Allied troops in Italy would be willing to fight alongside Italians who had spent the previous few years in POW camps and, in any case, the Badoglio government did not want Fascists arriving from all over the world to create chaos.

While the invasion of Italy was viewed in a positive light, it did make things in the Union more difficult, especially for the POW camp commanders. The UDF staff shortage, especially at Zonderwater, had been a sore point since the camp had opened its gates. When the 6th South African Armoured Division was called to action for the Italian campaign, it became a struggle to fill positions at camps all over the Union. To avoid complete anarchy, the camp command was forced to rely more heavily on Italian *carabinieri*. More of them were appointed and they took over from UDF guards during the daylight hours. They became known as the Italian Internal Security Police (IISP) and after a 14-month period they were considered to be an overall success: the crime rates had dropped and fewer men had been found in the prohibited areas.[16]

Prinsloo and Sonnabend knew that POWs had to get the 'correct' news about Mussolini's fall from power and about the progress that the Allied forces made as they battled their way north towards the Italian Alps. The unremarkable, rather dull memorandum that announced the armistice would do nothing to prevent rumours or lies from spreading, since it merely stated that

> there has been a change in the relations between the Holding Power and the Prisoners of War to this extent only – that the cessation of hostilities between the Allied and Italian nations necessitates from now onwards the closest co-operation on the part of the Italian Prisoners of War and the Union military authorities in regard to the provision made for their welfare and for the maintenance of discipline among them.[17]

For many in South Africa, including the POWs and some South African citizens, this meant that the Italians in their midst were no longer prisoners but were simply waiting and working in the Union until the war came to an end. There was also greater tolerance on the part of the UDF guards towards their captives, since many could not understand why they should force the prisoners to stay in a camp when their government was now on the side of the Allies.

The committed followers of Mussolini in the Zonderwater Fascist Block were now living a nightmare, though. With Italy no longer officially a Fascist country, they must have realised that they were fighting a losing battle of their own. Yet their actions did not show this: they remained determined to continue to fight for their ideals. Giovanni, for one, was completely against any form of cooperation. He did not accept the armistice and, making a remarkably stubborn choice, he vowed to remain a 'true prisoner', in other words, a prisoner who would reject his country's decision to make peace with the Allies. To convince others to follow his stance, Giovanni,

> [i]n this most critical state of moral disorientation, fought decisively and in every way to convince the weak to remain, as always, in their rightful place as prisoners. I stated and clarified that no cherished leader or superior of ours had come to visit us to shed light on the situation, nor to give us clear and categorical orders. I added that for no reason, ever, could we accept any type of order on the part of the enemy. I repeated to everyone that our rightful and legal position was that of being prisoners, and remain so until the great moment when, once arrived on the sacred shores of our beloved ITALY, our position and bond would be dissolved. Consequently, upon re-entering our Italian society, we could reclaim our positions as citizens in the Republic, as desired by the Italian people. And to dissuade good, though weak in body and morale, Italians from veering off the righteous path, I wrote: 'Every step outside the fence is a contribution to the enemy forces'.[18]

As a member of the Arditi Unit, Giovanni could not imagine working on the side of his enemy, even as a prisoner. The sacrifices he had made and the friends who had fallen during battle remained in his thoughts and he could not forgive those who supported the Allies. For him, crossing over to 'the side of the English as a friend, brother and ally, meant throwing mud, spit, and everything obscene onto all the dear, heroic and unforgettable deceased Arditi and all those deceased for Italy, as well as on myself'.[19]

Giovanni also believed that many POWs were cajoled into signing the declaration of cooperation:

> To think! ... that only a few days prior to [the armistice], actually a few hours prior to that, they spoke to us as hostile enemies. Then, all of a sudden ... they became dear allies, with their usual sugary smiles, inviting us, with apparent gentleness, to cooperate.
>
> But with all their acute and mastered tactics, they could not make the mass of prisoners move. So they changed their tone, and decided to pay the co-operators and treat them well economically. Many did bite in front of these tempting propositions, and so the number of co-operators steadily grew; [many prisoners] co-operated not out of an idea or faith or moral principle, and especially not because they thought well of the enemy, who had humiliated, despised and crushed them up to that moment, but in order not to suffer.[20]

It is true that the authorities increased the pay of those who made themselves available for outside work, but this was the standard operating procedure with POWs. It made sense to all Allied countries holding prisoners to incentivise those who volunteered to engage in work by paying them more. Another method with which to motivate POWs to work was to give them more food, because they would need more calories to carry out their work. In Britain, for instance, working POWs received 2 900 calories per day, whereas in the United States they were allocated between 3 000 and 3 800 calories per day, depending on the type of work they were doing. In South Africa, POWs on outside employment received an estimated 3 010 calories per day.[21]

True to his cynical attitude, though, Giovanni was convinced that money was the only reason the men decided to cooperate. But he was not entirely accurate. While some found the money attractive, many others

The declaration of cooperation signed by some Italian prisoners after the Italian armistice in 1943 (Photo courtesy NMMH)

wanted to explore the country, relieve the boredom of camp life, develop new skills, or simply feel as if they were of use to someone. Reflecting this attitude, Raffaello stated that it was 'in South Africa, despite being a prisoner ... I'd found the dignity of an occupation'.

Article 23 of the Geneva Convention states that POWs should be paid according to their rank. These payments were to be paid monthly, regardless of the work that was being done or not done. Giovanni had been getting his pay from the Zonderwater authorities because all POWs were subject to the same regulations, no matter what their political beliefs were.[22] Giovanni always found a way to be critical of 'the English', but even he admitted that the money he received made a considerable difference to life in the camp. As he wrote in his memoirs

A sort of trading store was created that sold various genres of items [and] we gradually recovered our strength. [I] was then able to buy: notebooks, still jealously conserved today, pens, pencils, rubbers, ink, etc, all to the detriment of the stomach. Such were my sacrifices for knowledge.[23]

Raffaello signed the declaration of cooperation, which meant that he could work in the kitchens of the Pietermaritzburg camp for the duration of his captivity. For him it was a case of being realistic about his situation:

> The majority, myself included, thought it right and apt to accept that request [to sign the declaration of cooperation] we by no means felt like traitors towards our homeland, considering how things had gone in Italy and how much useless rhetoric had surrounded fascism's inefficiency ... On the other hand, other prisoners, for reasons I respect to this day, refused to sign.[24]

To a large extent, the Pietermaritzburg camp experienced fewer problems with Fascists because they were sent to the Fascist Blocks in Zonderwater. Raffaello remembered that so many of his fellow POWs were eager for work that a type of 'recruitment agency' was opened in the command station of the camp.

Alongside Raffaello worked a prisoner by the name of Melani, who had decidedly different political views. Raffaello remembered how Melani

> would keep saying to the South Africans, half serious, half joking: 'We'll win the war, and I'll run after you and shove this knife point up your backsides'. He said it every time he offered a slice of roast. Now, after Mussolini's fall, the South Africans enjoyed making fun of him, though they did it good-naturedly. Because the truth is, *Duce* or no *Duce*, everyone loved him and held him in high regard. But Melani soon decided, before he lost his patience, to leave the kitchen and go work on a farm, where he ran no risks of getting upset.[25]

As it happened, Melani's departure turned to Raffaello's advantage: he was promoted to head chef and was also offered an assistant.

While Melani had the good sense to depart before he lost his temper, Giovanni was not able to remove himself from conflict in the camp as he was stuck in the Fascist Block. He began to think that the 'sold-out-to-the-English executioner squad' had set their sights on him and, being the Giovanni he was, he prepared himself. He wrote that

> [to] someone like me, ambush was more than logical, it was, so to speak, always on the cards ... One night, at about four in the morning, the great and decisive moment of my death sentence I stop ... He comes closer and asks: 'Sergeant! ... do you have a knife?!'
>
> I had already understood everything, and with Arditi steadfastness, I reply: 'Don't you know that Palermo always has a knife?!' and he rebuts: 'If you could lend it to me, I need to open a tin of jam ...'
>
> I confidently reply: 'Santoro! ... you know very well that my knife is not for opening cans, but for fighting men that are truly worthy of such actions'. Santoro, hit in his weak, Mafioso ego spot, spat out in a surly tone: 'Yes! ... and that's me!'[26]

What follows in Giovanni's memoirs is an elaborate two-page description of the fight between him and his attacker. Eventually, though, Santoro's breathing became 'louder and gasping, and his shortness of breath [made] him tremble'. Giovanni took this opportunity to inform him that he was still feeling

> fresh and cool, and in ten minutes or half an hour at the most you won't be able to take it anymore, you'll be on the ground, broken by your efforts and you won't hold up. Then I'll throw the two knives aside, and with you on the ground exhausted, I'll squash your face with my heel like a cockroach.[27]

Santoro gave up the fight, but he did tell someone about his confrontation with Giovanni. The next morning, Giovanni was escorted from his tent to the detention barracks or the 'Little Red House', as the prisoners referred to it. As he left his tent, his fellow Fascists saluted him in the Fascist way. Dressed in his Arditi uniform, Giovanni could not control a patriotic urge as he spurred on all of those around him with a 'Comrades! Salute the *Duce!*' And as he was led away to detention, he was proud to hear shouts of 'To us!' following him.

It is clear that the authorities suspected Giovanni of being one of the main instigators in the Fascist Block. He was searched and questioned about his 'writings', then he was sent to detention, where, according to him, he endured a torturous routine. His days started with a cold shower, followed by hard labour that consisted of pointless duties like filling wheelbarrows, running across ploughed fields and carrying heavy poles. Apparently, there were also beatings, whips and shouts that could only have been 'organized by cold minds and sadistic torturers'.

Unfortunately for Prinsloo, this punishment served only to strengthen Giovanni's resolve to maintain his Fascist pride. His hatred of the 'English' intensified. If Giovanni was a committed Fascist before, now he became radical in his beliefs and nothing the authorities would do could convince him to think or do otherwise.

The Fascist Blocks were supposed to separate the ardent Fascists, also known as Blackshirts, from the other POWs. Giovanni called it the Black Block, 'with none of the scum. It was an ideal Block, because it was homogenous and solid'. Here the Fascists POWs could live out their motto of 'we like the hard life' and when Easter drew near, they began to prepare for the celebration because they 'felt the Lord's Religion more than all the other prisoners, because with it, and through prayer, we strived towards the Redemption of all Italians and of the world'.[28]

Separating POWs into different blocks at Zonderwater may well have saved a number of lives. While the so-called Fascists were seen as stubborn hangers-on of a dying ideology, they also became victims of silent attacks, probably carried out at night, when non-Fascist POWs gained access to the forbidden blocks. On occasion, Zonderwater staff found the bodies of Fascist POWs floating in septic tanks.[29]

It is not known whether they included the 'English' or the Zonderwater camp command in their prayers. However, some time later, a Catholic priest was allowed into the 'Black Block' to serve communion to everyone there.

OSSEWABRANDWAG AND FASCIST PRISONERS

THE NEWS OF the armistice was carried in *Tra I Reticolati,* the main camp newspaper. Originally a leaflet advertising sporting events in Zonderwater, by 1943 it had become a proper weekly publication. By mid-September that year and, strangely enough, only a week after the armistice, the camp command proudly announced that *Tra I Reticolati* was so popular that it would be professionally printed in Pretoria.

It is true that the newspaper was enjoyed by many POWs and that early on its circulation grew from 6 to 300 copies since it was first published in 1941. However, when the Zonderwater command started to take an interest, circulation rose to 3 000 copies and it was sold at cost price to the prisoners.[1] It now became a handy tool with which to measure morale and to subtly, or sometimes not so subtly, direct POWs' thoughts in a desired direction.

The prisoners were encouraged to write articles for publication, but for the camp command it was a way to measure the atmosphere in the camp. The authorities read and evaluated all the articles destined for *Tra I Reticolati* and in this way they were able to judge whether it was necessary to intervene when Fascist propaganda or anti-Union propaganda became too prevalent. To no one's surprise, the armistice and later the peace agreement between the new Italian government of Badoglio and the Allied nations were favourite topics among the newspaper's Italian authors, with some encouraging cooperation and others raising the spirits of those who longed for a return to Fascism.

One such article, translated from Italian, cleverly 'criticised' the Allies for not trusting the Badoglio government:

> The democratic Italy of Badoglio has taken up such a positive attitude towards the Allies that this action has been defined by the

Nazis and Fascists as 'treacherous' ... when the Allies waged war against Italy ... they declared that they did not intend to make war against Italy but only against Fascism. It can be assumed, therefore, that Badoglio, after submitting to unconditional surrender and after having disbanded Fascism has done very much to demonstrate the democratic orientation of the new Italy. But General Badoglio has done still more, he has ... declared war against Germany [but] just now appeared a really curious feat in the Allied Press and propaganda [as they expressed] doubt towards the sincerity of Italian collaboration.

[T]he confusion of the new democratic Italy of today with the Fascist Italy of yesterday is still persisted on ... who is guilty? Fascism or Italy in general? Mussolini or Italy alone? ... the radio brings daily reports on anti-German manifestations in Italy and facts showing how Italians are doing their bit ... for the liberation of their soil and for nothing else [why then] in the light of these international events [is it] that Badoglio's Italy remains responsible and also under sentence for the crimes of Fascism? ... it is important not to forget [Italy's contribution during the First World War] as it was properly forgotten at Versailles and so set Italy adrift.[2]

The author of this article cleverly removed the blame from ordinary Italians and laid responsibility for the war at the feet of Mussolini and, to some extent, even attributed it to the Allies' handling of Italy's position during the 1919 Peace Treaty at Versailles. For those POWs who assumed that this article was written by a fellow POW among them, it certainly provided much food for thought; they may have been bystanders, but they were innocent of Mussolini's crimes. In fact, articles such as this were propaganda efforts to 're-educate' the Italian POWs, especially those who still had high hopes for Mussolini to pull a rabbit out of a hat.

A follow-up article presented the readers with a more direct message, one which would have appealed even to those POWs who were disillusioned by politics. Money was a scarce commodity in Italy, but the writer reminded the men that

Italy has never had a self-sufficient economic structure and even if she would have been victorious in this war, would have only played second fiddle ... we have to contribute to the reconstruction of the new world ... reconstruction and re-education must take the place of hatred which fills the minds of the warring people at present.[3]

In other words, if Italy were to be seen as a loser in the war, the least its citizens and returning POWs could do was to work towards rebuilding the economy, because there was no time for political interference. They had to choose money, not hate.

Less cynical POWs used *Tra I Reticolati* and other camp newspapers as a creative outlet, writing poems and essays on their experiences of war and captivity. For Sonnabend, however, the thoughts expressed in the paper remained a source of investigation and he became fascinated by the 'mental make-up of men behind barbed wire'. According to him, the articles threw 'considerable light on the Italian character and the psychological effects of two decades of Fascist rule'.[4]

Not surprisingly, themes of homesickness, family, wives, girlfriends and home-cooked food were popular, and as long as politics was omitted, writing helped many POWs to come to terms with their situation. As is still the case today, however, politics was all-pervasive and divisions between POWs increased at the time that the Allies were fighting to liberate their country from the Nazis.

Despite the developments on the war front, the Zonderwater authorities had no choice but to carry on with their work. The need for POW labour remained strong and the call for cooperators increased after Italy's surrender. After all, the South African economy had to grow and the Italians were an important part of the labour supply.

In fact, by 1944, the authorities had become impatient with the Fascists who refused to sign the declaration of cooperation. A year after Mussolini's fall, one of the welfare officers wrote to Prinsloo, stating the case for a renewed effort to get the Fascists working. According to him, it had been impossible to distinguish the real Fascists from those who were simply wearing Fascist paraphernalia. The officer believed that with greater effort

on the part of the camp command, the true Fascists and those who were
being intimidated could be separated from one another. He argued for
a 'radical revision' of the Fascist Block system for the following reasons:

> At least half of these men could be usefully employed if they were
> to be separated from the agitators and submitted to an intensive
> course of enlightenment. As long as they remain with others, they
> will just be a burden on this country and their labour could never
> be utilised.
>
> Humanitarian considerations must prompt us to reduce the
> number of men who will return to Italy with the Fascist label. I
> always felt that such men will, upon return to their Fatherland,
> finish in another and much less comfortable concentration camp.
> It is safer to give the Fascist salute in Zonderwater than it is to lift
> the arm in the Roman style in Rome.

What he meant was that the Fascists were treated so well at Zonderwater
that they were given the false impression that their belief in Fascism was
valid and that they would be able to live out their Fascist way of life once
they had returned to Italy. The aim, according to the welfare officer, was
for the Fascists of Zonderwater to be made aware of how much things had
changed in Italy. Most of the people of that country no longer supported
the ideology Mussolini had held up and now that the Fascist leader was out
of the picture, hardly anyone still felt obliged to support his political views.

To drive home his point, the officer mentioned a letter from a UDF
captain stationed in Italy at the time. According to this man, the
Zonderwater authorities should not hesitate to be firm with the Fascist
POWs, because

> ultimately it will be in their interest not to come back [to Italy] as
> Fascists. If this is not done they will be hurt much worse by their
> compatriots who will deal with them very harshly indeed ... one
> should conduct an intensive campaign of enlightenment through
> the printed and spoken word and those who still seem hesitant
> should gradually be sent to the Fascist Block.[5]

To put in place the so-called 'campaign of enlightenment', the camp command first had to find and destroy Fascist propaganda that was being written and spread by the Fascists themselves. While Giovanni wrote long essays on philosophy, others were more direct in their efforts to maintain Fascism among the POWs. Fake news reports were produced and distributed among the Fascist POWs, all of which were aimed at strengthening the resolve of those who held on to Fascism.[6]

One such document made it clear to the camp command that the Fascists at Zonderwater were being treated too kindly and that their extreme political views were being tolerated at the expense of the good of the Union and of Italy. In the document, a prisoner writes that in the month he had spent in Fascist Block Camp 8

> my body has become stronger and my soul has rested, because here, apart from the inevitable infiltration of a few men of doubtful loyalty, one lives in the atmosphere of the new revolution. This is really a corner of Fascist Italy, where, by dreaming with open eyes, we can again find the new Italy of Mussolini.[7]

As if this was not enough to spread alarm among the camp command, they also found propaganda material written by *Ossewabrandwag* members, with one writer declaring: 'To the Fascist comrades of Zonderwater. I hope that these few lines of mine will reach you. I am a modest member of the South African OBs and I am proud to feel close to you in spirit'.[8]

In his message, the *Ossewabrandwag* man also falsely claimed that the American forces in Italy were abandoning their positions because their morale was very low. In yet another propaganda message, the writer warned the Fascists at Zonderwater not to donate their blood, as it was being used 'to the exclusive benefit of British soldiers [and] there are people who are speculating and making money at our expenses'.[9]

At the Kroonstad camp in the Orange Free State, members of the *Ossewabrandwag* and Fascist POWs also found ready comrades in each other. The camp was known, at least by Prinsloo, as one that was not managed effectively and where discipline was a great problem among POWs and staff. Almost three years after it had been established, the

Kroonstad camp was in a terrible state, with an inspector describing the staff kitchen as a 'quagmire', while the POW kitchen was even worse, an 'eye-sore' with 'vegetable peelings, and general filth ... strewn about the kitchen floor and within yards of the kitchen ... the conditions generally present a most repelling picture'.[10]

It was not only the physical state of the camp that needed attention, though: some of the POWs and possibly the UDF staff, were also in need of inspections and improvements.

All the POWs at Kroonstad were sent out to work on harvesting schemes in the vicinity. Some of them were sent to Klerksdorp, where the mayor was a member of the opposition party and he himself employed a number of them. In a letter to the United Party, the Organiser of the Vigilance Committee asked that the military authorities be made aware that POWs who were working for the mayor were enjoying excessive privileges. The letter also claimed they were a bad (Fascist) influence on the other POWs in the area. Apparently, the local police were powerless and too afraid to take action against the men because, according to the writer of the letter, the opposition party held powerful sway over the town's inhabitants.[11]

Apart from outside influences, many cooperators who had been on outside employment were experiencing pressure from Fascist prisoners. One man, who had been working on the Orange River project in Upington, reported his experiences to the camp command on his return to Zonderwater. Apparently, his work party was enlarged to cope with the workload, but one man who had joined them was determined to convert all of them to Fascism. The POW said that when the 'Blackshirt' joined them in Upington, he began 'an intolerable Fascist campaign'. First he limited his propaganda to those POWs in the work party, but later the man became increasingly daring and tried to influence civilians in the vicinity.

The POW also claimed that a group of Fascists were plotting acts of sabotage

> to be carried out at a suitable moment. These gentry who, with their vile and cowardly leader Mussolini, once sold Italy to the murderous Germans are now ruining the peace enjoyed by the poor prisoners working on the farms. Moreover, many of these infamous

followers of the swine Mussolini are scattered among the working camps in South Africa, particularly at Kroonstad. These should go the way of all the others at Zonderwater.[12]

Sonnabend realised that he would have to refine his propaganda techniques if he wanted to make any progress among the POWs. Not only did the Fascists infiltrate the outside employment schemes, they were also working to spread their message to the civilians, many of whom were already against the Smuts government and its support for the Allies.

While Sonnabend thought up new propaganda techniques, the Zonderwater command took practical measures to limit the influence of the Fascists. First, it was decided to erect an additional fence around the block that housed the so-called 'ardent' Fascists. Another plan was to build a new camp at a distance from Zonderwater, but some thought it would be best to move all of them to the Pietermaritzburg camp. But because these ideas were all considered to be impractical and expensive, a new approach was needed. In the end, Sonnabend and Prinsloo realised that moving the Fascists to a different location was not the solution: they would have to change the way these men thought about life and politics.

It was a formidable task and all that Sonnabend could do was to rely on anti-Fascist propaganda. The camp radio substituted rumours with authentic news and no outward signs of Fascism were allowed, including badges. Furthermore, no singing of the Fascist anthem was allowed and the 'Roman salute' was banned. Finally, an appeal board was established. This enabled those who felt that they had been wrongly segregated from the main POW population to petition the camp command. The idea was to apply strict disciplinary measures with a sense of compassion, as Sonnabend stated:

> It was not right to confine the POWs into a special Block and at the same time make them feel that there was no possibility of redemption as far as they were concerned. The fact that they knew there was a way out accelerated the process of independent thinking and reduced the power of the Fascists terrorists over the other Blackshirts ... it must be remembered that the POWs know

that they will return to an Anti Fascist Italy and they dread the possibility of going there with the stigma of Fascist obstinacy. It is for this reason that one must be very careful when giving to a POW the label of 'unrepentant Fascist'.[13]

Yet the camp command nevertheless found it very difficult to distinguish real Fascists from those who only pretended, for whatever reason, to hold these beliefs. The camp command knew, for instance, that some POWs may have held personal vendettas against others and used the fall of Mussolini as a reason to put paid to such feuds. Others thought the harsh treatment meted out to Fascists would turn them into martyrs and heroes and in this way they would achieve a certain status among the POWs. Another reason why a POW might have declared himself Fascist in order to be moved to a different section could have been the Italian marshals who were helping the UDF staff with disciplinary duties in the camp. Many POWs viewed the marshals as cooperators since they worked alongside the camp authorities. It was especially the non-cooperators who refused to take orders from the marshals and this led to punishment and further resentment.[14]

By this time, Prinsloo and Sonnabend had a very good sense of how daunting their task was. To make matters worse, Smuts continued to put pressure on them to supply more POW labour. The labour shortage in the country, and perhaps Smuts's personal priorities, now caused the prime minister to think differently about the outside employment scheme. In the early days of 1941, Smuts was adamant that employers had be vetted before they were allowed to take on POWs for labour purposes, but by 1943 he had apparently changed his mind, believing that 'it couldn't be helped if POWs are hired to Nazi or anti-war sympathisers'.[15] This did not sit well with those in Smuts's political circle and eventually the matter was dealt with by implementing new rules for the treatment and behaviour of POWs on outside employment.

10

ARMISTICE JITTERS

AT THE TIME the armistice commenced, Prinsloo had been in command of Zonderwater for eight months and he had a tremendous amount on his plate. It didn't help that Smuts kept a close eye on Prinsloo's performance to ensure that his imperial masters were not disappointed – and, of course, the POW camps also had to adhere to the Geneva Convention.

Prinsloo was therefore not only responsible for ensuring a constant supply of labour for local employers and sending POWs to Britain, but also for keeping order among the POWs and staff, maintaining high morale and preventing escapes from the camp. While he was aware that the UDF authorities were not in favour of sending POWs back to Italy to fight alongside the Allies, he still put in a request to form a Prisoner-of-War Corps (POW Corps). To make his request more palatable, he suggested that these men could serve in Italy under a UDF officer in the 'back areas'. He believed his plan was practical because many of the POWs had expressed a wish to serve under UDF officers: 'their recent experience in this camp has shown how UDF officers take an interest in those under their command'. According to him, the Italian officers apparently 'took little interest in the prisoners of war'.[1]

Despite answers not having been forthcoming from his superiors, Prinsloo persisted with his requests and naively went ahead with his plans to form the Italian Corps. He even made an announcement to the POWs on the camp broadcasting system, saying that

> it may be that one day some of you will again have an opportunity to render a great service to Italy by bringing to Italian shores food and other necessities of life. I want to assure you that, whatever happens, there will be no direct or indirect compulsion. Should really the time come to ask for volunteers, only those who will be

genuinely willing will be called upon to come forward.[2]

The authorities remained silent on this matter, however, and so Prinsloo was forced to explain to the POWs that he had not received any orders from the UDF or the new Italian government regarding the formation of the POW Corps. He nevertheless kept the hopes of the prisoners up by saying that 'until such time as I receive orders in this matter, I expect you to remain disciplined and at your posts, waiting and carrying out orders like good soldiers'.[3] In the same announcement, he asked them to submit written applications to volunteer for military service, and these soon swamped his desk.[4]

Based on Prinsloo's broadcast, POWs started to look forward to an active period of soldiering again. One of them was Sub-Lieutenant Carlo Majetta. In his well-composed application, Majetta stated that he had served in the Italian Navy for five years 'with the utmost diligence and willingness'. He also expressed his wish to be 'formally released for service in the Allied Merchant or Auxiliary Navy Forces'. In response, he was advised to wait until the Badoglio government decided to participate in the war against the Germans. If so, the Italian POWs would then fight alongside 'their own people'.[5]

As it happened, Badoglio declared war on Germany in October, but Sub-Lieutenant Majetta was never called up for duty. He and others at Zonderwater who wanted to fight against the German forces were labouring, and hoping, under a misapprehension. While Prinsloo raised their hopes, their own government remained silent. The new Italian leaders issued a memorandum on the matter only in 1945, but it was frustratingly vague:

> The Italian Government understands very well how hard it is for so many of Italy's sons who are champing at the bit because they cannot fight or work directly for their suffering Fatherland, but who, even while waiting, know how to keep their military pride and their faith in the destiny of their country.
>
> Understanding this fate of the Italian POWs is its constant care, now and in the future, as is the lot of all Italians who have been involved in the tragedy and misery of this war.[6]

The pages of *Tra I Reticolati* were also full of letters and articles from POWs who expressed their desire to fight for the Allies and against the Fascist forces. In one of the summaries of the newspaper penned by Zonderwater welfare officer Captain JA Ball, he describes how one prisoner wrote on the topic of patriots. For this man the Partisans, who carried out 'subversive activities behind enemy lines' in Italy against the German forces, were heroes who were no longer fighting 'a war of oligarchy but a war for the cause of justice and decency'.[7]

Yet despite heroic calls to arms such as these, it soon became clear that the prisoners' hope to fight for the Allies was misplaced. The Deputy Chief of Staff informed the Deputy Adjutant General that the status of the POWs was to remain as it was before the coup d'état in Italy and that until an armistice was agreed upon between Badoglio and the Allies, no applications for Italian POW participation in the conflict could be considered.[8] When the armistice was signed, the Deputy Adjutant General tactfully wrote to Prinsloo, saying, 'it would be better to wait until events in Italy have crystallized and it can be seen in what manner the services of Italian POW who volunteer to join the Allies can be best utilized'.[9]

Yet, a week earlier, on 23 September, the High Commissioner in London had sent a telegram to the Secretary for External Affairs indicating that the signing of the armistice with Italy did not change the status of Italian POWs. He emphasised that while they would continue to treat the Italians with respect and consideration, discipline had to be maintained and orders obeyed.[10]

If Prinsloo did try to explain why the POWs in South Africa could not return to Italy to fight, something was lost in translation. Some POWs mistakenly believed that the non-cooperators, or Fascists, among them, were the cause of their not being able to fight for Italy. As one POW wrote in *Tre I Reticolati*:

> We have been overwhelmed with the reaction and stubbornness of those still believing in Fascist [cooperators]. But the heaviest thing is that these irresponsible ones are doing harm to our country and to ourselves. Most P.O.W.s are accused of not agreeing with the Baloglio's government. This is the reason why the Allied Governments distrust

and do not interest themselves in us ... Do you think the detaining power is not aware of what is happening in the camps? She is fully aware of what goes on. She is informed of Fascist attitudes, the old and the new ones ... How can we be trusted?"

Others, like Sergeant Petrosillo, found it particularly difficult to accept that they would never be trusted again, and that they would have to allow others to fight for their country's liberation:

This barbed wire in which I have been enclosed for three years has never reduced me to exasperation because one of the ex-leaders of the Axis had made me understand that he required great sacrifices from the Italian people, for the greatness of Italy. Under these illusions and being an obedient soldier, I was never shaken by hardships and humiliation.

But the well-known events in Italy of 1943 and later made me disbelieve his theories and compelled me to think of all the things of the past and of the many promises which had all gone up in smoke. And so, seeing all with clear eyes, I turned my thoughts away from that Fascism which in 20 years had ruined the Italian nation.

Ever since Italy declared war on Germany I was pervaded by new spirit: the desire of freedom, so that I might follow my comrades who are sacrificing their lives side by side with the allies in order to free Italy from the Germans and the Fascist traitors. I have been patient and I have heard from the radio of all the atrocities committed by the Germans against the Italians. Later their cruelty was confirmed by letters from our mothers, wives and sisters in liberated Italy.

My contempt of the Germans increased and so did my pride of being a soldier and I had hoped to be called one day, to play my part in the war ... the Allied government announced that the Italian ex-POWs in England, America and Australia had been organised in proper military formations ... not even the POWs in South Africa were neglected. In fact, it was announced in TRA I RETICOLATI.

We are not trusted ... soldiers of the King may become the joke of these madmen (Fascists) here in this cage ... I absolutely cannot resign myself to remain inactive, I feel that I am not inferior to my comrades (ex-POWs) and I do not want to be humiliated by those who, although not Italian, are fighting and dying for the freedom of my Fatherland.[12]

When a 'Captain C' brought these articles to the attention of camp command, he stated that such articles were considered harmful to the general morale in the camp. It could only have been the Fascists who were offended, so the Captain's note might be taken as evidence of camp staff having Fascist sympathies. Indeed, three weeks later, POWs in the Fascist Block expressed their wish to produce their own newspaper because *Tra I Reticolati* was viewed as being too political.[13] Their wish was granted.

Back in Italy, young men who had dreamed of fighting for liberty on the side of the Allies were also disappointed. Even when they demonstrated their willingness to assist the Allied effort, their participation was viewed with some suspicion and they were considered better off joining the Partisans. Operating on their own initiative, small groups of Partisans were able to carry out acts of sabotage and provide the Allies with information about German troop movements. Only in mid-1944 did the Allies start to call on the Italians to resist the German army with military force and, in fact, in August that year they played a significant role in liberating Florence. Given that many Italians remained loyal Fascists, the Partisans were often having to fight against their fellow countrymen and -women.[14]

Mountains and rivers made Allied progress slow, yet the front lines between the Germans in the north and the Allies in the south moved slowly towards the Alps. Each town and city presented its own challenges, the German retreat leaving devastation in its wake – as, inevitably, did the Allied advances. In August 1944, in the Italian town of Lucca – the home town of Raffaello Cei – German troops found themselves attacked from two sides: by Allied troops south of the River Arno and by Italian Partisans to the north of Lucca.

Knowing that they were stuck in South Africa while brutal fighting continued in Italy caused great frustration and engendered fear among all the POWs, cooperators and non-cooperators alike. Raffaello received his first letters from home in 1942 and, although, in hindsight, he realised that 'nobody told me how things really were at home in Italy', he became very concerned about his family's safety – 'two women alone and defenceless in the war'.[15]

By 1944, however, Raffaello had become increasingly worried about his family. In his memoirshe wrote about his fears:

> [H]ow could I not worry? How could I forget the risks my dear ones ran, alone in a war-stricken country? Every morsel of food, every sip of water or beer inevitably brought to my mind the hunger and thirst they were probably enduring at home. I could only thank the Lord for the abundance and security I enjoyed, but at the same time a deep sense of guilt took my breath away. What had become of my mother and sister? The news I received from home through the Red Cross was both scarce and too old for me to feel at peace about their fate. Their words and the few photographs I got showed two apparently smiling women whose faces were gaunt, perhaps from hunger, with frightened eyes and mouths distorted by superficial smiles that existed to reassure a prisoner rather than express a joy for life. A constant feeling of inadequacy made me restless. I, the man of the home, instead of defending them as would have been my duty, was so far away from them, and they were probably suffering.[16]

Although Raffaello did not have up-to-date information about the war in Italy, he was right to be worried about his family. With Lucca becoming crammed with refugees and war pressure mounting, the scene was set for carnage. On 12 August 1944, German frustration with Partisan activities boiled over and they took it out on the civilians, killing 560 civilians as they searched for Partisans.

Genoa – Pietro Scottu's home town – lies 162 kilometres to the north of Lucca. Although it had been cut off, the German forces were ordered to keep it secure the following month. In September, the Canadians took

An artwork of a prisoner receiving bad news from home.
It was drawn by another prisoner. (Photo courtesy NMMH)

Rimini, the town where Paolo Ricci had gone to join his regiment four years previously.[17] During the first week of October 1944, the German 8th Battery was stationed near Savignano, Paolo's home town. Just outside the town, the New Zealanders and the Canadians engaged them in battle.

Between September and December 1944, the area around Reggio Emilia and Parma was being bombed by Allied aircraft. Between these two places lies the small town of Gattatico, where Luigi Pederzoli spent his early years and first made his acquaintance with the harsh realities of life.[18] However, at this point, Luigi and Pietro had not yet arrived in South Africa and it is not known whether they received any news from home in the temporary camps in Africa where they were held.

By the end of 1944, many POWs would have heard about the destruction of their home towns and they began to realise that they would have been in the thick of things had they returned after the armistice. Had they been repatriated in 1944 or even in 1945, they would have been met with scenes of utter devastation. After the war, as more and more POWs contacted the Red Cross and the Prisoner of War Information Bureau to help them obtain information on their families in Italy, the reply was often 'Family wiped out'.[19]

When the Allies occupied Rome on 5 June 1944, news quickly reached the Union, but Prinsloo was careful not to cause further divisions, given the different views on the war among the POWs. The POW camp representative asked for permission to celebrate the event, but Prinsloo allowed only church services, no festivities. It was thought that the excitement among some and the disappointment felt by others could lead to emotional outbursts that in turn could develop into a full-scale riot.[20]

Some of his officers may have thought he was being overly cautious because the first report on the political situation in the camp following the fall of Rome stated that the event created a general sense of relief and enthusiasm among the POWs. Also, anti-Allied Fascist propaganda had 'practically ceased' and many Fascists had apparently changed sides. Only Block 5 was still 'under the absolute domination of the Fascists'.[21]

Despite the optimism of the report, though, Prinsloo was wise enough to suspect that it did not contain the whole truth. The Fascists may have been on the losing side in Italy, but this only served to inspire the extremists at Zonderwater to fight harder for the ideas they had grown up with. After all, many Fascist POWs had the support of sections of the local population who, like former Prime Minister JBM Hertzog, wanted the Union to remain 'neutral'.

Nevertheless, many civilians showed through their actions that they were not, in fact, neutral. By participating in demonstrations against the war, confronting soldiers on the streets or spreading rumours of Axis victories, they showed that they were on the side of the Axis dictators, Hitler and Mussolini. Just as the anti-war faction clung to their convictions throughout the war, so did the hardline Italian Fascists: after all, both groups had grown up with more or less the same world view.

A case in point is Giovanni, who became increasingly determined to resist cooperation, even when it became clear that Mussolini's days were numbered. The outspoken Fascists continued to provide the camp command with daily headaches. Giovanni, still offended by the 'English propaganda' and the 'traitors' who had signed the declaration of cooperation, related the story of one 'true prisoner' – a 'cultured man, a purist without comparison' – who was assaulted by prisoners whom he called Judas followers. Giovanni relates how the man was beaten on various parts of his body and that the beating was so severe that his teeth fell out: '[B]loody and dying, they left him there like a dog,' he writes, although the exhausted prisoner 'carried on yelling, until the end: "Long live Italy! ... Long live the *Duce*!"'. [22]

According to Giovanni, the prisoner was admitted to hospital in a critical condition but survived after many months of hospitalisation. As if this were not enough, Giovanni and his friends 'collected the batons and knives we had built ourselves ... to save oneself: it is barbarity, incivility, anti-Christianity and anti-humanity ... about ten of us, prepared to confront hundreds or thousands of insignificant beings'. [23]

Fights with fellow POWs, especially those who did not want to listen to the Fascist reasoning of their compatriots, was one way to vent frustrations. Another was to arrange protests and, for good measure, to damage camp buildings. From the time of the armistice until the last POW returned to Italy, every celebration came with a warning. In May 1944, for instance, the camp staff were reminded that 24 May was a holiday for the Italians in commemoration of their entry as an ally into the First World War, but 'under no circumstance will demonstrations of any kind be tolerated'. [24]

Later in 1944, POWs 'wilfully and through lack of discipline' damaged a number of the barracks in camp. A memorandum pointed out that before the armistice it was

> impossible to apportion blame or fix responsibility for such damages ... in future all OCs [Commanding Officers] of blocks will ensure that the strictest vigilance is observed ... with the view to establish individual responsibility in respect of any future acts of this nature. [25]

POWs who were found guilty of an offence found themselves locked up in the detention barracks. Their punishment allowed them only three blankets in winter and one spoon. [26] It is ironic that after Italy was no longer formally an enemy the UDF authorities were obliged to keep a closer check on their Italian prisoners than ever before.

Christmas 1944 was difficult for Raffaello, as it must have been for many other POWs in South Africa. The sadness and uncertainty of that time remained with him, and when he wrote his memoirs years later, he recalled without any enthusiasm that

> Christmas of 1944 came. I celebrated it in the canteen with the few soldiers that had stayed on. By then, none of us even hoped for an approaching repatriation. We knew little or nothing about the fate of our wretched country. But we carried on hoping. How can one stop hoping at the age of 24?[27]

Those who did not have strong family ties started to consider staying behind in South Africa. Many of them realised that South Africa was, at least compared to Italy at that time, a far better option. There was enough food, the climate was mild and the country was still intact, since it was so far removed from the theatres of war. Italy had been destroyed, its people continued to be impoverished and the only prospect for a returning POW was hard work and, on top of that, possibly misplaced blame by civilians.

Already in October 1943, the Zonderwater camp command became aware of a rumour circulating among the Italians that 20 000 of them would be allowed to stay in the Union when the war came to an end.[28] In response, orders were sent to all the POW camps to inform POWs that there was no truth in this rumour. Yet many remained hopeful and wrote directly to Prinsloo. One of them, Boccardi Onofrio, wrote:

> You are certainly aware of the wretched conditions in which Italy has been plunged by war. Even in pre-war time, prevailing conditions in Italy for the working stratus of the population were very low, unemployment and destitution being a plague that never could be healed. Under the circumstances, it may be assumed that the state of affairs is still worse and I dare not look forward to what will be in store for working classes and especially for those who, by spending long years abroad, have lost many chances and will find all the vacant places filled by those who were lucky enough to stay at home ...
>
> I therefore wonder, why should I carry on a living in my country, where the grim grip of unemployment and want is at hand and not emigrate to a country that may offer a chance of a decent and

honourable living? ... your benevolence will be met by my deepest gratitude and that of my whole family, which you will have helped with me.[29]

At the time, Prinsloo would not have been able to do anything to help Onofrio, as repatriation, much less immigration, was still a long way off for most POWs. Those who suffered from severe homesickness and who wanted to return regardless of what awaited them had no choice but to sit it out until the war had ended. Meanwhile, Prinsloo and his staff continued with their attempts to maintain order and good discipline by lifting morale and creating a relatively pleasant environment for the prisoners that would not induce them to rebel or escape – although if ever there were a season for escape, it was now.

11

FREEDOM AT ANY COST

PIETRO SCOTTU DID not give a hoot about politics. Unlike many POWs in Zonderwater, he had no wish to return to home to rejoin the war. He arrived in South Africa in 1944, just as Mussolini was being removed from power in Italy. And he did so determined to make the most of what he had; and so, as soon as he set foot in Durban harbour, he began plotting his next move.

Pietro knew that he would have to rely on his own initiative. Growing up without a father in the coastal city of Genoa and having to work from a young age to help his mother, he had matured very quickly. He was also not afraid of taking risks, which might explain why he became a repeat escapee after he was captured in Eritrea. No matter how good the camps in South Africa were supposed to be, Pietro had no intention of becoming a meek and complacent prisoner: the hellish POW camps in North Africa had made him determined to follow his own mind and carve out his own escape route.

His first impressions of the 'Boers' who gave him the thumbs-up on their arrival at Durban harbour could not have instilled in him too much confidence in the locals, although this, of course, was the result of a cultural misunderstanding. Like everyone else, Pietro was sent to Zonderwater, where he considered

> the food was better, though not abundant. There was, in addition, a systematic distribution of fruit and cigarettes, which I'd never experienced before, and this made me very pleased because, having never been a smoker, it allowed me to barter my ration of cigarettes with the heavy smokers' ration of fruit, which I'd really missed up to that point. This way I had double and sometimes triple what would have been my regular ration.[1]

The barbed wire and the watchtowers did not make him feel welcome; and although his later recollection of 'soldiers armed with machine guns' was an exaggeration, he no doubt felt heavily caged in.[2] Not one to procrastinate, though, he 'immediately started to think about how to escape at the first opportunity. I therefore needed to learn something useful in case I decided to flee'.[3] As part of his plan, it was a logical decision for him to improve his English language skills and, together with that, he also gathered information that would later be useful to him, because

> whatever was said about the camp ... was considered as a free and useful lesson to facilitate the future I had in mind, and news regarding external events and names of foreign places were like music to my ears. I had become a South African Geography student preparing for an exam, other than being obsessed with language.[4]

Pietro's ultimate plan was to escape to Mozambique – then Portuguese East Africa, a neutral country during the war.[5] He befriended a fellow inmate and the two of them sat together in their tent making elaborate plans. As a skilled goldsmith, Pietro's friend (whose name he never shared) made rings from mess tins, and 'precious stones' crafted out of red or green toothbrushes. Because Pietro was a fast learner, his English improved considerably after his arrival, and so it became his job to sell the rings. Their main target market was the 'black soldiers who were on guard duty and that displayed a certain sympathy towards us', he explained.[6] Although trading goods with guards was still forbidden, Pietro found a way to keep the cash flowing in, their friendship growing into a useful partnership for both men.

A third tent-mate, Gilio, expressed a desire to live out his passion for wool, and as he found himself in a country that produced it, he wanted to serve an apprenticeship that he could apply upon his return to his homeland. Obviously, Gilio's ambitions were severely curbed by his status as a POW, but not his dream.

Pietro had also developed a taste for money and, here again, the strictures of camp life presented a problem. He could only exploit the guards for so long before his illegal trade would be uncovered or before one of his

Pietro Scottu (sitting), with his fellow escapee, Gilio (Photo courtesy Pietro Scottu)

buyers would discover that the 'precious stones' in the rings were nothing more than cheap plastic. So the three of them agreed, 'there was only one option: ESCAPE, at that point, all our actions only had that objective, and we were very, very motivated to attempt it', he writes in his memoirs.[7]

But Pietro and his tent-mates were not the only prisoners who were hell-bent on escaping from Zonderwater. Luigi Vivaldi and Sergio Dodi shared the same ambition to regain their freedom in neighbouring Mozambique. On 10 November 1943, the two men decided to climb onto the back of a truck that was about to leave the camp. Even though the truck was inspected by the guards at the gate, they did not see anything suspicious under a strategically placed canvas sheet at the back. However, Vivaldi and Dodi's plans had been put together rather hastily, and once they found themselves outside the camp, they really didn't know what to do next. For one thing, they were hungry but they were unable to find a source of food. In the end, they surrendered themselves to the Witbank police.

When questioned, the two men gave the same reasons for their escape: first, they wanted to get out of the Fascist Block and, secondly, they had both applied for outside employment but had not received any feedback. One of them even volunteered to fight in Italy, but when his request was denied, he took matters into his own hands.

The court of inquiry found that the two UDF sentries were responsible for the escapes as 'a certain degree of carelessness was displayed by the gate duty staff ... due to too long spell of duty'.[8] While the matter was settled at Zonderwater, letters flew between the British Consul General, the Consul General for the Union and the Police Commissioner until mid-December about who was supposed to inform whom about the two escapees who were 'seen near the Portuguese [Mozambique] border' on 25 November. (Witbank is about 315 kilometres from the border and it is unlikely that the escapees would have been able to walk that distance in ten days.)

However, Vivaldi was not deterred by his first failed attempt and in May 1944 he tried to escape again. This time he escaped from the camp hospital with a new friend, Gaetano Savarese. They set off for Mozambique and they managed to reach Komatipoort, a town at the border. This time, though, Luigi was better prepared and somehow the two were able to ensure that they would get food and shelter on their way to the border. But they were discovered by an undercover constable who had been hiding under coal in a train truck.

The two pretended to be French citizens, but the authorities did not fall for their ruse. Once it became clear that they were escapees, they gave the names of two farmers who had helped them. But Luigi's escapade only served to confirm the police's fears that 'some of the escaped prisoners of war endeavour to enter Portuguese East Africa via the Zululand-Portuguese border'.[9] From this point onwards, therefore, all coal trains were searched at the border. While the court of inquiry found that none of the UDF staff were to blame for the escapes, the authorities took note of the involvement of the farmers and decided to investigate the matter. They did not like what they found.

A certain Professor Albrecht had set up a group of farmers to assist POWs who wanted to return to Italy via Mozambique. The damning evidence came from an intercepted telegram, sent by Albrecht to a POW at Zonderwater. The message 'When do you leave?' was cryptic but meaningful. Albrecht himself employed POWs on his farm in the Letaba district, close to the border. The investigators informed Colonel Prinsloo that 'quite a number of POWs have succeeded in crossing the Portuguese frontier'.[10]

A few days later, the same investigator expressed his concern that the police in the area actually admired the daring spirit of the escapees, writing that

> any escapees from [Albrecht's farm] would have to make their way to Komati Poort and cross the Crocodile River near Ressano Garcia. The police suggest that any POW who succeeds in crossing the Game Reserve would deserve his freedom as the odds are 100 to one that he would be killed and eaten by lions. And moreover, there are now special patrols in this area on the look-out for emigrants attempting to leave the Union without passports.[11]

It is certainly true that those who made it to Mozambique were quite gutsy, to say the least. One of them – Sebastiano Compagno – escaped from Zonderwater via this same route to get to Mozambique in 1942. When he arrived in Lourenço Marques, he wrote to Prinsloo, introducing himself before making a rather audacious request:

> Hopening [sic] you are not blaming me for my escaping for, the right of freedom is sacred to everybody all the World over and; in getting away from a stage of captivity, I did nothing but my duty. Likewise any other POW, of whatever nationality, who has done the same thing under whatever sky. Certainly you are very acquainted with the risks I went through, but in the same way, I'm sure you'll realize that, for a soldier, there aren't enough when personal freedom is in the bail and, surely had you been in my cloth, you would have done the same thing I did …
>
> [K]indly let me get back that correspondence which, I know, has arrived, addressed to me at my former POW address, since the date of May 1st, 1942 … I've to informe [sic] you that that correspondence

is of great value to me and of no value at all to anybody else because it came from my dearest, mother, father, brothers and fiancée of whom [I] am in the darkness about their whereabouts.[12]

A dramatic search for information ensued after Prinsloo received the letter. First, Sebastiano's friend in Zonderwater was interviewed to find out if he had kept his letters. When this didn't deliver useful information, Prinsloo, the camp inspector, the Secretary for External Affairs, the Consul General in Mozambique and the Red Cross all became involved. They must have spent hours on the matter, as is evidenced by the number of letters and telegrams that sped up and down the lines.

In the end, the Geneva Convention was consulted and the matter was settled at last. The POW authorities, according to Article 77 of the Convention, had no obligation to forward mail to escaped POWs; in fact, mail was to be kept at the POW camp until the escapee had been recaptured or until the war came to an end. At the same time, Prinsloo wondered why Sebastiano was not communicating directly with his family from Mozambique.[13]

Obviously, the escape network over the Mozambiquan border ran far deeper than was first thought to be the case. Escapes from citrus farms in the Nelspruit area (today's Mbombela) were not uncommon and, in some cases, the escapees even used trains to cross the border. In these instances, it became clear that Smuts's emergency war regulations were perhaps not as effective as they were intended to be, because they didn't seem to stop POWs from receiving help from civilians.

The emergency war regulations were mostly aimed at putting a lid on the *Ossewabrandwag*'s anti-war campaign. For one thing, its members were not allowed to work for the state, including the police and the railway police. And although the leader of the *Ossewabrandwag*, Hans van Rensburg, released all state workers from their membership of the organisation, some continued with their anti-war efforts.[14]

Despite these regulations being in place against *Ossewabrandwag* members who worked for the state, the authorities started to suspect collusion between POW escapees and members of the railway police. In one case when two POWs escaped from the Union and arrived in Lourenço

Marques, it was clear that they had travelled by train. Furthermore, the authorities knew about their arrival in Mozambique because they had intercepted the postcards that the escapees had sent from there to their farm manager.

With Albrecht's influence and the trains offering fast escapes, 'especially if some official on the train is sympathetically inclined'[15] it seemed ill advised to send POWs to work in that area, but the work camp at Sabie still required labourers for its forestry project.

However, not everyone in what was then called the Eastern Transvaal believed that escapees should be assisted. A few months before, the authorities were alerted to another escape in the same region. This time, black civilians helped the authorities to track down, capture and detain the men. In the light of the lack of acknowledgement of their efforts, a certain Captain Ingle wrote to the Secretary of Native Affairs, stating:

> In the latter part of December, 1942, some 15 Italian prisoners of war stole a Government lorry and 40 gallons of petrol, with which they escaped from Sabie forestry work camp. They were at liberty for quite a number of days in the area (Sabie and Bushbuckridge) … we finally rounded up the lot.
>
> I would like to mention the names of the following Natives as being in my humble opinion due to some sort of recognition by your department at least for the loyal help given by them … I feel that this is the only way in which the loyal help given by these Natives is likely to be recognised at all, as all local officials have seemingly forgotten to do so … perhaps a few thanks 'when thanks are due' may be of great help in letting the local Native know that when he does a good deed the Government recognises it.

The individuals Ingle was referring to were Mafuta Servellam and his wife, Marichep, and also Mokkies Mafone. According to the captain, whereas Mafuta 'showed great pluck and resource in this matter and was primarily responsible for the complete capture by the way he put out his scouts', Marichep 'pluckily helped to guard the 6 Italian prisoners and prevent them from breaking out of the old hut we had put them into – although she was only armed with an old sword'. Mokkies had helped to guard the prisoners and rounded up those who were left in the bush, 'of which one escaped and was afterwards tracked down and then run down and captured by Mokkies Mafone single-handedly, although he was only armed with a stick'.[16] They were rewarded with £2 each.[17]

Despite this successful episode of recapturing escaped prisoners, and others, the POW authorities eventually decided to close down the outside employment camp near Sabie: it was simply too close to the Mozambique border and presented too great a temptation to the prisoners of war.[18]

For the duration of the war, the UDF was very concerned about any possible interaction between Fascist POWs and like-minded South Africans. One way to try to stop the anti-war segment of the population from gaining greater influence was to keep some of them in internment camps until the war came to an end. Many members of the *Ossewabrandwag* were consequently interned at camps such as Koffiefontein and Andalusia.

Italian civilians from defeated Italian colonies also passed through the Union on their way to internment camps in what was then Southern Rhodesia.[19] Like the POWs, they arrived in Durban, and on their way to Rhodesia they spent some time in the same internment camps that housed *Ossewabrandwag* members and others who were not in favour of South Africa's war effort.[20] Although the Pietermaritzburg camp was mainly used for Italian POWs, it was a transit camp initially, and many others also moved through this camp.

In January 1942, for instance, a group of about 5 000 evacuees were accommodated there. They were on their way from Ethiopia to Southern Rhodesia and most probably included the wives and children of some of those prisoners already in the Union, although the men and women were separated. Perhaps the authorities did not expect the evacuees to share any extreme Fascist thoughts or they simply did not have room in any other camp, but it cannot be denied that this contact offered an opportunity for Fascist ideas to spread.[21]

In 1978, Hans Trümpelmann, a former inmate and leader of the internment camp at Leeuwkop, wrote in his memoirs that the authorities were wrong to place Union internees among Italian evacuees, since in many cases those contacts served to establish ties that weren't broken after the Italians moved on to other camps. Trümpelmann recalled how he was put in charge of making a large group of Italians feel welcome at Leeuwkop and, although he viewed the Italians as 'big boys' who looked at him 'with tame dog eyes', he became very fond of them. He was very amused when they depicted Mussolini, Hitler and 'Smats' in an artwork, with Smuts portrayed as a 'box of troubles' carried aloft by Mussolini and Hitler, who were on their way to put him in the ground.[22]

After the Italians were moved to separate camps, the two groups maintained contact, mostly through letters that were smuggled in by sympathetic guards. In one such letter, a man named De Jager wrote to the Italian POWs, expressing his wish that relationships between the two groups should continue, especially since they were all 'victims of British Imperialism' and that 'the Boers were united with the European nations in a life and death struggle'.[23] In another letter, he wrote that the Italians would achieve their aim of a 'free Fatherland' and that the 'Boers' supported their gallant cause. He ended his letter with an invitation, writing that 'when the banners of our Boer cause rise triumphantly and the flag of freedom is hoisted, I ask you to return to our Fatherland [the beauty of which is] hidden and obscured by rusted barbed wire'.[24]

The response from the Italians was positive; they expressed the hope that the communication would continue and that

> we are all united by the bonds of alliance in the greatest crusade of all time, which will end with the overthrowing of British Imperialism all over the world ... You and all Boers should be assured that all Italians, and particularly those who have lived in S Afr for a number of years, follow with the keen goodwill of true friends [your efforts] towards the attainment of freedom ... the day will come when side by side with your Boers we shall have a chance of fighting the British.[25]

In another instance, the message from the Italians to the Afrikaner internees included a request to send a message to the German state and to the Italian Socialist Republic, supplying information on the lineage of the

POWs who had penned the message and asking that they be repatriated as soon as possible. The Italians also stated that they had access to a radio, which allowed them to receive messages, presumably from their supporters in the Axis countries. The Union government viewed the practice of internees and POWs mixing as a threat, but it seems that they were unable to prevent it.[26] Many of those who were interned were members of the *Ossewabrandwag*, old adversaries of the Smuts government.

In at least one case, Military Intelligence informed Beyers of a potential concern. The Censorship Controller warned them that Buffa Buccellato, a Fascist leader in Lourenço Marques whose three sons were interned in the Union, had apparently approached the Portuguese Red Cross and suggested that his sons be repatriated to Mozambique in exchange for three British POWs. The Intelligence Service suggested that the UDF should not comply with this request as Buccellato was a 'most pugnacious Fascist' and that they should first establish whether his sons were indeed being held in the Union.[27] The administrative system was in such a parlous state, though, that it was an impossible task to track Buccellato's three sons. But Beyers nevertheless agreed that they should not be released to Lourenço Marques.[28]

When camp guards were implicated in assisting escapees, things became complicated. The staff shortage forced the authorities into a corner and they had no choice but to use the available men, loyal or not. Besides, it was often difficult to prove that guards were actively complicit in escapes. For example, on 14 January 1944, Antonio Lo Presti escaped from Zonderwater, apparently by bribing a guard. When the escape failed, the usual court of inquiry took place and, according to Presti's sworn statement, he offered to pay the sentry £2 if he allowed him to escape. Presti managed to crawl through the first perimeter fence, but he was spotted by another guard when he arrived at the second fence, and therefore 'could not pay the sentry the £2'.[29]

When asked why he had attempted to escape, Presti answered, 'I was tired of staying in the camp after 3 years'. The guard vigorously denied that he had colluded with Presti and claimed that he 'chased him with his bayonet' as soon as he realised Presti was trying to get out through the fence behind the sentry box. With no other witnesses, it was one man's word against another and, as usual, the inquiry found that 'no person was directly or indirectly to blame for the occurrence' and that 'the occurrence was due to a lack of discipline on the part of the POW concerned'.[30]

Despite the best efforts of the *Ossewabrandwag*, Trümpelmann and Professor Albrecht, though, relatively few POWs made it to Mozambique. Those who were captured en route were returned to Zonderwater and they must have shared stories about their adventures with other prisoners.

Presumably, some of these stories must have reached Pietro, because he changed his plans and abandoned Mozambique as a destination to escape to, deciding instead to try his luck elsewhere in South Africa. As he told me in an email in 2017, 'We learned that many POWs had been caught trying to cross the Limpopo because the route was kept under control. My decision to go south proved to be successful'.[31]

Pietro did not share with me the details of how he, the maker of the fake jewellery, and the wool-obsessed Gilio managed to escape from Zonderwater, except to say that he was 'one of the lucky chaps that managed to leave the cage and run off the camp, spending almost all the free time in hotel rooms'.[32]

When Pietro and his fellow escapees arrived in Port Elizabeth, they settled into the comfortable Saint George Terrace Hotel. Their next step was to set up a business making toys and it was not long before they secured a deal with a prominent sports retailer in the city. What they did not consider was the space they would need to produce large orders from the shop. As luck would have it, an airman serving at the Port Elizabeth airport offered them a solution. It is likely that this UDF man did not realise that he was helping escaped Italian POWs to establish a successful business when he allowed them to use his house as a toy factory. Pietro and his friend quickly began selling their toys, the first clients being Chinese men 'who fell in love with the little toy and without further question' decided to purchase more.

Their success was satisfying, but also scary, not least because, technically speaking, they remained escapees on the run. Pietro later wrote in his memoirs:

Although getting such an important client made us rejoice in our success, because it guaranteed more clients in the future, thinking about it carefully, we realized that it could also represent a threat to our freedom. Firstly, because we weren't at all equipped for production on a large scale, and secondly, because if anyone had had the idea, thinking to do us a favour, of finding out who we were and where the toys were made, and made it known to the press, whether local or not, we would have run the risk of finding ourselves back at Zonderwater. Our decision was sudden and perhaps a little hasty.

Consequently, they quit their enterprise and departed for East London; but good fortune seemed to follow them, and especially Gilio, as Pietro remembered:

Gilio had not forgotten his passion: wool. There was no business dealing in leather and wool that he would not visit to talk about current products … the British Wool Commission was, in fact, in East London, and here, after a competency exam, he was hired as a Wool Appraiser. This became his fortune, not so much during his stay in East London, but after his return to Italy … when he finally returned to Italy, he started to sell wool with so much skill and ability that he immediately became successful, and in 1951, the large corporate, Bielletti, already a client of his, chose him as a consultant. They even brought him along when, by government request, the company had to visit South Africa to agree on wool purchases in order to properly revitalize the Italian wool industry.[33]

But Pietro had other ideas and so the two friends parted ways. It was now about a year after his escape from Zonderwater and Pietro was having the time of his life. Having left his friend in East London, he soon found himself in an isolated part of Natal, working for an Irish woman who managed a trading post, 'where one could haggle as well as trade'.[34] Except for the odd mamba that caused excitement, there was not much to do there, and so it was not long before Pietro felt as if he 'had arrived at a tranquillity convent because of the calm that reigned all around'.

Things, however, became interesting when, in July 1944,

> on a cooler evening than usual, I found my boss in my bed, candidly telling me that, if I don't mind, seeing the cold, we could perhaps warm each other up! How does one respond to this type of demand? I told her it was not a bad idea, and that on top of things we would be saving on firewood! And so, for the first time, I also worked nights.[35]

As always, Pietro was open to new adventures, but either he or his employer did not know or, what is probably more likely, did not care that 'fraternisation' was against the rules: the regulations clearly stated that captives were not allowed to

> fraternise with the public, travel on public vehicles other than local busses, visit any place of public entertainment, bars, cafes or dances, public or private, enter any private house, except with special permission of employer eg to visit a priest or fellow PW employed elsewhere.[36]

In any case, by this time Pietro no longer considered himself a prisoner, and who knows what thoughts were in his employer's mind?

By 1944, however, the authorities should have known that only the pernicketiest of men would follow these rules. Despite the new arrangement with his landlady, though, for Pietro 'life seemed very monotonous, and the thoughts of total freedom came back to [my] mind.[37]

12

'WHAT ARE YOU DOING IN MY BEDROOM?'

As MORE AND more POWs went out to work on farms and on larger projects, many of them began to feel more at home in the Union. Most of them became fluent in English and others in Afrikaans. This, together with a convenient loss of memory that they were actually once at war with the country they were now enjoying so much, led to a greater sense of familiarity.

After the armistice in 1943, many Union citizens also assumed that the Italians were no longer prisoners. What they did not understand was that Italy had become a co-belligerent and not an ally, which meant that the POWs would remain POWs until the peace agreement was signed at the end of the hostilities. As a consequence, the POWs on outside employment remained subject to the same rules that had applied before the armistice.[1]

But the civilian population tended to ignore these details and so those who employed POWs started treating them like fellow citizens, friends and, in some cases, family members. Several POWs began dreaming about settling down in South Africa, marrying a farmer's daughter and starting a new life in the country. Unfortunately for them, CF Clarkson, the Minister of the Interior was not amused, thinking otherwise, and so when in March 1944 he was asked in Parliament if the POWs in the country were allowed to become Union citizens, his answer was a clear 'no'.

The follow-up question, however, produced a slightly more ambiguous answer. The issue at hand was marriages between POWs and Union citizens. The minister explained that each province governed these laws, but that no overall ban existed which prohibited such marriages. He concluded by saying that such marriages were to be 'discouraged in every possible way'.[2] He was naive to think that such polite discouragement would have any effect. After all, the outside employment scheme had been introducing POWs to civilians for the past five years and it was only natural that romantic relationships would develop, especially since the South Africans were known for their hospitality.

Evidently, the communication between the government and the public on this very issue was not very effective, as most citizens seemed to have no idea that relationships with Italian POWs were against the rules. Each time a liaison was uncovered, criminal proceedings followed, yet the news did not reach the public.

Being unfenced, the camp at George gave ample opportunity for POWs and citizens to socialise. In December 1942, the camp held 505 POWs with a further 1 500 on their way. The camp commander there apparently held the rules in low regard and did not do much to restrict the movements of POWs.[3] The locals, however, were split in their views on the foreigners in their midst: while some civilians found their presence exciting, others felt threatened by them. Thanks to the latter group of residents, the George police soon found themselves swamped with complaints and accusations about the Italians in town, but, strictly speaking, this was a matter for the military authorities to deal with. So, in a magnificent display of bureaucracy, the Deputy Police Commissioner of the Cape Western Division wrote to the Police Commissioner who, in turn, wrote to Beyers at Defence Headquarters in Pretoria. The commissioner stated his concerns in no uncertain terms:

> These prisoners are intended for work on road construction. Owing to the fact that the camp is unfenced these prisoners wander about as they like and it is no uncommon sight for them to be seen strolling along the roads in the vicinity in the company of European and non-European females ...
>
> [T]he following facts have been ascertained: visits to the [POW] camp are not restricted; so far they have been visited by a large number of people ... local civilians (Europeans) invite Prisoners of War to their homes and actually convey them from and to camp. These civilians are all, I understand, of the anti-Government element. Mostly members of the OB [*Ossewabrandwag*]; Prisoners of War attend public functions such as Bazaars. etc at Blanco and they have been seen parading the roads with European and Coloured

women who reside at and in the vicinity of Blanco.

This state of affairs I submit is very unsatisfactory and if allowed to continue will probably result in serious complications. This state of affairs is not sound, more particularly adjoining a village such as Blanco ... with a population of approximately 500 whites of the 'poor' type and some 1 800 coloured and native; and within four miles of George where there is a large flying school ... the law-abiding residents are now becoming perturbed and agitating for a Police Station at Blanco on account of the Prisoners of War camp there ... in order that there may be no unforeseen happenings as the result of the apparent free intermingling of these Italian Prisoners of War with the poor white, unloyal element and non-Europeans. I strongly recommend that steps be taken to have more strict supervision exercised and more stringent regulations issued governing [their] freedom.[4]

Beyers was not impressed with the content of this report and so he acted swiftly. A camp inspection was followed by a stern telling-off, leaving the camp commander – who was not a military man but a road engineer – in no doubt about the possible risks when POWs were left to their own devices. The engineer was soon replaced by a UDF officer, a Captain Fletcher, who the authorities hoped would have a better understanding of military discipline.[5] Fletcher's report to Beyers' deputy shortly after his arrival shed light on some of the issues:

There appears to be a general agreement that Capt Joubert [UDF officer at George camp] has shown himself to be most efficient, under almost impossible circumstances, and that without his excellent influence on the POW, the situation would have been far worse ...

It is pointed out that the POW strongly resent being controlled by a civilian, and further that the Engineer in local charge is himself a blustering and bullying type, unsuited to have control of Military labour and most deficient in tact ... The Magistrate reports considerable trouble with the local population, a section of

which openly defies his instructions regarding the taking of POW
into their houses ...

A further problem is presented by the conduct of women towards
POW. Many of these, both white and coloured, openly solicit them
in the area around the Camp. Instances constantly occur of car loads
of women parking near the Camp and calling to any POW in sight.[6]

Clearly, Fletcher blamed the civilians for many of the problems at George,
but perhaps he did not realise or want to acknowledge that fraternisation
was not a one-sided affair. According to him, the initial reports were
'exaggerated and misleading'. In his investigation, he found that the
POWs were not guilty of serious offences and that 'only three cases of
Venereal Diseases have occurred, which under the circumstances must be
considered as satisfactory'.[7] Nevertheless, from then on, no outside work
camps were without a military officer, who took charge of security and
controlling the POWs. Even so, the system remained flawed and prisoners
and civilians continued to find ways to meet and mingle.

As could be expected, the armistice of 1943 complicated matters. In
Oudtshoorn, for instance, four cases of fraternisation against Union
citizens were heard even before the armistice. When news of the armistice
reached the Union in August, seven new cases followed and by the end of
the year there were a total of 17 cases. It was almost as if the armistice had
served as an inspiration for fraternisation. The most common charges were
those of keeping company with a prisoner and conveying or harbouring a
POW in a motor vehicle. In one instance, a man was accused of allowing
a POW to attend a dance at his house, while in another a woman was
accused of entering the POW camp. Of all the accused, five were male
and 11 female and they were either fined between £5 and £15 or sentenced
to three months in jail.[8]

As for the POWs who participated in these offences, not all of them
were sent back to the Fascist Blocks at Zonderwater; neither were they
all declared unfit for further outside employment. Instead, the POWs
were simply placed with new employers or, as was the case with a farmer
in Lindley, the employers were allowed to retain the POWs who had
committed the offence.[9]

One of the reasons why socialising between prisoners and civilians carried on unabated was that many civilians didn't understand what the word 'fraternisation' entailed or what conduct qualified as 'fraternisation'. For instance, many did not realise that they were breaking the law when they hospitably invited POWs into their homes. For many POWs, fraternisation was a means to an end – whether it was for better living conditions on a farm, to create an opportunity for escape or to find a way to remain in the country. While many occurrences of contact between POWs and civilians were nothing more than innocent chats, from a military perspective even they were classified as 'fraternisation'. In fact, it was often these informal, often spontaneous, tête-à-têtes that landed prisoners and civilians in trouble.

In one example, a farmer took along three of his POW workers when he went to town to attend church. While the farmer was worshipping, the three men wandered around town. However, their seemingly innocent behaviour was in contravention of the War Measure Act 47 and 49 and so they were apprehended and charged.[10] While they were simply cautioned, others did not get off quite so lightly. In Paarl, a young woman was brought before the court along with her mother as both were accused of fraternising with POWs. The daughter was fined £15 or two months' hard labour; the case against her mother was withdrawn when the daughter accepted full responsibility for the offence.[11]

By 1945, however, the POW camp authorities had had enough of farmers, civilians and POWs breaking the law. As they saw it, everyone was taking advantage of the somewhat fluid and uncertain situation. To add to the administrative burden, many POWs wrote letters of complaint or tried to explain their transgressions. In particular, many wrote about the bad treatment they were receiving from their employers. Giuseppe Calicuiri, for example, did not get any food on Sundays because he was told 'no work, no food'.[12] What made matters worse was that his cranky employer would also not allow any of the POWs to go to town to buy their own food.

In another case, a farmer complained that he did not understand why he was no longer allowed to be supplied with POW workers. After all, he wrote to Beyers, he was only using the POWs on his farm to serve drinks to his guests at dance parties and allowing the Italians to dance with the guests. Blaming the inspector of outside employment, the farmer wrote that he felt he was 'treated unjustly because of a complaint of a person, who for some reason or other is after me'.[13]

In some cases, feuding farmers reported each other for breaking the rules and for mistreating their POW workers. In the Bethlehem district of the Orange Free State, two farmers drove one inspector of outside employment almost out of his mind with their constant complaints. The inspector became so annoyed that he told one of the farmers that if they did not resolve their differences, he would 'sweep the whole Bethlehem district clean of Italians'.[14]

This was not the end of it, though, and the aggrieved farmer – one Bruwer – wrote to Beyers that he was under the impression that the inspector's job was to investigate the 'doings and misdoings' of the POWs. He was greatly offended that he, as the farmer, seemed to have been the subject of an investigation. He wanted his POWs back because, as he said, 'neither I nor any of the Italians in my service have made the slightest misstep'.[15] The inspector's report showed that Bruwer had allowed the POWs on his farm 'to fraternize with his women guests, and [allowed] them to attend dances'.[16] Beyers, who really had better things to do, was no doubt annoyed by these types of incident, yet each case demanded the attention of the authorities as the threat of subversion from Fascist POWs and anti-war or pro-German civilians hung like a cloud over the country.

To complicate matters, there was no gainsaying that the POWs on outside employment continued to play an important role in food production. The UDF could therefore not simply withdraw them from service. After all, the main reason for their being in South Africa was to fill the labour gap left by South Africans serving in the war. Smuts was purposely and productively employing the Italians to help build infrastructure and assist with food production. Without the country enjoying these substantial benefits arising from their presence, he would probably not have offered to take in so many prisoners.

For their part, the military authorities tried different methods to deal with the constant headache presented by interactions between POWs and civilians. Zonderwater camp commandant Prinsloo also believed that many of their problems originated with civilians. In a letter to Beyers in February 1944, he reported how the inspector had struggled to convince civilians that they were violating the law when they fraternised with the Italian POWs in their area:

> Experience has shown that in quite a number of cases of frater-
> nisation where the POW is brought back to Camp and penalised for
> his actions ... the approach of fraternisation was made by civilians.
> If publicity could be given to one or two successful prosecutions,
> I am sure the whole question of control of POWs on OE [outside
> employment] would be considerably lightened.[17]

Just as Fletcher had done, Prinsloo considered civilians to be the root of the problem, but at least he also realised that their ignorance of the rules was playing a role. Efforts to stop fraternisation had clearly not been effective and the authorities were finding it increasingly difficult to remain patient with civilians who expressed only wide-eyed and dumbfounded innocence when they were arrested for this offence.

After Prinsloo asked for publicity on the matter, the Commissioner of Police wrote to Beyers suggesting that 'a suitable notice [be published] in newspapers ... warning members of the public against violating these regulations [49 of 1942 and 47 of 1943]' which prohibited fraternisation.[18] If civilians knew that they were committing an illegal act with a prisoner, the argument ran, then they could, of course, be held accountable, brought before a court and sentenced for their misdeed.

Unfortunately for the authorities, many of the cases against civilians did not succeed because several of them claimed they did not know that their 'friends' were POWs. One example was a young woman from Johannesburg who was accused of fraternisation. However, during the investigation it came to light that the POW had misled her. He had claimed that he was a Greek citizen in the process of immigrating to South Africa and that he intended to marry her. The woman became aware that he was a POW only when he was arrested. The upshot was that while the POW in question was returned to Zonderwater and served 28 days in detention, the young lady went unpunished because no evidence could be obtained that she knew her lover was an Italian POW. Although the docket was submitted to the Senior Public Prosecutor, they declined to prosecute.[19]

While the *Rand Daily Mail* did publish an article on the topic of fraternisation in July 1943, it was not enough. Another effort was made in 1944, when the same newspaper made it clear that it was the Department of Defence that had drawn up the rules about the 'control of prisoners of war'.[20] The article was in fact an official statement by the department in which it explained that the agreement between an outside employer and the military authorities placed specific responsibilities on the employer. These responsibilities included giving a written pass to POWs before they left their place of employment for whatever reason. Without these passes, POWs could not use public transport or visit cafés, swimming baths, zoos or any other places of entertainment. The statement also warned that POWs dressed in civilian clothing would be arrested. Furthermore, it asked for the public's help:

[M]embers of the public can co-operate with the authorities in maintaining proper discipline over prisoners of war, realising at the same time that very heavy penalties may be imposed in cases where individuals are found guilty of fraternisation ... instead of making general allegations, it will be appreciated if members of the public bring specific instances of breaches of the prisoner-of-war regulations to the appropriate authorities.[21]

The Star newspaper also warned against fraternisation, reporting on the cases of a number of civilians who had been prosecuted and given heavy fines or jail sentences. In addition, the article tried to clarify the meaning of the armistice by stating that there

appears to be an erroneous impression that the status of Italian prisoners of war has changed since Mussolini's downfall and the Italian armistice. This is incorrect; the treatment of Italian prisoners of war continues to be governed by the provisions of the

Geneva Convention.[22]

However, these two newspapers were preaching to the choir: both were aimed at English-speaking readers who mostly supported Smuts's stance on the war. And many of the farmers who made use of POW labour were Afrikaners who were unlikely to be readers of those newspapers.

Later in 1944, an amendment to the War Measure Act 47 was adopted. According to this new regulation, small parties of POW labourers were allowed to visit towns while on outside employment, but they had to be escorted by UDF guards. Those POWs who worked in smaller work camps were allowed to visit towns only if they had a pass from the camp officer. These visits were for essential shopping only and the men were not allowed to enter private houses, bars or places of entertainment or to use public transport.[23] Moreover, if POWs did not comply with these regulations, their conduct would be viewed as an effort to escape if they did not carry the requisite pass. They would also be suspected of fraternising with civilians if they were found in a house or a bar.

Between April and September of 1944, three cases of fraternisation between civilian women and POWs were investigated at Zonderwater, leading to two convictions and one allegation that was withdrawn. Although this appears to be a low number, arriving at an allegation actually involved inspections and control over 18 000 prisoners per month, which meant that a total of 108 000 POWs had had to be monitored or investigated during the period April to September for the purposes of compiling the report.[24]

At other camps, including Paarl, Storms River, Robertson and Rustenburg, incidents of fraternisation were a fairly common occurrence.[25] The work camp at Standerton also had its share of trouble that required 'energetic investigations' by the UDF staff. They found that the POWs were 'perpetually committing offences [and] contravening' rules. POWs mixing with 'Native women and certain elements of the European community' caused concern, but when it became evident that POWs were 'supplying Natives with wine', met 'Native girls' and also had relationships with them, the authorities realised that stricter control was necessary as the 'passive means to curb this nuisance is futile'. It didn't help that UDF members were reluctant to apprehend offenders, especially when, as was the case with one unfortunate corporal, the Italians 'ran away, halted and pelted the Cpl with stones'.[26]

In Johannesburg, another corporal endured similar bad treatment, but this time from a furious local woman after he had arrested a POW who was working on the property but was accused of fraternising with the owners. The woman lashed out at the corporal, shouting, '*Waar is die donder, ek gaan hom doodslaan*'. ('Where is the bugger, I'll beat him to death'.) She proceeded to threaten the corporal with a length of wire.

Meanwhile, the POW took advantage of the situation and acted as if he was having a fit. Eventually the hapless corporal let the POW go, but he recommended to the authorities that the property was unfit for outside employment as 'it no doubt will prejudice the discipline of the prisoners of war'.[27]

POWs who worked on the fruit plantations in the Elgin district were apparently also tempted to flout the rules. A number of them were caught in the company of 'immodest' women and it was decided that they had to serve 21 days in detention but would then be allowed to return to the farms. However, when ten POWs were caught with 'undressed Coloured Women in their beds', the Grabouw police station commander was unhappy with the different treatment the women and the POWs received.[28]

The station commander wrote to the camp commandant at Worcester who was in charge of the POWs that, given how severely the women had been dealt with, 'the Prisoners should not be allowed to get away with it. They have also contravened War Measure No 47 of 1944 and should be severely dealt with'.[29]

The women were all prosecuted and two of them, who had been found guilty of fraternisation in the past, were sentenced to three months' hard labour. The other women were each sentenced to between £10 and £15 or hard labour ranging from two to three months.

In response to the Elgin station commander's missive, the camp commander at Worcester felt that 'in view of the POWs' long service ... it is proposed to comply with the Employers' requests and permit the defaulters to return to their service on completion of their sentences'.[30] Beyers was of a similar mind and decided that they could stay in Elgin. Under normal circumstances, they should have been returned to Zonderwater, where they would have been reclassified as non-cooperators and housed in the Fascist Block – which meant that they would also have been denied the opportunity to go on outside employment again.

Although some investigators became frustrated with having to police POWs' and civilians' interactions, in at least one case they helped to protect a prisoner from exploitation. One of the cases the Special Investigation Officer at Zonderwater, one Atkinson, was looking into during April 1945 was not so much a matter of fraternisation but of possible collusion between a POW and his employer. The POW was employed for agricultural work but the officer became suspicious that he was being used in a different capacity. The officer decided to set a trap by placing an order with the farmer and his wife for two paintings. When they were ready, the farmer asked the POW to indicate his price for the artwork. The officer relayed part of his conversation with the farmer's wife in his report:

> 'I suppose this quite a profitable side line with you – selling these pictures'.
> 'Oh yes,' replied the lady, 'we make plenty money!'
> (This detective business is a cruel job. Truth lies at the bottom of a deep well. Our function is to uncover every facet, so we put a final question.)
> 'Aren't you afraid that the authorities at Zonderwater may object to this arrangement?'
> 'No, because they are not likely to find out'.[31]

The officer recommended that the POW be withdrawn from employment as he was being exploited for his artistic talent.

The same officer who found his work so 'cruel' submitted a second report to the Zonderwater authorities on the same day. In this case, an informant had told him about fraternisation between a POW and his employer on the Eikenhof estate near Rietvlei, south-east of Pretoria. Upon his arrival at the property late at night, he entered the house and found a man wearing an overcoat over his pyjamas. In the bedroom was a woman, still in bed. Again, the officer described part of the conversation that followed:

> The woman: What are you doing in my bedroom?
>
> Your IO [investigating officer]: This man, madam, has just admitted that he is a prisoner of war, and that gives me the legal right to enter this room. Will you now explain why I find him in your sleeping quarters at midnight?
>
> The woman: I am very ill and he is looking after me ... I haven't had a doctor.
>
> Your IO: Why not?
>
> The woman: Because I don't need a doctor; I am a doctor myself.

The POW was reported and the officer was asked to return to Eikenhof to investigate the matter further. He found that the woman was married to a German man who had been interned at the Baviaanspoort internment camp when the war began. The officer established that the woman frequently brought young girls from Johannesburg to 'associate' with the POWs and that a young girl from a neighbouring property had been sexually abused by one of the POWs. The neighbour also stated that 'on one occasion an Italian entered her kitchen and made an indecent exposure of his person, at the same time demanding that one of the Native women be sent to his room to alleviate his condition'.[32]

Another case of abuse was brought before the Robertson Circuit Court in April 1946. The POW was charged with breaking section 2(1) of the Girls' and Mentally Defective Women's Protection Act 3 of 1916. More specifically, the POW was accused of having had an 'unlawful carnal connection with ... a girl under 16 years of age'. Because this was a criminal offence, he was not sent to Zonderwater for detention but was given a sentence of two years' imprisonment with hard labour.[33]

In the Zonderwater archives, there are many boxes with hundreds of files dealing with what the authorities referred to as cases of fraternisation. The way in which these most human of relationships were policed foretold the injustices that were to come under the apartheid government that forbade relationships and marriages between blacks and whites. Even just a small measure of reflection might have made the lawmakers of the day realise that it is impossible to control human needs and emotions. After all, among the authorities themselves there were those who openly 'fraternised' with the prisoners in their charge.

13

LOVE BEYOND THE RULES

THE KIND-HEARTED RAFFAELLO saw things differently from most other POWs. If he could make someone's life more tolerable, he did. He did not see those around him as compatriots or even as so-called 'enemy captors': for him, everyone was human, fallible and deserving of goodwill.

As the chef at the Pietermaritzburg camp, he was entrusted with the regular task of going into town to buy supplies 'for both the bar and kitchen extras, from the butcher, to the cigarette wholesaler, to the brewery, to the Ross & Co department store'.[1] At the department store worked a local girl called Mabel and she had taken a liking to his friend, Gregorio Fiasconaro, after they met at one of the concerts organised by Gregorio.

'They'd given me the role of love messenger, a role that didn't excite me all that much, but that I did willingly anyway in the name of friendship,' Raffaello wrote in his memoirs: 'Every day I went to the counter where Mabel worked with the excuse of buying or exchanging a packet of colourant, and instead I left or picked up messages. Gregorio's life was a lot more bearable than ours. He had music, and now he also had love'.[2]

But Gregorio had more than music and love: he had also found the country where he would spend the rest of his life. In the meantime, though, the war was still raging and it remained illegal for POWs to socialise (or fraternise) with South African civilians. Gregorio was fortunate, though: he had Captain Rogers on his side, and when Raffaello was not in town, Gregorio was able to go, also with the pretence of exchanging packets of dye with the girl behind the counter at Ross & Co.

As Gregorio and Mabel's relationship blossomed, they devised a plan to see more of each other. It was a cunning plan: Gregorio would escape from the camp on specific nights and hide in a ditch next to the road where Mabel would come along with a taxi. The car would stop and Gregorio would jump in before the taxi driver could ask 'where to?' On one occasion a drunk taxi driver asked for a bribe not to report them to the camp command, but before he could make his demands, he crashed the car, leaving Gregorio and Mabel with having to make plans for their homeward trip in the back seat! At that time, Gregorio's English was rudimentary, but language did not get in the way of the two love birds, and so in 1947 they got married. At the same time, Gregorio's career in music took off, and he eventually became the most well-known voice in the South African opera world.[3]

Luckily for Raffaello, his role as love liaison was never uncovered and he was able to continue to build on the good terms that he had already established with the UDF guards and officers in Pietermaritzburg. As time went by, the relationship between Raffaello and the officers developed an interesting dimension, thanks to their love of fishing:

> Captain Van Zeal [probably Van Zyl], a fishing aficionado, would oftentimes take me out with him on fishing trips from which we came back loaded with small iridescent fish that I believe were pumpkinseed. One afternoon, a friend popped into the kitchen and said: '[Raffaello], make three large steaks, some sandwiches, get a few beers and a grill for the captain. We're going fishing'.
>
> While we were fishing in a lake about forty km from the camp, I made a fire while waiting for them to come back. But time went by and nothing was getting caught. There were many swearwords and curses going round, and it looked like the expedition would be unsuccessful. Suddenly I heard a cry. A very big fish must have bitten, and after pulling all the fishing line away, it had pushed the float all the way to the middle of the lake. The fishermen couldn't find a way to get it back. So, Captain Van Zeal took off his shoes and shirt, dove into the water and swam all the way to the centre of the lake, where he retrieved the float as well as the 'monster' that had pulled it so far from the line ...
>
> I went out on other occasions to prepare well-received refreshments for the officers and soldiers. Their appreciation made me feel useful, though not indispensable, despite my prisoner status.
>
> There were times when the English, whether simple soldiers or

officers, stopped being in my eyes the 'enemy' that had defeated us and imprisoned and relegated me to that faraway, inhospitable land. What I saw in front of me were human beings, with qualities and flaws just like everyone else. I don't know whether this attitude exposed me to my fellow prisoners' criticism or should be considered unpatriotic behaviour.

I've always cared more about substance than appearance, and even then, despite my young age, I tried to learn all the good things I saw from the enemy. I had no prejudices outside the common feelings of like or dislike that men routinely experience and that influence their choices.[4]

Perhaps the officers abused their position in making use of Raffaello's services in this way or perhaps it could even have been classified as a type of fraternisation. Whatever the case may have been, these fishing trips gave Raffaello reason for reflection. In general, his experiences at the Pietermaritzburg camp show that, at least in his case, even officers would sometimes ignore regulations regarding interactions with prisoners:

I became friends with [Sergeant Rogers, the bar manager at the camp], or rather established the kind of friendship that can exist between a prisoner and his jailor, in any case, a loyal relationship based on mutual respect. Many times he asked me for a sweet treat to make up with his girlfriend ... They often argued because he liked beer a little too much and he would collapse onto the canteen floor blind drunk. I took him home myself many a time in the wee hours of the morning, when he wouldn't have been able to find the way.

Sometimes I slept outside the camp, hosted by Mabel, who had become my friend Fiasconaro's girlfriend ...

Corporal Rodger [Sergeant Rogers] himself once wanted to take me to a museum where he showed me a magnificent specimen of mammoth in the palaeontology section. He was like that, nice and friendly, a beer lover but also a culture lover. Once he dragged me to an assembly in the city hall. The speaker, representing the South African Union, was General Smuts.[5]

In the meantime, Raffaello developed a close friendship with Dora, Mabel's friend at the department store in town. Raffaello was smitten, but careful, since he was never one to overstep his boundaries. When Dora offered to send a package to Italy on his behalf, Sergeant Rogers took Raffaello to her family home to deliver the package. When they arrived, her parents asked Raffaello to stay the weekend.

It seems that Sergeant Rogers was a helpless matchmaker, and he took great risks with his exploits. He had only Raffaello's word that he would not try to escape or participate in any other illicit activities. Leaving Raffaello at Dora's house was itself an unlawful activity as it amounted to fraternisation. In the end, Rogers agreed, leaving Raffaello to spend the entire weekend toing and froing about whether or not to 'declare' himself to Dora. In the end, he said nothing, 'and when Rodger (sic) came to fetch me I greeted him with the same deference I used to say goodbye [to] the other members of her lovely family'.[6]

The case of Gerli Ferdinando was an exception to most other instances of fraternisation. After he was captured in February 1941, he willingly signed the declaration of cooperation as soon as he could. During his imprisonment, he studied medicine. At an unknown date, he met and married a South African woman. At the time he wrote to Prinsloo, they already had one child.

Gerli informed Prinsloo that 'it has been my dominant pre-occupation throughout to make adequate provision for my family and to endeavour to obviate, if possible, the cruel necessity of separation'.[7] The cruel separation he referred to was, of course, his impending repatriation to Italy, from where he would be able to apply to emigrate to South Africa.

Gerli had been offered a position at the University of Milan and so he asked Prinsloo 'that a special dispensation be made in my case whereunder my wife and child may be permitted to accompany me on the ship in which I shall, in due course, be repatriated'. To strengthen his case, Gerli gave the example of the Red Cross delegate, Dr Grasset, who had been allowed to travel with his family on a repatriation ship.[8]

Prinsloo, impressed with the fact that Gerli had 'conducted himself honourably throughout and in a manner consonant with the behaviour of a gentleman', gave permission with his 'strongest recommendation on compassionate grounds'.[9] It is strange, though, that Prinsloo had nothing to say about Gerli's marriage to a South African woman, something that was not permitted at the time.

In another case, Beyers responded to a request that had been forwarded to him by Smuts. The anxious woman was informed that 'there has been no relaxation in the law governing marriage and fraternisation with POWs. It is regretted, therefore, that we can be of no further assistance to you'.[10] The woman had written to Smuts, stating that she wanted to marry a POW and asking his permission. She wrote:

> As a widow with two children, I am applying to you with the hope that you will give me some sympathy & help. I have written to the Immigration Officer & the Camp Commandant about an Italian Prisoner of War whom I wish to marry.
>
> As you see I am prepared to pay the deposit for permission for him to remain in the Union. I am quite independent of anyone & would be no trouble to the Government. We wish to stay in this country, and as my husband [the Italian POW] would wish to become a Union national. Should he have to go back to Italy it might be years before he could return, & why waste our lives like this for nothing.[11]

In their desperation, some women appealed directly to Issie 'Ouma' Smuts, the wife of the prime minister. In one instance, Mrs Smuts received correspondence from a young woman who wrote to her that her 'big sin was to fall in love with an Italian prisoner'. The lovers had tried to obtain permission to marry, but apparently it was not granted:

> Two years and six months passed, and we really tried to keep our love clean and if we only had permission [to marry] our lives would not be the great tragedy that it is today. Two years ago we began expecting a baby, but even then we could not get permission and our son is still without a name ... And now the prisoners are going away ... Oh, Ouma, what can we do? Can they not give us a helping hand?[12]

The woman also made it clear in her letter that the POW had sincere intentions, although she had not seen him because he had been in the POW camp for the past two years.

Beyers responded on behalf of Mrs Smuts but he was stern and unsympathetic in his answer. His office could do nothing to help her, he wrote, and he made it clear that the law against marriage and fraternisation was there to protect South African women. She could have been fined or sentenced to a year in prison, or both, he said. Beyers concluded his correspondence by warning her that a number of convictions have been made in this regard.[13]

At the opposite end of the scale, a number of POWs decided to stay in South Africa and many of them married South African women.

Some South Africans did not approve of family members' connections with POWs, though. As was the norm at the time, the entrenched patriarchy often dictated the reaction among local men to a relationship between one of their family members, whether it be a sister or a daughter, and their Italian friends or lovers. For example, when a young woman married a POW in 1945, her brother saw it as an insult to his family and he wrote to the authorities complaining about the 'clandestine marriage' and asking them to get the Italian out of the country:

> I should like your assurances that this person is going to be re-patriated with the rest of the Italian prisoners of war, and not [be] allowed to remain in the country as my sister's husband. If he returns to Italy and then re-enters the Union as a regular foreign immigrant, it would only be fair to the thousands of British, American and other allied groups, who are at present de-barred from entering the Union until South African nationals are fully repatriated, and re-established in civil life. I am an ex-serviceman, having served for five and a half years with the RNVR and SANF and naturally feel this unfair marriage very keenly.[14]

The brother was most probably hoping that the POW would not be allowed to make his way back to South Africa once he had been repatriated. In a follow-up letter, the brother wrote to the South African Legion, stating that he, the brother, wanted to see the marriage certificate. According to him, his sister was not aware that he was making these enquiries. Apparently, he wanted to protect her two sons 'from any unfavourable consequences of their mother's marriage'. Her sons, from a previous marriage, were 20 and 15 at the time, the elder of the two a volunteer serviceman in the UDF.[15]

As with the brother in question, many South Africans did not approve of the authorities' lenient attitude towards Italian POWs. They also believed that it was far too easy for POWs to become citizens.

An easy way for the authorities to identify and find evidence of instances fraternisation was for them to intercept letters between POWs and civilians. More often than not, these letters made for interesting reading. Between December 1944 and February 1945, for example, the official censors found a number of suspicious letters between a young woman, perhaps the daughter of a farmer who had employed POWs, and a POW who had been returned to Zonderwater after having been found guilty of fraternisation.

Once back at Zonderwater, the POW and the girl started writing to each other, with the girl expressing her devotion and longing in no uncertain terms:

> My darling, I am doing my best. I wish that I may go to you, but dearest, I can't … oh! It is so long ago, since I saw you for the last time … I wish that I may go to you to take you out of prison, dear, but what can I do? I hope always that the day when we'll meet again may come soon, my dear, and you darling?'[16]

In another letter, she wrote despairingly that she was convinced she had not received all his letters. Regardless, she remained committed to him, writing that she would 'wait until my death. Forever'.

Possibly to avoid exposure, in their letters the two referred to each other as 'brother' and 'sister', but, upon investigation, the authorities concluded that these descriptions 'can be relatively discounted'. When interrogated, the POW in question baffled the authorities by stating that he only met [the girl] on two occasions: that he once wrote to her requesting her to use her influence to get him on outside employment [and] he denies that he ever entertained a 'sisterly' affection for her or that he was on any other terms of intimacy.[17]

Censors also intercepted letters intended for families in Italy. In one case, it was clear that the POW concerned had no idea of the rules about freedom of movement or of those about fraternisation. The descriptions in the letter were closer to those of a travel writer than a wartime correspondent. He wrote:

I am well enough off, above all I enjoy the freedom. There is little work and not many amusements but I tell you that I spend some evenings dancing with some lovely ... during the rest of the day I can go out into the country: and I find everything that I need, and there is no shortage of wine.[18]

The idea that love could conquer all was also a popular theme in letters written by desperate lovers who had been separated from each other. However, appeals by lovesick young Italian men to stern Calvinist fathers were often ignored, as the following letter by a POW shows:

Surely you forgive me everything I did to [your daughter], but you must understand that it happened just through love that existed between me and her. And still today I have the same feeling towards [her] as great as in the past and nobody may prohibit our promise. And therefore I wrote to her almost twice a week, but I am very discounted with her mail, which never arrives.

Please, Sir, forget my wrong deeds and satisfy this sad heart, and tell me where [she] is, and why she does not write, so that I can say that you made me feel happy till the last moment. I am in Zonderwater.[19]

The many intercepted letters are ample evidence of emotional hardship, secret marriages, lustful liaisons, divorce, young innocents with naively open hearts, and unplanned pregnancies. In 1944, a member of the Union's Women's Auxiliary Army Service (WAAS) even asked for a transfer to

Zonderwater so that she could be closer to a specific POW.[20] In another case involving UDF servicewomen in Wellington in the same year, two POWs were caught giving a lift to the women on the handlebars of their bicycles. The women were each fined £3 or one month's imprisonment with hard labour. It took until April 1945 for the matter to be resolved.[21]

It goes without saying that Giovanni would not fraternise with Union citizens even if his life depended on it. One can only wonder what would have transpired if he had ever had the opportunity to meet up with *Ossewabrandwag* supporters, but that never happened.

Luigi's love for his wife, Barbara, was enough motivation not even to consider fraternising with local women.

Paolo, who was still sewing theatre costumes at Zonderwater, became bored with camp life, but apparently felt no need for female companionship of the illegal kind. His main aim for signing the declaration of cooperation after spending most of the war in the camp was so that he could put his skills to use outside Zonderwater. He, together with two friends, Lotti and Gambuti, were sent to work for a 'Dutch' family near Pretoria, where they stayed until the end of the war.

In Natal, the serial escaper, Pietro, became increasingly dissatisfied with his work at the trading post and with finding his employer in his bed. He felt caged in and perhaps a little threatened by her expectations of him. Also, the day-to-day boredom got the better of him. He wanted adventure and excitement, and it was not long before he found a way to 'leave my job without any obligation to return'.[22]

An opportunity presented itself when Pietro and his employer went to Durban on business. They had agreed to meet again at lunchtime at the place where she had parked her car. 'Instead, the first thing I did was go to the station by taxi and get on the first train [back to] East London,' he wrote. Here his old friend Gilio introduced him to the 'Lions Beer Agent', who in turn appointed him as a barman at the Queenstown Hotel Windsor. This time, Pietro stayed put for two years.[23]

14

THE LONG WAIT TO RETURN HOME

EVEN THOUGH HE had been deposed, Mussolini remained hopeful that there was still a future for Fascism. He was appointed the President of the Italian Social Republic in the German-controlled northern parts of Italy. Trusting his advisors, Mussolini formed the Black Brigades after the armistice was signed in 1943. The men in these units were loyal Fascists who would protect Italy from the Partisans who were fighting for the Allies. Unfortunately for Mussolini, the Partisans grew in number and with their support the Allies continued to push north.[1]

Eventually, with the arrival of spring in 1945, the German forces in Italy realised that they could no longer hold back the Allies. Mussolini grew concerned for his own survival and tried to escape across the Alps. But his disguise as a German general was not convincing and he was recognised by a group of Partisans. He was summarily arrested and shot dead in a small village on 28 April along with his mistress. Their bodies were taken to Milan, where they were first displayed in the Piazzale Loreto square there before they were strung up ignominiously by their feet.[2]

At the time, Hitler and a small group of his most loyal supporters were hiding in a bunker beneath the streets of Berlin. As the Allies entered the city at the end of April, street-by-street fighting began and the last German bands of resistors, made up mainly of old men and young boys, were overpowered.[3] Overcome by paranoia, Hitler suspected almost everyone of treason and handed out execution orders in between fits of rage.[4] When the Fuhrer could see no way out, he married his long-time companion, Eva Braun, and, a day later, on 30 April, they both committed suicide.

The war in Europe was over, but the official end would come only once the German command had signed the surrender. This did not happen before another war of words broke out between the Allies: Russia wanted to claim victory because Joseph Stalin of the Soviet Union believed his

Red Army had sacrificed more than the others. In the end, victory was postponed for several days and Victory Day in Europe was announced late at night on 8 May.[5]

Everyone at Zonderwater followed these events as closely as they could. On 7 May, the camp's senior chaplain, Don Rosario Napolitano, announced that a mass would be held to celebrate victory in Europe. Another mass was planned for the 'Glorious Dead who with their blood have contributed to the realisation of this long-awaited day of Victory'.[6] Depending on individuals' personal views, the end of the war brought either relief, joy, resentment or a sense of anticipation.

Those POWs who had assumed that the end of the war in Europe – the war in the East would continue until 2 September 1945, when Japan surrendered – meant a return to their homeland would soon discover that they were mistaken. While South Africa was protected from the worst impact of the war due to its distance from the main theatres of war, now that the war was over that distance became a great disadvantage – at least for the Italian POWs.

Almost the entire population of Europe was displaced and thousands of newly liberated Allied POWs began to emerge from their camps across German-occupied territories, all looking for a way home. Alongside them were refugees from bombed-out cities who were searching for, but not necessarily finding, their families, homes or even their towns. The deadly concentration camps where the Nazis had exterminated thousands of European Jews, Roma, Sinti, homosexuals and political adversaries were liberated, but collectively they still held about 700 000 inmates.

In Italy, the Partisans wanted revenge for the destruction of their country and their people, in consequence of which thousands of suspected Fascists were executed. This meant that the formal end of the war in Europe did not mean the end of killing: reprisals continued for many months afterwards.[7] It is impossible to estimate how many Italians still believed in Fascism after the war, but some academics hold the view that Fascist ideas dwindled in the aftermath and never posed a serious threat to the new Italian government.

The memory of Mussolini and the destruction he caused in Italian society led to a strong Communist presence in the post-war politics

For security reasons, the end of the war was a quiet affair at Zonderwater
(Photos courtesy NMMH)

of the country.[8] But while the Italian government tried to establish a 'new culture' and a 'new society' after the war, some still clung to the Mussolini-era style of politics. Many of the country's intellectuals started writing about the war, but it is not always possible to determine whether they 'sought to conceal or to confront their Fascist past'.[9]

Back in the South African POW camps, the men grew increasingly impatient and restless. Considering their many years of captivity, it is no surprise that rumours started spreading about repatriation and how the prisoners would be welcomed back in Italy, or not. False assumptions and misunderstandings flourished among the inmates and yet again the camp command was kept busy with distributing the 'correct' news and preventing extremist ideas from influencing those POWs who held more moderate views.

Repatriation itself was a complex operation that required logistical skill, accurate record-keeping and the careful management of people. It was not simply a matter of loading men onto ships and sending them home: for one thing, the British government wanted all its Dominions to adopt the same policy on the repatriation of prisoners. Discussions in Parliament went round in circles as conflicting interests clashed. Yes, POW labour was still necessary to bring in the harvests and complete the road-construction work, but it would have been unfair to keep the cooperators back while the non-cooperators went home first. In the end, the deliberations reached a stalemate and the POWs remained in limbo.

Overall, the repatriation process started slowly and proceeded in dribs and drabs. At first, only a selected group of POWs were chosen to return to Italy; among others, they included those who could fulfil the 'special needs of the armed forces', those older than 60 and those over 50 who had been prisoners for more than two years. Also included were those considered essential to contributing to civil reconstruction and those who were thought to have compassionate reasons for returning home.[10] Among the cooperators, the opportunity for repatriation was determined by the date on which they were first captured. But this opportunity was denied them if they had been found guilty of escaping, fraternisation or any other misconduct during their captivity.

Prisoners leaving from Zonderwater station, possibly being
repatriated after the war (Photo courtesy NMMH)

Whereas the majority of the POWs in the Union couldn't wait to be repatriated, in one particularly poignant case an Italian prisoner declined an offer to be sent home early. Tomaso de Lellis refused to sign the declaration of cooperation, even though every effort was made by a UDF soldier who had been captured in Italy to ensure his early return to his homeland.

Tomaso's family lived in Gerano in southern Italy. Stanley Smollan was a member of the 2nd Transvaal Scottish who had been captured at Tobruk in June 1942, along with almost 30 000 Allied soldiers. When the armistice was announced in 1943, Stanley and three of his friends escaped from their POW camp. They survived in the Italian countryside, thanks to the goodwill of peasant families – Tomaso's family was one of those that offered Stanley a place of refuge.

When Stanley arrived back in the Union, he wrote a number of letters to the authorities, hoping to secure Tomaso's early repatriation. He felt he had a debt to repay to Tomaso's family. However, when the authorities approached Tomaso, he refused the offer because he was unwilling to sign the declaration of cooperation. In a letter to Stanley, Tomaso wrote that he would sign it only if he could be withdrawn from Zonderwater – indicating that he feared a strong reaction from other non-cooperators. He explained that his unwillingness to sign the declaration was because of the 'personal humiliation he would have to suffer in deserting principles he has stood by for so long'. Tomaso assured Stanley that Fascism, 'its emblems and all it stands for', meant nothing to him and that he 'would gladly desert them if only he could return to his wife and children'.[11]

Zonderwater was the only camp at the time where Fascist POWs were held and so Tomaso could not be moved elsewhere. Following a discussion with Tomaso, the camp command informed Stanley that Tomaso 'resolutely declined to abandon his adherence to Fascist principles and designation [and] there is nothing further to be done in the matter'.[12]

Tomaso may have had the courage to wait patiently for his return home, but others became increasingly despondent and frustrated. In May 1946, a medical officer at Zonderwater, Lieutenant Shlugman, was called out to attend to a POW in the Fascist Block. When he arrived, he found the man hanging. The death of this prisoner prompted the angry POWs in the block to surge forward, shouting and jumping into the ambulance while Shlugman tried to manage the situation and remove the body. Remaining remarkably calm, he realised that 'in the event of a rising the greatest difficulty and tact would have to be displayed', not only by himself in that moment, but also by the camp command to 'prevent the loss of unnecessary blood'. Writing to Prinsloo later, Shlugman emphasised that

> These men have been away from their families for periods varying from six to eleven years and during that period they have had to undergo both the strain and hardships of military and POW life, coupled with the fact that the vast majority of these fascists are middle-aged ... the fact that they have lived solidly and continuously during their stay in Zonderwater behind barbed wire must lead to a 'barbed wire' complex.

Their living conditions conform without a doubt to that laid down by the Geneva Convention, but leave much to be desired, as judged by our standard of living. Their lives are bound up with monotonous routine. However, one must not lose sight of the fact that a death always tends to set people a bit haywire as in this instance, but in this particular instance it was far in excess of that normally displayed.

Shlugman warned that the cumulative effect of psychosis or 'barbed wire complex', as he labelled it, and their circumstances had to be taken into account and guarded against. Most of all, it was the waiting for repatriation that 'amplified a thousand-fold the minutest detail important to them'.[13]

In the meantime, the war in the Far East continued and shipping remained both expensive and scarce.[14] Returning servicemen were given priority when space became available on ships and so POWs, however impatient they were, simply had to wait for such opportunities, irregular as they were. For the 27 070 POWs still in camps across South Africa, apart from those still on outside employment and the escapees, repatriation would necessarily be a slow process.

For once, the South African press was cautious in its approach. In May 1945, an article in *The Star* stated that arrangements for repatriation formed part of the peace negotiations and that POWs should not expect to return to Italy until such time as an agreement could be reached. No timeframe was given.[15] In Parliament, the same information was given in response to a question related to repatriation.[16] The Geneva Convention of 1929 states that belligerents should enter into the peace agreement provisions for repatriation, that is, subscribe or agree to them, or 'enter into communication with each other on the question [of repatriation] as soon as possible'.[17]

In the meantime, though, Italy's former enemies, including South Africa, Canada and Britain, began to establish links with the new Italian government. Just like its counterparts, South Africa wanted to institute direct relations with Italy, because until then all communications had been directed through the War Office in London. Considering the large number of Italian POWs in South Africa, the Italians apparently believed that it would be helpful if a representative was appointed who would have jurisdiction over their POW compatriots.

In December 1945, therefore, Ubaldo Rochira became the new Italian Consul General in South Africa and set up office in Pretoria. Earlier in the war, Mussolini had fired Rochira when he refused to cooperate with the Fascist regime; and then, when the Allies liberated Rome, he was promoted by the new Italian government to Minister First Class.[18] However, it seemed that Rochira was kept so busy that the Italian POWs did not receive much of his attention.

One of the main sticking points in the peace negotiations was what to do with the former Italian colonies in Africa. The United States was in favour of a United Nations trusteeship for the colonies under the control of a governor. Smuts was against this and did not want to rush through any decisions. For him, it was important that Italy be given some 'administrative' role over the former colonies and that Britain oversee control over Cyrenaica (the former name of the eastern part of Libya).[19] But while London understood Smuts's point, they did not want to offend the United States.

Eventually, the matter was discussed in the Dominions Office and the High Commissioner for South Africa was given another chance to state Smuts's view. In essence, the forward-thinking Smuts saw the Mediterranean as a buffer zone against Russian Communist expansion. In the end, the Dominion representatives stood with South Africa and agreed that 'if Russia once got a foothold in Africa, it would be a great menace to the British Commonwealth'.[20] The Cold War between Communist Russia and Western democracies was already brewing.

Naturally, the Italian POWs could have had no idea of what the peace negotiations entailed, but this only added to their difficulty in understanding the reasons for the delay in sending them back home. Someone had to carry the blame for the slow progress and for the POWs it was natural to blame the camp staff. For the Zonderwater camp command, therefore, there could be no respite in their efforts to maintain control and discipline. The system of separating cooperators and non-cooperators continued as before. Those unfit for work, escapees and Fascists remained in the same blocks and they would also be last on the list for repatriation.

For those on outside employment, returning to Italy was not an immediate prospect either. Many prisoners escaped to try to find their own way home. Others escaped to avoid repatriation, because they wanted to remain in South Africa – although they would then have had to live undercover, because at that time no formal arrangement had yet been made by the Union government in that regard.

In October 1945, the Zonderwater authorities received a letter from a Mr Anthony in Geysdorp, asking why the Defence authorities did not search for escapees in Johannesburg and other big towns, asking if POWs were allowed out. Evidently, there were so many POWs in this man's vicinity that he was under the impression that they had all been set free. Prinsloo's reply, in which he asked Anthony to 'furnish information which will lead to the recapture of the escapees to whom you refer', showed that the authorities had little or no information on these escapees.[21]

At some point after the war ended, Prinsloo decided to entertain the Fascist Block with a special lunch. Giovanni was one of those who attended and, although he was an ardent Fascist, this event made a significant impression on him even though it was not enough to persuade him to abandon Fascism. He recalled that as Prinsloo arrived at the long table that had been prepared for them, they all stood to attention, without being ordered to do so. According to him, Prinsloo gave a speech in which he said:

> Gentlemen! I am happy to be among you even though you consider me your enemy, and I thank you for the kind and hospitable gesture. I am English, and you Italian. Wars are won and lost, but the homeland always remains! War is what it is; we are soldiers and we fight, each of us, to defend our homeland!

Following a pause, Prinsloo continued:

> With all honesty, I must appreciate you! Why? Despite the war being over and long lost, you have stayed faithful to your principles and ideology of old, even though we tried to bend you in every way,

without success! Well! in all honesty I have to say that if all Italians were like you, I mean every single one, I don't know how the war would have ended![22]

Prinsloo's South African War memories, specifically those of the so-called *bittereinders* (bitter-enders), who fought on even after the British had occupied the Boer republics of the Transvaal and the Orange Free State, and his own love for his homeland, could have encouraged him to speak so passionately. Or it may also have been Giovanni's attempt to convince the readers of his memoirs that they, the Fascist POWs, had won the propaganda war in Zonderwater.

It was not only Prinsloo who seemed to have developed a soft spot for the POWs, though: many citizens had become so used to seeing the Italians on the streets, moving about as if they were free men, that they resented any attempt at discipline from the military authorities or the police. Just a week after the war came to an end in Europe, a POW was stopped in Jeppe Street, Johannesburg. A Special Investigation Officer asked to check his permit, without which the POW could not be on the street. One of the civilian onlookers did not like this and saw the incident as harassment. The man, who gave his name as 'Captain Johnson', began telling other bystanders that the officer had no right to 'interfere with the POW'.

When Johnson was informed that he would be reported to the Military Police, he

made use of an obscene expression which he repeated three times in a loud voice. The words used were, in effect, an invitation to 'salute the sanguineous terminus of his rectum'. The objectionable expression was uttered sufficiently loudly as to be heard by passing pedestrians, one of whom was a lady.[23]

Upon investigation, it was found that Captain Johnson had given a false name and the senior public prosecutor declined to take the matter any further.

As POWs waited and waited to go home, their morale dropped. At the same time, the camp staff also became despondent and less motivated to perform their duties. Many no longer regarded strict control of POWs as that important and, just as the POWs did, the camp staff wanted to move on and continue with their lives.

A number of the POWs who tried to make their own way home attempted to do so via Mozambique. On 11 March 1946, one such attempt took place: three POWs escaped from outside employment near Potgietersrus (the present-day Mokopane) by stealing the farmer's vehicle. The escapees were arrested at Komatipoort, yet in this case the POWs were accused of theft and the offence of escape was considered less important.[24]

Clearly, keeping control over the POWs had become a secondary concern, perhaps because the number of escapees was considered to be very low at that time. In March 1946, the camp command reported that

> whilst it is recognised that there may have been an increase in the incidence of escapes in proportion to the decreased POW population ... the number of escapes, other than those on Outside Employment, is remarkably low.[25]

By 1946, the POW population stood at 16 000 and, of them, only 0,033% escaped. This was seen as an achievement because among the 16 000 there were 4 400 Fascists in separate blocks and the remainder were being guarded by fellow Italians.

Later the same year, Prinsloo wrote to Beyers asking if he would accept sworn statements from witnesses when inquiries into escapes were being made. This was because the authorities' insistence on oral evidence, given in person at a court of inquiry, placed a financial and administrative burden on the authorities because escapees had to be transported from far and wide. At this stage, POWs were mostly escaping from the farms or the outside employment camps that were scattered across the country. The face-to-face interrogations simply required too much effort and money. Prinsloo also stated that 'circumstances are now very difficult [due to] considerable reduction in the strength of the Staff [and] owing to the speeding up of repatriation, all matters must be expedited'.[26]

Two months later, in January 1947, measures were put in place that removed this burden for Prinsloo. At the time there were still more than 90 escapees at large, but as some of the smaller camps were closing, the decision was made that all recaptured escapees would be handed over to the Military Police,[27] who held them in military custody before they were deported as 'undesirable aliens' by the Department of Immigration, which would claim the expenses from Britain.[28]

Meanwhile, many POWs were still awaiting repatriation two years after the end of hostilities. The most severely affected were those in the Fascist Blocks, as they were held back until all the cooperators had been returned home. Another reason the Fascists had to wait was that the authorities hoped they would renounce their Fascist beliefs before their return, since in Italy Partisans were actively carrying out reprisals against Mussolini supporters who refused to let go of Fascism, even after the war had ended. At Zonderwater, the opposite was happening, though.

Indeed, the reluctance of Fascist POWs to escape caused some staff at Zonderwater to look more kindly upon them as they were causing less trouble. As these closer links developed, sympathy for the Fascist POWs grew, and in one case an officer even asked Prinsloo to protect the Fascists against cooperators of 'bad character'.[29]

15

THE END — BUT NOT YET

IN ITALY, THE end of the war did not necessarily mean the end of Fascism, since many Mussolini supporters still clung to Fascist ideas. In South Africa, the Zonderwater authorities had unwittingly created a 'paradise for Fascists' by keeping Fascist non-cooperators separated from more open-minded prisoners.[1]

The Fascists at Zonderwater didn't feel the humiliation when the German army made it clear that the Italians were subordinate to the German nation; nor did they witness the death and destruction as their homes and towns were obliterated. They may have read about it, but printed words place reality at a distance, and so many of them remained convinced that Fascism was a good thing.

They could also not benefit from contact with Allied soldiers in the way that many Italian Partisans did who had fought with the Allies against the Italian and German Fascist regimes. At least the cooperators in South Africa had the opportunity to associate with men who held different views from theirs.

The new Italian government knew that Fascist POWs could pose a danger to the young democracy they were trying to put in place and so they issued instructions that all returning POWs be screened 'from a political angle', making it clear that Fascists were not welcome back in Italy. Beyers made it clear that South Africa's reputation was again at stake and so he wrote to Prinsloo that

> it is obvious that the Italian authorities are most anxious not at this stage to re-admit to Italy any persons who still hold strong Fascist sympathies. Care must therefore be taken when reclassifying POWs even to the status of non-cooperator.[2]

This meant that the pressure was on the Zonderwater authorities to select for repatriation only those POWs who were free of Fascist ideas. Using the camp newspaper, *Tra I Reticolati,* the welfare officers reported on the changes taking place in Italy in an effort to give the POWs a better idea of the true state of the country to which they would be returning. Prinsloo and Sonnabend hoped that such knowledge would convince the Fascist POWs to start thinking differently.

As had been the case with selections for outside employment, it was a great challenge to distinguish genuine cooperators from committed Fascists. To make things easier, the men were given yet another opportunity to sign the declaration of cooperation, which, if they did, would mean that they could go home sooner rather than later.

For many POWs, though, it was not simply a matter of signing a piece of paper. Many of them believed that signing the declaration would have real consequences when they eventually returned to Italy. Many were under the impression that the Fascists still had some measure of power and that they would be blamed for cooperating with the enemy. Others feared that they, or their families, would be punished by the new Italian government for their Fascist activities during the war.[3] Furthermore, there was still the danger of ending up in a Fascist Block as a result of something other than political ideology, and how would they withstand the threats from those who would never sign the declaration?

Regarding the signing of the declaration, one Zonderwater censor hit the nail on the head when he wrote that, although many POWs

> expressed their relief and enthusiasm for this 'new privilege', some are still hesitant lest they may even now jeopardise the position of their families in Italy. There is still an under-current of anxiety about making any decision for fear of not being free from the grip of the former Regime'.[4]

Yet, even for cooperators, repatriation was a slow process. Most POWs had to wait until the peace treaty was a done deal before they could begin to return home. While the peace treaty was being discussed, Allied soldiers had to stay in Italy to keep the order between those who had supported

Mussolini to the bitter end and the Partisans who had fought alongside the Allies.

In 1946, though, Italy became a democracy and by the summer of that year the Allied soldiers had started their homeward journeys.[5] However, it was not until February 1947 that a peace treaty was formally concluded and Italy became an autonomous country again.[6]

At the time, however, no one knew how long it would take to settle after the war and so, understandably, the prisoners became impatient and frustrated. By June 1945, a censorship summary reported that 'much bitterness' was expressed in letters as repatriation was postponed until the start of spring in Europe.[7] The Red Cross, on behalf of the POWs, also expressed its unhappiness with the delays in repatriation to the military authorities. They were concerned about the morale among the men, which was already very low. Accordingly, quoting Prinsloo in their correspondence, they wrote that 'the Prisoners of War at Zonderwater are in the enjoyment of more than ordinarily favourable treatment: but this, of itself, cannot be held in any way to compensate for the sickness of heart engendered by deferred hope' to return home.[8]

The Smuts government did not complain about the slow peace process, though, because it suited it that the POWs remained in the Union until that season's harvesting was completed.[9]

Most prisoners who worked on farms were eager to return home or to get away from the conditions they had to work under, but some farmers were reluctant to give up the cheap source of labour they had in the Italians. This was the case with Giuseppe Vaccaro, who tried to explain his predicament to the authorities in March 1946.

Vaccaro's employer had reported him missing from work for four days, implying that he had escaped. Vaccaro had in fact been trying to get away from the difficult circumstances on the farm:

> I was forced to leave the farm and go to the Police Station since I could not endure any longer the strain of the working-time imposed on me by the farmer and because of the scarcity of food which was, for the truth, inferior to that prescribed. He had previously refused to take me back to Zonderwater when I asked him for it.[10]

Vaccaro had walked 24 miles from the farm to the police station to report the matter. There he was given a letter that instructed the farmer to send Vaccaro to Zonderwater. After Vaccaro had walked the 24 miles back to the farm, the farmer ignored the instruction and kept him there for a further six weeks. Because the farmer had reported him missing, Vaccaro was considered to be a suspected escapee. In his defence, he wrote to the authorities: '[T]hat means that I have lost my repatriation turn ... so that I am hereby begging of you to take my case into due consideration, hoping that your steps will enable me to be repatriated with the first draft leaving Zonderwater,' signing his letter with the valediction familiar in UDF circles: 'I am, sir, your obedient servant'.11

At the bottom of his letter, someone wrote in red pencil that Vaccaro 'should not have been reported as escapee ...' He was reinstated as a cooperator from the day that he had set off to the police station, but it is not known when he returned to Italy.12

To ensure that no Fascist ideas were fed back to Italy, the welfare officers at Zonderwater checked all outgoing mail. If any evidence was found of prisoners promoting such ideas, the writers of those letters were classified as non-cooperators and put last in line to go home. Many of the younger POWs, who for their entire lives had known nothing other than a dictatorial Fascist regime, were tormented by confusion and indecision. One POW sought advice from his wife:

> Several times I have asked you to tell me about the internal situation of our beautiful Italy, but you have never told me anything. In my letters recently I told you that I was not going to sign as a cooperator, but if you think I am wrong in not doing so, you can let me know. I do not know what is happening in Italy and as long as the Italian Government does not call me I will do nothing of my own free will.
>
> Let those in Italy judge me as they like, but I swear to you that there are very few that love their country without self-interest as I do, because my country means my family. Write and tell me if I am doing wrong. Should it be so my life is finished.13

This letter was written in January 1945, while parts of Italy were still under brutal German control; yet those at Zonderwater still relied on their government to tell them what to do. Whereas the war had changed Italy and its people, many inmates at Zonderwater remained stuck in the Fascist era. Loyalty to Fascism was not easily discarded, especially for those who had not seen firsthand the changes the war had wrought in Italy.

Letters telling prisoners of 'those Allied gentlemen who will soon be victorious' gave birth to lasting family feuds.[14] In some cases, Fascists became even more determined to save Fascism, as was the case at the Pietermaritzburg camp, when they decided 'to carry on the "good" work by stepping up the Gestapo vigilance' against liberal and democratic ideas.[15]

However, when the war in Europe did eventually come to an end, the censorship summaries that were compiled at the end of each month showed a slight decline in the number of Fascist phrases in the inmates' correspondence. But this did not necessarily make control and discipline easier, because, yet again, staff problems cropped up when the UDF guards stationed at Zonderwater were demobilised and sent home from the camp.

As a result, Prinsloo was eventually forced to place cooperators and non-cooperators in the same block at Zonderwater. Some of the POWs even helped with the heavy load of administrative work needed for the smooth running of the repatriations.

Meanwhile, the usual disciplinary headaches continued. With the prospect of POWs returning home, black market activities flourished as they tried to make some money to take back with them. A few days after the chaplain's announcement of peace in Europe, for instance, the Pietermaritzburg camp publication, La Carretta, began advertising black market goods for sale. When word of this reached Prinsloo, he was not impressed, writing in a memorandum that 'a Black Market would appear to be in operation on a sufficiently lucrative scale to warrant advertising energy'.[16] He accordingly reminded the Pietermaritzburg camp command that these 'scandalously rampant' activities had to be investigated and stopped.[17]

As if the selection process, the slow repatriation and the ongoing disciplinary problems were not enough to frustrate everyone, the Italian government decided on a new policy with regard to the Italian POWs. From November 1945 onwards, the government announced, all POWs still in foreign countries would be allowed to marry local women in those countries. All the POWs had to do was to inform the Italian State of their marriage by sending a copy of the marriage certificate. Both the Red Cross and the Swiss Consul General sent this information to the Union authorities in November 1945, asking for it be published in camp newspapers or made known to the POWs in some other way.[18]

However, Beyers did not think this was a good idea and replied that 'it is not considered advisable that this should be brought to the notice of POWs, in view of the existing regulations on the subject in the Union'.[19] Of course, he was referring here to the fact that fraternisation between POWs and locals was still illegal.

In August 1946, the Immigration Board in South Africa insisted that all Italians who wanted to immigrate to South Africa first had to return to Italy and apply from there. The board believed that this would sort the men of good standing from the others, because by first returning to Italy a man who could show that he 'kept alive [their] affection for his family, is one giving promise of becoming a loyal and steady citizen'. It was believed that many of the Italians would be welcomed back as permanent labour on the projects and farms they had worked on during their captivity.[20]

Three months later, it became clear that the need for labour was so great that it could even negate the new policy on immigration. Accordingly, in December 1946, the Secretary for the Interior wrote to Beyers informing him that the repatriation policy had changed and that

> where it was in the interest of the country, particularly in the production of food, applications for permanent residence in the Union by Italian Prisoners of War will be considered by the Immigrants Selection Board after careful enquiry [such cases] will be permitted to remain in the Union without the necessity of their first having to be repatriated.[21]

It was exactly at this time, though, that South African soldiers who had fought in the Italian campaign started to return home. Many of them found that their jobs had been taken by Italian POWs and this was the cause of great dissatisfaction. The nationalist opposition under DF Malan and his Purified National Party seized this opportunity to try to win votes. An article appeared in *Die Transvaler* claiming that Prinsloo had ordered his subordinates not to supply the press with any answers regarding the immigration statistics of Italian POWs, hinting that thousands might stay behind and that the Smuts government did not trust the judgement of its soldiers, who would in the future have to compete with Italians for jobs.[22]

At the same time, the returning ex-servicemen did not receive much support from the government in this regard. Understandably, they found it distasteful when they started working to discover that their new colleagues were former enemies. Many UDF veterans viewed the Italians with scepticism and distrust; others no doubt felt anger and hostility towards them. So while many of the local farmers and building contractors viewed the Italians as a valuable and cheap workforce, the UDF veterans wanted to see the back of them.

In support of the returning UDF soldiers, the Memorable Order of Tin Hats (MOTH), a veterans' society, informed the government that they would prefer immigration from countries that had fought on the side of the Allies during the war. They also pointed out that while the Italian POWs were a cheap source of labour during the war, they would expect the same rate of pay as citizens once the war was over. A particularly sore point was the knowledge that several Italians already had jobs earmarked for them once their immigration paperwork had been dealt with.[23]

The Smuts government's official stance was that the Italians had 'honest, industrious habits' and were able to adapt to agricultural work. Furthermore, they were considered to be proficient artisans. The average Italian prisoner of war was 'attached to the soil and is satisfied with his status ... accustomed to climatic conditions [and] he would likely continue indefinitely in [agricultural work] and not join the drift to urban areas', one memorandum read.[24]

With no fanfare whatsoever, the Zonderwater prisoner-of-war camp closed its gates on 1 March 1947. In typical military style, though, its closure was accompanied by a certain amount of contradiction.

Three officers at Zonderwater, Colonel Prinsloo in the middle
(Photo courtesy NMMH)

For one thing, Prinsloo remained camp commandant and a number of POWs who were still waiting their turn to go home stayed behind. Officially, Zonderwater was transformed into a care and maintenance camp to relieve him of the responsibilities attached to security. Still, for him it was not security that gave him sleepless nights: it was the fact that Zonderwater 'undertook a very considerable task in the organisation, despite a depleted staff, of an immigration Section'.[25]

For those Italians who were still on the run, things were about to change, too. It was now up to the police force to ensure that all escaped POWs were recaptured and so it became a matter of urgency to find those escapees who were still wandering around the country. To this end, Prinsloo issued an amnesty in March 1947, shortly after Zonderwater had closed. The amnesty stipulated that should the escapees surrender themselves to the police before the end of that same month, they would be repatriated without punishment. But if they refused to give themselves up, they would be arrested as 'prohibited immigrants, and will be dealt with by the Civil Courts and deported on conviction to their country of origin'.[26]

Maro Tomasso Scarcella, who had been working in Bloemfontein as a bricklayer, was determined to remain in the Union. On 3 May 1947, his attorney wrote to the military authorities to begin the process for

There was never a dull moment for the administrative staff
(Photo courtesy NMMH)

his immigration, but a month later the Secretary for the Interior and the Acting Adjutant General realised that Scarcella was an escapee. This was a potentially embarrassing dilemma because the Secretary for the Interior decided on 29 May 1947 that no escapees would be granted temporary residence. Instructions were immediately issued that Scarcella be recaptured.[27]

He was arrested in Kroonstad on 6 June.[28] If it hadn't been for his attorney's enquiry, he would most likely not have been recaptured as the enquiry made his whereabouts known to the military authorities. Tomasso was sent to Durban to be repatriated to Italy on the *Dominion Monarch*, but he was determined to stay in South Africa.

During the last week of June 1947, the *Dominion Monarch* sailed from Durban, supposedly with 29 POWs on their way back to Italy. On 3 July, however, the Sea Transport Officer informed the Quartermaster General that seven POWs were missing from the ship and were presumed to be still in the Union.[29] On 10 July, the authorities were given the names of the escapees, among whom were bricklayer Tomasso Scarcella, Vito Cinito, Dante Martini, Salvatore Silvestrino, Pietro Testa, Egidie Vicchiet and Desiderio Panico.[30] They had in all likelihood replaced their POW uniforms with civilian clothes and slipped off the ship.

The year 1948 brought great change in the country and especially for Smuts. The Afrikaner nationalists had long been waiting for a chance to take political control, and especially DF Malan, as leader of the opposition, looked forward to getting rid of Smuts and his British imperial ideas. As far back as 1940, Malan had tried to reach an agreement with the *Ossewabrandwag*, but for them Malan was far too liberal. The main concern of the *Ossewabrandwag* was to limit Smuts's pro-war efforts, but when it became clear that South Africa was on the winning side in the war, they lost their will and their raison d'être.

On 26 May 1948, Malan and his National Party won the general election.[31] So Smuts was out, the war was over and Zonderwater was no longer a prison camp. Yet several Italians were still waiting to go home; others were trying to escape repatriation and either immigrate or marry their lovers. Someone had to sort out the mess, but it would not be easy. The escapees were very determined, with some having been arrested as many as four times.

The new Acting Adjutant General made it clear that POWs who had been evading recapture were not to be treated in the same way as illegal immigrants. It seems as if the new Minister of the Interior, Dr Eben Dönges, was planning to allow former POWs to remain in the country by asking them to surrender themselves to the authorities before the end of January 1949.

However, according to the Acting Adjutant General, the UDF remained responsible for escapees and for keeping records of those who were to be repatriated. He made sure that Dönges understood this, pointing out that some escaped POWs had civil offences recorded against them, while others wanted to remain in the country to 'continue the questionable and dishonest, or immoral occupations into which they have drifted' since their escape from the camps.

Beyers asked that the Department of Defence be given an opportunity to inform the board of the POWs' records before any cases were decided on by the Immigration Selection Board. It is not known what Dönges' response was to this request and for this reason it is not possible to determine how many escaped POWs, some of them with criminal records, may have remained in South Africa.[32]

Of those who had escaped from the *Dominion Monarch,* Vito Cinito was the first of the seven runaways to be recaptured and transported back to Pretoria, where he awaited repatriation.[33] Salvatore Silvestrino, a convicted rapist, was next, followed in October 1948 by Pietro Testa, whose real name was Nucci Ulderico. The new authorities recommended that he be 'repatriated to Italy at the first opportunity'.[34]

Dante Martini was recaptured on 17 March 1949 but released on the same day on a special permit issued by the immigration authorities. In November 1951, the Red Cross wrote to the War Records office enquiring about Martini's whereabouts. This enquiry probably originated from his family, who sought to contact him. Evidently, he never let them know that he was staying behind in South Africa.[35]

All this time, Scarcella had been working for the Du Plessis Brothers, a building firm in Bloemfontein. They were 'anxious to retain his services' whether or not he was arrested, but it seemed that he was not found until 1949, when he reported to the authorities following the announcement of a concession regarding escapees.[36]

In 1940, the Du Plessis brothers won the tender for the completion of the Voortrekker Monument, which had been started, ironically, by an Italian firm in 1937.[37] Scarcella eventually obtained a temporary residence permit to remain in the Union – after all, the war had postponed the completion of the monument for long enough.[38]

Gradually, the number of escapees began to decline as they were arrested and deported, and when Zonderwater closed in 1947, 86 POWs were still at large. Most of them chose to assimilate with the South African population to the extent that the authorities 'had nothing but an Italian appearance to work on'. Those who were questioned by the police apparently replied in fluent English or Afrikaans, leaving their interrogators frustrated.[39]

The list of escapees included those who made it to Mozambique and, of those, only one man, Giovanni Morrasutti, managed to reach Italy. The authorities were mystified as to how he achieved this, but speculated that

it is probable that he impersonated one of the Prisoners drafted for repatriation in the ordinary way who wished to remain in South Africa. It is not possible to identify the impersonated man at present, but should the SA Police [find] any suspected Italian who is not in possession of documents and giving a name not included in the above nominal roll, the matter may be cleared if this office will be notified.[40]

16

'I ALSO NEED SO MUCH TO CRY'

RAFFAELLO REMEMBERED HOW a UDF officer tried to prepare them for their return home. The officer's task was to tell them about the many changes that had taken place in Italy during their absence and how they should accept the changes and become part of a new democratic Italy. It goes without saying that many of the young POWs could not imagine Italy without Mussolini. Many could not even dream that they would be able to live their lives without the state interfering in some way – they were that used to doing what they were told, whether growing up in a dictatorship or living in a prison camp. In any event, a prison camp is not where one learns about the practical aspects of democracy.

Yet the officer carried out his task and the POWs listened as he spoke about the rebirth of the Italian nation. 'But this didn't make us feel better,' Raffaello wrote in his memoirs:

> A sense of pessimism loomed above us if only we stopped to think about our future. We felt abandoned by our homeland, abandoned by everyone; degenerate children, forgotten children. In early 1946 repatriation began to be more frequent and the groups leaving Africa more consistent. Life in the camp was definitely no longer controlled by our ex-jailors, although a certain respect of British-style norms remained.[1]

Like many others, Raffaello experienced the end of the war as an anti-climax. The war was over, but his circumstances remained the same – he was still in captivity, unable to live freely. Perhaps he knew that what he would find in Italy would be hard to bear. All over Europe, feelings of distress and devastation continued among citizens and servicemen alike long after the German commanders had signed the surrender documents.

Raffaello Cei at the Pietermaritzburg POW camp in 1946
(Photo courtesy Elisa Longorato)

Everyone realised that things could not go back to the way they once were. The war had come and gone and in its wake everything was different.

In Zonderwater, Giovanni and his mates still held on to their dream of a Fascist Italy. To them, signing the declaration at this late stage was as ridiculous a thought as it was at the start of their captivity. Even if it meant that they could go home earlier, they would not become cooperators. After all this time, he still saw the Zonderwater command personnel as tormentors who were out to make his life hell:

> The war had ended on all fronts many months before and WE! PRISONERS languished in SOUTH AFRICA under the English. They sarcastically stated it was our fault, because we didn't want to cooperate. The careful reader might now ask: 'Cooperate how, if everything had ended?!'
>
> The reply is as follows: they wanted at all costs to humiliate us, bend

Giovanni Palermo in his uniform
(Photo courtesy Elisa Longorato)

Defiant prisoners giving the Fascist salute (Photo courtesy www.zonderwater.com/it)

us to their will and subjugate us. But after all the vicissitudes and dangers suffered and sacrifices of all sorts made, WE! PRISONERS, real and worthy ITALIANS, saw no gain or advantage in signing for the enemy, even while knowing that this signature no longer counted for anything or served any purpose.[2]

The months following the end of the war were a true test of Giovanni's character, and it does seem that his stubborn adherence to Fascism won the day. In a desperate effort to convince non-cooperators like him of the benefits of democracy and also to get them to sign the declaration of cooperation, the camp command organised talks by Italian government ministers, who appealed to the POWs' common sense. In Giovanni's case, he became only more determined to hold on to the principles that had shaped his life since childhood. He definitely did not believe one word of the

pseudo-colonel [who] arrived and began to speak in a placid and suspicious manner and I would rather say sweetly undecided, because he knew who he was dealing with. He explained to us in brief the situation of a semi-destroyed ITALY where everything had changed, etc, etc, that the English were not our enemy but our allies and as such they only wanted the best for us. But they needed us to change, that is, to forget the past and erase everything, and every now and again he would state that: 'Now, there is nothing left in ITALY!'

[H]e concluded his speech with these profound and sentimental words: 'Dear ITALIAN brothers! ... Do you see? Since the war has ended, why stay inside the fences and suffer? ... With a simple signature, you will be repatriated, and be able to soon embrace your loved ones, who are waiting for you with open arms!'

With this significant and profound conclusion, he wanted to strike a chord of feeling towards our families and ITALY. But WE PRISONERS, with aching hearts and without hesitation, gave our reply in unison: loud and solemn. We all snapped to attention, and a powerful voice rose: 'SALUTE TO THE *DUCE*!' ... 'TO US!' ... we replied, united and compact, with an echo reverberating into the distance. He dismounted the stage, humiliated, and left the hall with his tail between his legs.[3]

The 'pseudo-colonel' could have been Captain Ball, who apparently told individuals in the Fascist Blocks that the chronically sick POWs would be repatriated regardless of their political attitudes. The Fascists did not believe a word and the self-appointed representative of the block, Guerra Emilio, wrote to Prinsloo and the Red Cross, pointing out the many examples of ill POWs who were Fascists but had been sent back from the hospital to the Fascist Blocks and had not been repatriated. It was true, the camp command had received instructions from a 'higher authority' to delay the repatriation of Fascist POWs, regardless of their health status.[4]

In the same letter, the aggrieved Fascists also pointed out that a UDF commanding officer had told them that the Italian government wanted the cooperators to be repatriated before any of the Fascists were sent home. While this was indeed the case and Prinsloo was obliged to hold back the Fascists until they had signed the declaration of cooperation or at least had become less hardline about their political beliefs, the Fascists at Zonderwater did not believe this was true. They stated that their 'political ideas, whatever they may be, are a matter for the Italian Government when we get back to Italy'.[5]

The Fascists believed they were being manipulated by the authorities at Zonderwater because they could not accept that their own government would not want them back in Italy. What they did not realise was that the new Italian government had turned its back on Fascism and as long as POWs refused to sign the declaration of cooperation, they would remain unwanted in Italy.

In these ways, the Fascists steadfastly held on to their principles while the Zonderwater command was putting policy into practice. The two sides were deadlocked, which led to trust between the Fascists and the camp command deteriorating. As a result, when the Italian government representative, Rochira, visited the camp in April 1946, his request to speak to the Fascists was denied, since the camp command could not guarantee his safety.

Meanwhile, the Fascists had started their own camp newspaper, *Il*

Punto, in which they hoped to counter the perceived 'anti-national and anti-Fascist campaign' of the camp authorities. In reaction to Rochira's visit, an article in *Il Punto* pointed out in an elaborate and metaphor-rich style that the representative did not in fact represent any of the Fascists at Zonderwater. '[I]f we, who have done our duty, are inside here, he, who is outside, has probably not done it [his duty]'. The article then went on to ask, 'So then, with what right could he consider himself as our representative?'

They were also especially aggrieved at the thought that Rochira had tried to convince them that Italy had a role to play at the peace conference. According to them, Rochira knew 'quite well that his opinion at the peace conference table is worth less than the squeal of a small drawing room dog'.[6] Most of all, however, the Zonderwater Fascists did not trust Rochira because although he had been in Mussolini's cabinet, he was now working for the other side. They were apparently unaware that Mussolini had dismissed him when their views clashed.

Giovanni and the other Fascists were equally passionate about returning to Italy as they were about their political beliefs. Right up to the end, they remained committed to spreading Fascist propaganda. When a group of Fascist prisoners was repatriated in January 1947, the *Sunday Times* reported that while they 'could not get away [from the Union] quickly enough', their Fascist 'sentiments' caused various fistfights on the train all the way to Durban, which then continued once the POWs had boarded their ship.[7] They even found the time to carve out a printing block and print thousands of pamphlets with an ominous message – 'if they kill me, avenge me'. These papers were tossed out of the train windows on their way to the Durban docks.[8]

The Officer Commanding who accompanied the POWs on this same train reported that the POWs had started throwing pamphlets out of the train just after they left Pretoria. The atmosphere on the train was tense and the POWs were described as 'insolent' and 'truculent' and showed signs of getting out of hand.[9]

When Giovanni and his Fascist camp mates were transferred to Pietermaritzburg, they had a similar idea when, along the way, they saw what they thought was an educational institution and 'immediately we thought about communicating with the students as a propaganda tool'.[10] They carved messages into the rubber heel of a shoe, printed it onto paper and let fly the leaflets as far as they went.

According to Giovanni, the 'English' thought patronisingly of the Italians as 'children' and that is why they decided to tie the leaflets together to look like kites. He believed it would make the guards think they were being playful, while in reality they were distributing propaganda. They continued flying their kites when they arrived in the Pietermaritzburg camp until the authorities realised what was happening and decided to disallow any paper to be brought into the camp. For Giovanni it did not matter: they 'were truly happy to have fooled the English gentlemen, the masters of propaganda'.[11]

During the time Giovanni and five of his most committed friends, known as 'the six', spent at Pietermaritzburg, they made life hell for the camp command and the guards. First, they collaborated with a like-minded prisoner who pretended to be a cooperator. This man arranged for one of them to escape. Apparently, the escape was successful, but what became of the man is a mystery.

Emboldened, 'the six' refused to obey any and all orders, which led to extreme frustration on the part of the guards. As if this was not enough, 'the six' then went on a hunger strike because their food was prepared by a cooperator. The strike was eventually resolved when one of 'the six' pretended to lose all control of his faculties and was taken to hospital. When the doctors realised that he was faking insanity, he was returned to his friends.

Until the day they were taken to the harbour to board their ship, 'the six' continued with their disruptive efforts. In Giovanni's words: 'Our battle in prison continued without rest, because every day we would do one thing and think of another hundred, all studied to annoy the English'.[12] The most common and satisfying way to irritate the camp command was to paint 'Long live the *Duce*' on every wall and pillar they could find, especially if these were in full view of as many of the 'English' as possible.

Giovanni believed their propaganda messages hit home. When he wrote his memoirs in the 1970s, South Africa was no longer part of the British Commonwealth but a republic. He was happy to report that we can say with pleasure that the [anti-British] seed that was sown then, as well as we could and with no historical expectations, has borne fruit, because SOUTH AFRICA is the only ex-English colonial state that has its own physiognomy,[13] autonomy and freedom in the national sense, and it is anti-English on top of that.[14]

Once they arrived in Italy, the Fascist POWs continued with their propaganda efforts. The *Rand Daily Mail* correspondent in Naples reported that 'Italian soldiers returning from POW camps in South Africa landed here yesterday singing the Fascist hymn, *Giovanezza*, and strewing leaflets vowing vengeance for Mussolini's death'.[15] Some of those leaflets displayed Mussolini's face while others were printed with skulls and crossbones and with the letters 'COSI' printed on them. According to the news article, COSI was an abbreviation for a new Fascist movement that had emerged in Italy after the war.[16] It would seem that the stronger the commitment was to Fascism, the greater the reckless bravery.

Most POWs, however, did not see their return journey as an opportunity to spread any kind of message. They simply wanted to return home. What awaited them in Italy was the shock of seeing how their country had suffered under Mussolini's ill-advised war plans, then under the Nazis' vengeance for the 'treasonous' armistice. As if this was not enough, the people of Italy were now divided between those who fought with the Partisans and those who remained Fascists. A new political dispensation may have been important for some, but most returning POWs probably just wanted to seek out any living relatives first before finding work and a place to stay.

For those who had spent the greater part of the war in POW camps, the experience of post-war Italy was somewhat different from that of those who had fought on the front lines or who had remained on the home front. When Raffaello wrote his memoirs, he reflected

> I cannot forget the fact that I was raised under Fascism, which had accustomed a whole nation to a particular type of thinking that had been decided elsewhere, but I also know that Italian people have deeper sentiments than the superficial conventions they may

have learnt because [it was] imposed on them with coercion.

I thought I faced the worst of the war with the same flippancy as everyone else, and I tried to obtain an awareness and degree of maturity from my prisoner status that would allow me to have the most authentic judgement possible in that situation. I mean an objective one in the face of everything that had happened to my country and to me in particular.[17]

Raffaello was held back in Pietermaritzburg until 17 February 1947. One UDF officer incorrectly informed him the reason for this was that the POWs in Pietermaritzburg had lived in comfort compared to those in other camps, and that that 'had to be paid back somehow'.[18] The officer was misinformed: Raffaello's late repatriation had nothing to do with the conditions under which the POWs lived; it was because his cooking services were sorely needed in the kitchen.

Ultimately, Raffaello saw his captivity as an experience from which he could take the good and leave the bad: 'I tried to learn as much as I could from that adventure that had catapulted me to the other side of the world, trying to direct my destiny towards goodness'.

He had suffered from severe toothache since he was conscripted into the Italian army and he lived with the pain until his teeth were removed, at the age of 25, towards the end of 1945. He even tried to view this development in a philosophical way:

Pain in the body is sometimes symbolic, a real sign of a deeper pain on the inside, pain that crosses the soul. For me, toothache was almost a means to redeem myself for the most pleasant aspects of life in the camp and force me to reflect on a more general woe that afflicted the whole of humanity. I had no treatments to stop the increasingly lacerating pain with which my teeth reminded me of a suffering world.[19]

During the last days at Pietermaritzburg, Raffaello continued to carry out his duties in the kitchen, but handing out food was no longer as important as it was in the early days of captivity. Instead, he was now able to hand out coffee, tea, soap and pepper to those who had space in their suitcases. It would be some time before Italy's economy would recover from the war and these 'luxury' items must have been a welcome treat in Italy.

For many POWs, even suitcases were a scarcity and they improvised by soaking pieces of leather in water. Once the leather was pliable, it was hammered onto wooden frames. And once they had dried, these containers became sturdy hold-alls that were to last for many years. Some men began to make these in 1943 when they heard about the armistice, but the opportunity to use them arose only in 1947 when they finally went home.

When at last it was Raffaello's turn to go, he suddenly became indecisive. Having been in South Africa for so long, it must have felt as if he was leaving home, albeit to return to his childhood home. He remembered that he and his fellow POWs

> wanted to go back and face life, to carry on living as free men after years of knowing the weight of imprisonment. But I cannot hide the fact that, in some instances, my restlessness tempted me to stay in that African land that held a certain fascination for me, and perhaps also represented a desire to avoid the reality that awaited at home. None of us, including myself, expected to go back to a country without ruins and conflict.[20]

In the end, he decided to turn down an offer of employment at a local hotel and return to Italy; and so, after having spent seven years in the Union, he left with two suitcases, two suits, two shirts, underwear and soap. He felt frustrated with the repatriation process, saying: 'It wasn't easy, not even for the victors to organize their victory'.[21]

Luigi Pederzoli, who had endured hardships in East African camps and arrived at Zonderwater in 1944, ended up in the Fascist Block. But, unlike many other Fascists such as Giovanni, Luigi did not see his imprisonment as a demonstration of loyalty to Fascism. He became very impatient to go home, having no interest in making any political statements and prolonging his captivity: all he wanted to do was to return to Barbara, see his son and carry on with a normal life.

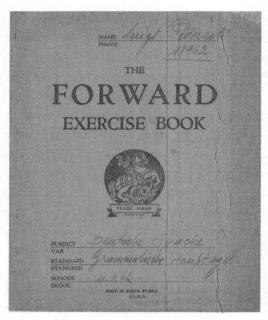

Luigi Pederzoli's notebook for his German language studies at Zonderwater
(Photo courtesy Emilia Pederzoli)

For Luigi, the waiting period was 'torture' and he did not think that the military authorities were really intent on sending them home. As he wrote to Barbara, he was

> still awaiting repatriation, that repatriation which is becoming a real torture. Again this month there were few departures, only 3 000 men and we are about 20 000 left. If they really wanted to get serious, we could all be home in just a couple of months.[22]

As his impatience turned to frustration, he looked for ways to take action, to make repatriation happen, yet he was a prisoner and could not even demand answers from the camp command. In his letters to Barbara at this time, he wrote only of going home:

> This is a very hard experience and only the determination to make use of this experience is giving me confidence in tomorrow. You say

that you can go crazy, well, if I had not the certainty to see you again
and to live again with you and our son, at this time, madness would
be a sad reality. It is true that we have sacrificed our youth apart from
each other, but we must not ruin the rest of our lives, we are 32 years
old, so don't be sad. I also need so much to cry and forget this hell.[23]

He wanted to be home before winter, but he had no way of knowing when
he would be able to leave. He had heard that in Italy some families had
begun to believe that those POWs who were still in South Africa most
probably did not want to leave the country of their captors. For Luigi, this
was utter nonsense and he angrily wrote that he would have liked to have
met 'some of these guys on my return and I would not regret to spend five
years more in prison, just to make him limp for life'.[24]

To pass the hours, Luigi had continued with his language lessons; but
when Prinsloo presented his language certificate to him, it could only
have been a small consolation.[25] The best he could do at this time was
to write letters and have them hand-delivered to Barbara by friends who
were on the repatriation list before him. By October 1946, Luigi was still
in captivity, but this time his message was cautiously optimistic:

Maybe 4 or 5 percent will leave [the camp] at the end of this month!
We are still more than 15 000! and I am probably among the first
5 000 leaving. A large shipping is expected before Christmas, so
the situation would be solved. In my opinion, an acceleration
could take place in case the peace is soon signed ... I also will be
repatriated and then we will start living again, finding the joy and
serenity that we left over there. If we are not going well in Italy,
we shall go far, far away in a country where it is possible to live in
peace and honestly earn our living. Do not cry ...[26]

On 7 November, he finally received the news that he would be on his
way soon. Hopeful that he would be home for Christmas, he nevertheless
wrote to Barbara that he would only believe it when he saw his home
again. He also warned her that he was suffering from gastric disorders and
that she may 'find me a little disoriented and lost because I come from a

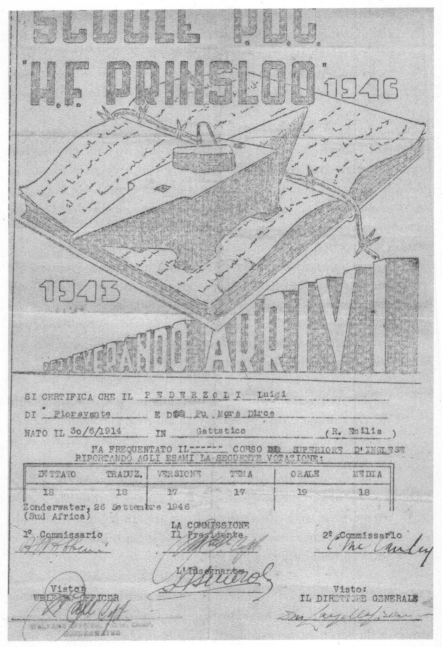

Luigi Pederzoli's Zonderwater school certificate, received from Colonel Prinsloo in 1946 (Photo courtesy Emilia Pederzoli)

A graduation ceremony at Zonderwater with Colonel Prinsloo handing out certificates (Photo courtesy NMMH)

very different world, where life is not life, but darkness'.[27]

As was the case with so many of Luigi's wartime experiences, yet more disappointment awaited him: he set foot on Italian soil at Naples only on 3 January 1947. When his train reached Treviglio, he was met by a sight of utter devastation. Bombing raids had destroyed much of the town and it would be years before it could be rebuilt to resemble anything like what Luigi remembered from his childhood. When he and Barbara were finally reunited, he heard about the ordeals she had endured in East Africa following his capture. She told him how she rescued Ennio from 'cannibals' and was then moved to a camp in Addis Ababa, where women and children died of hunger and disease until the Pope arranged for the remaining prisoners to be returned to Italy. Her story convinced Luigi that it was she who had fought the real war.[28]

For Giovanni, who was held at Pietermaritzburg for the final months of his imprisonment, repatriation could also not have come soon enough. However, the conflict and anger that had marked his captivity from the start continued to the end. In Pietermaritzburg, the POWs were asked to clean their accommodation, but as Giovanni believed that this was not in accordance with the Geneva Convention, he and his friends refused. For them, it would amount to labouring for the English. He was wrong: the Convention did not allow detaining powers to demand any war work from captives, but cleaning sleeping quarters was not seen as that. Regardless of the misunderstanding, he and five others decided to use their old tactic again: they went on a hunger strike. However, when he looked back on this experience, he realised that

> our extremism was paid at a high price, with imprisonment, special cells, days without food, hunger strikes, etc, etc, by our homogenous little group; it initiated the long imprisonment in Pietermaritzburg, with all its grave consequences, at our sole expense, of course.[29]

When 'the six' were eventually confronted by an interpreter about their behaviour, Giovanni explained that for the Italians the war was lost and so they would rather 'die heroically, fighting the enemy'. What Giovanni still did not realise was that, in saying that, all they achieved was the postponement of their repatriation. The dilemma for the authorities was that they could not keep the POWs in the Union indefinitely, and with Giovanni and his friends not giving up their fight, it would seem that the decision was made that if the six of them could be persuaded to do some work, they could be classified as cooperators and be repatriated.

In a desperate attempt to convince them, two chaplains were sent in. Following an exasperating negotiation process, they eventually convinced Giovanni and his friends to do some work outside the camp, in line with the ruling that UDF officers also had to work out their punishment. So, after enduring many ordeals, Giovanni and his friends eventually went on 'outside employment', which officially made them cooperators. To Giovanni's way of thinking, 'it was not really work, but its purpose was solely that of applying their rules, and with this insignificant job they were incredibly satisfied because they had managed to make us work and had therefore won morally'.[30]

The work involved straightening a stone wall. And when it was done, they returned to the main camp, where they awaited repatriation with the rest of the POWs. The fact that the words 'Long live the *Duce*' were found painted on that wall did not seem to deter the authorities, who were by now very eager to be rid of them.[31] Giovanni eventually arrived in Naples on 21 January 1947, dressed in his Arditi uniform.

It is highly possible that, of all the POWs in South Africa, Pietro spent the least amount of time in a prisoner-of-war camp. He was a free spirit who knew how to use any opportunity to his advantage. By the time he secured a job at the Hotel Windsor in Queenstown, he had become a skilled entrepreneur.

He settled in and was very happy at the hotel and in the town itself. He almost immediately formed a close friendship with the owner: apparently, he resembled the owner's son, who had been killed in action 'up north'.[32] And so it was not long before Pietro was promoted from barman to bar manager, giving him a chance to live out his entrepreneurial spirit. To be on the safe side, he changed his name to Alex Rendy and pretended to be a Frenchman in exile. With his new identity and a driver's licence to match, he was able to 'move more freely', as he put it. On the side, Pietro ran a gambling business, known as a 'bucket shop', taking money from clients and giving it to a bookie. No doubt he took in healthy commissions when his horses or clients won. Hosting these betting and dance parties at the hotel bar, he also provided extra drinks, specifically for two ladies who were 'avid drinkers ... so whenever they liked to have access to their favourite "nightcap", even after hours, namely, the Gimlet for one and the Horseneck for the other, which I was happy to deliver to their rooms after 22:00. They were the most loyal residents in the hotel'.

It was during these escapades that Pietro met Doreen and he saw in her something more substantial than he had seen in anyone before.[33]

However, after 18 months, the owner and Pietro's benefactor, retired and sold the hotel. The new owners did not share the same affection for Pietro and he was soon demoted to a mere barman. In response, Pietro decided to seek out a new life elsewhere. Apparently, Doreen felt 'great regret', but understood his desire to be on the road again. It was Chippie, Pietro's little dog, that 'really paid for it [but he] remained in good hands'.[34]

Pietro then became a professional in the betting world in Klerksdorp, and at his first race he made £60. But the POW on the loose had bigger ambitions, and being in a mining town gave him an opportunity to

Pietro Scottu's driver's licence showing his name as 'Alex Rendy'
(Photo courtesy Pietro Scottu)

Pietro Scottu living the good life (Photo courtesy Pietro Scottu)

follow his dream of making more money. When he arrived in Klerksdorp, as luck would have it, he met a man whom the 'press had identified as the Vice Governor of the South African National Bank'. With the man's love of horse racing, Pietro quickly 'judged his personality' and set about making use of the opportunity to win over a new friend.

'On three separate occasions, I gave him advice on a suggestion (when I knew the race was fixed), which he regularly bet on,' Pietro wrote. In return, Pietro wanted advice on the stock market. The man promised to give him shares at a 'low cost that will do well in the future'.[35] In this way, Pietro's initial investment of £3 500 increased to £12 500 over a short period. But, as luck would yet again have it, just when he thought things could not get any better, everything changed again:

> I was not to enjoy the taste of my success, as during a visit to Johannesburg, upon entering a 'tearoom', I encountered an old acquaintance from the concentration camp in Zeidab 21 (Sudan). I

*Pietro Scottu at the entrance to the Hotel Windsor in Queenstown
with a young friend (Photo courtesy Pietro Scottu)*

Chippie, Pietro Scottu's beloved dog (Photo courtesy Pietro Scottu)

offered him a drink and asked why he was in Johannesburg and he replied that he had escaped Zonderwater, but had no idea how to find a job since he didn't speak any English.

Without stopping to think, I asked if he would settle for a job in a kitchen, in which case I could help him seeing I'd made some contacts in the hospitality industry and had some useful connections. I gave him my phone number and office address and told him to call me in a few days so I could tell him whether I'd been able to find him a job. I commended him to not use my real name but the one I'd taken on after my escape, Alex Rendy: that was the end of my freedom.[36]

The next day, a military policeman showed up at Pietro's office and arrested him. He believed he had been betrayed: 'I had thought I would be helping a fellow national, not realising that he was out to act as bait in order to capture escapees, and his remuneration, other than food and lodging outside of the camp, was £5 a head'.[37]

Things could not have looked any worse for Pietro, but he was not about to give up. Back at Zonderwater, he smuggled in whisky, perfumed soap, sugar, tea and cigarettes – all of which were scarce commodities at the time. He used these to tempt one of the officers at the camp, presumably to get off lightly at his trial. Apparently, the officer refused to take any of the items, but when Pietro asked if his wife would be interested, the officer changed his mind. The next day, as Pietro recalled, the officer's 'response was positive, so I gave him everything except the sugar and the tea'. For once, though, Pietro's tactics did not work and he was sentenced to 28 days in the detention barracks. He was granted 482 shillings for his uneaten camp meals, but for Pietro this was scant comfort: his shares had been confiscated! The officer told him it was the law.

Pietro eventually arrived in Italy on 16 February 1947. He was ordered to appear before the Marine Commander for a 'discrimination' process. There he was questioned about his time in South Africa and his reasons for escaping. Pietro recalled:

The question seemed so puerile to me that I asked the officer posing it whether he had ever been to a concentration camp. The answer was: 'no'. I commented: when you have a chance to go, you'll find the answer. Nonetheless, 'discriminated against', I left for Genova [Genoa].[38]

The next morning, at his sister's house in San Fruttuoso, on the outskirts of Genoa, his mother greeted him with a 'long embrace, after almost nine years apart'.[39] However, Pietro soon sought out excitement and it was not long before he met a group of UDF servicemen of the 6th South African Armoured Division who had been fighting in Italy. He was still wearing his South African outfit and spoke with a South African accent, so he blended in well with the group. Ever the opportunist, he walked with them as they went back to their headquarters in Genoa. There he met an officer who knew him as Alex Rendy, the French exile. When questioned, he casually informed the officer that he 'was French only while in South Africa, but now, being Italian, I've come back home'. Listening to his story of escape and of his 'vicissitudes in the various regions', the UDF men had a 'fat laugh'.[40]

When he was informed about Pietro, General Poole, the commander of the 6th Division, was also amused; 'at the end of the questioning, he asked: "Do you have a job?" No, I replied, I arrived in Genova yesterday. "Then stay with us and work in our translation office." Said and done, I stayed with them until the day they left Genova'.[41]

Pietro's meeting with General Poole, as described in his memoirs, is best taken with a pinch of salt, though. It is unlikely that General Poole would have spent time interviewing ex-POWs, but perhaps Pietro was fortunate or had spoken to another army officer.

According to Emilio Coccia,[42] President of the Zonderwater Block ex-POW Association, about 870 Italians never returned to Italy and thousands returned to South Africa in the post-war years. One of them was Paolo Ricci, who had enjoyed considerable freedom during the last two years of the war when he was on outside employment. On one of his and his friends' sightseeing walks through Pretoria, they met an Italian woman who owned a tailor shop:

She was a lovely widow and every now and then Lotti and I would go and visit her and help her sew to pass the time. At the end of the war, she made us a proposal to remain in South Africa and work for her in her shop. Lotti said to me, 'Why don't we stay in South Africa a while longer? You know by us, in Italy, the war is over, but Rimini has been razed to the ground. We shall return to Italy once Italy is back on her feet'.[43]

Paolo followed the advice of his friends and the three of them decided to make a living in South Africa. Waiting for Italy to get 'back on her feet' would in all probability take years. Italy was a poor country before the war started, but by mid-1945 workers earned half of what they had done before the war. Food rations were also in place well after the war came to an end and those who were unable to grow subsistence crops were forced to weather the high prices on the black market. It was only in 1949 that the situation started to improve, but then only marginally.[44]

In 1953, Italy began a process of industrialisation, and the effect it had on the economy became known as the so-called 'economic miracle'. The period of growth slowed down again only in 1973.[45] In contrast, the economy in South Africa was doing very well and 15 years after the war only Japan's economy was growing at a faster pace.[46] Although nobody could predict the future, especially after the war had wrought so much havoc, Paolo and his friends made the right decision, at least financially. At an emotional level, though, it was not such an easy decision to make, and Paolo found it very difficult.

Paolo and Lotti worked for the dressmaker for 18 months, but for them things moved too slowly. Ultimately, they wanted to do their own thing. It was only when by chance they met a 'Jewish gentleman' that things started to change. With the man's help, they were able to establish their own workshop in a basement of a hotel. But after months of watching shoes pass by on the pavement above, they convinced their benefactor that a basement was not the place for them.

A first-floor room in a building on the corner of Pretorius and Van der Walt Streets,[47] large enough to be divided into two sections – one for sleeping and one for working – gave Paolo and Lotti the opportunity they

Paolo Ricci at his home in Pretoria, 2016 (Photo courtesy Paolo Ricci)

had been waiting for. They hung a sign from the balcony advertising their services: 'Lotti and Ricci Italian Tailors'. Their business grew and, with it, their premises improved. For Paolo, life without his Italian family became more bearable when he

> met a wonderful girl who came from one of the most renowned families in Pretoria. Within eighteen months of meeting each other we got married and as a wedding gift Nonno Pietro (Mom's father) paid our trip to Italy. In those days there were no planes, and so we travelled by ship. The ship was called *Jerusalem* and it took twenty-six days to travel from Durban to Venice. Our honeymoon lasted five months![48]

In 2016, referring to their honeymoon, Paolo jokingly recalled that 'the only thing when you come back, the honey was finished it was only a moon'.[49] Paolo and Fosca were married for 60 years.

Yet when I asked Paolo about his decision to stay in South Africa, he became emotional: he was never quite convinced that he had made the right choice. His vivid memory of the day the last repatriation train left the station without him remained with him for many years:

> I was a [South African] civilian already and I was living near the station and so I said I want to go see these Italians, my friends leaving, and I tell you when that train started to shweeesh, I went on my knees and I cried. I think that cement is still wet today.[50]

Epilogue

When Jan Smuts died in 1950, the new National Party government of South Africa had already begun to break down that which Smuts and his supporters had been fighting for during the war: democracy, freedom and progress. When the war began in 1939, Smuts tried very hard to convince everyone in the country that Fascism had the potential to destroy everything that stood for freedom and progress – and, goodness knows, South Africa had quite some progress to make in that direction. Yet, when the Nationalists under DF Malan came to power in 1948, his supporters set about steering the country in the opposite direction. Whereas the former Allies were striving towards democracy and liberty, South Africa's new leaders sought out discrimination and oppression. Smuts was a complex character, and his record on racial equality is obscure, but he did at least have the foresight to reject Malan's apartheid policy as both foolish and disastrous for the long term.

While the country was beginning to move in a new direction, most of the former Italian POWs were settling in to a new life in Italy. Others remained in the country that was once their prison. As time went by, their stories spread, although in different forms and variations. Some of these stories are closer to the truth than others. Today, many South Africans with some knowledge of the Italians look back on that time with a sense of wistfulness, almost as if longing for friendships lost and an enchanting past. Somehow, over the years, reality made way for myth and the idea took hold that the Italians' story is one that is wholly positive – for instance, that every Italian prisoner loved being in South Africa, that each benefited in one way or another from the experience and that there was mutual respect between them and also between them and all the UDF staff. One historian describes this process as 'mythologising', that is, the manipulation of POW stories to serve the purposes of the wider community.[1] Italians and South Africans created myths in the post-war era for different reasons: acceptance, justification, accountability and appeasement, among many others.

These chapters have, I hope, shown that there is good and bad in every man, every group and every country. And whereas a myth may make for a good story, it would be wise to remember that a myth is much like a millipede: it stands on the truth with only one of its many legs.

Yet there is no doubt that the Italians enriched South African cultural life with music, art and theatre. It was especially the case in the years after the war: those Italians who decided to return to their country of captivity, to make it their home, certainly made their contributions, some of them enduring. Some achieved fame. Among them were Aurelio Gatti, the gardener-turned-ice-cream man; Edoardo Villa, the renowned sculptor who was awarded an honorary degree by the University of Pretoria; and Gregorio Fiasconaro, the singer and director who made a significant contribution to the opera world in South Africa and further afield. Most Italians who returned to the Union after the war worked quietly at improving their lives and, in so doing, brought about development and progress. I am sure there were many more former prisoners of war who made important contributions to the development of this country, and I invite the families of these men to share their stories, as without it, historians are not able to do their work.

The history of the POWs in South Africa is as much about the Italians as it is about the camp guards, the welfare officers and the larger UDF hierarchy, and also those South Africans who made use of their talents and services. As with the Italians, I have tried to convey their versions of events in detail and to remain faithful to the truth – at last as far as the documents in the archives allow. And as was the case with each of their charges, each man's unique personality influenced what he did or did not do while guarding prisoners. To place these men in categories would be to ignore the complexities that made them human. They were as we are today: each one thinking he had the perfect solution to a difficult situation. Smuts's approach to equal rights was characterised by contradictions, but so was each UDF guard's view of the work they were doing. Some guards saw their task as caring for the prisoners, others as guarding them, educating them, tolerating them and so on …

Whether their hearts were in it or not, though, the men of the UDF fought – or worked at Zonderwater – to keep the country safe from the dangers of Fascism and to ensure freedom from the Fascist dictatorships that threatened to bring about a new world order. Despite the day-to-day frustrations of their work, the staff shortages, escapes and Fascist propaganda, though, the UDF men managed to show many Italian POWs what personal freedom looks and feels like. With the truth (hopefully) revealed, it is possible to give these war-time men their due for their efforts to preserve humanity in a time of war. Yes, mistakes were made, but who among us can say that they are perfect?

It is a shame, then, that those Italians who returned to the Union found themselves in a country where the personal freedoms of many citizens had been suppressed and their basic rights ignored. One can only imagine how the apartheid policies must have reminded the post-war Italian immigrants of their childhoods under Mussolini's stern gaze.

In contrast to what was happening in South Africa, those who remained in Italy joined a larger movement towards democracy and began building a country that Mussolini would never have recognised, one where democracy and freedom emerged from the poverty and destruction wrought by the war.

South Africa benefited from the legacy of the POWs, but the POWs in turn also benefited from the hard work of the likes of De Wet, Prinsloo and all the others who showed them the value of freedom. A myth, like any other story, may give us all a nice fuzzy feeling; but a millipede with only one leg will not carry you into the future.

NOTES

AUTHOR'S NOTE

1   The Union of South Africa became a republic in 1961.
2   Pietro Scottu, email correspondence, 12 March 2017.

INTRODUCTION

1   Also known as *Squadrismo*, it was the military arm of Mussolini's Fascist movement which he established in 1919. The Blackshirts were in no way affiliated with the Royal Italian Army, and they were used by Mussolini to take power in 1922.
2   Ironically, when Italy signed an armistice with the Allies in 1943, it was again the younger generation who formed the resistance movements that fought against the Italian Fascists and the Nazi occupation of Italy.
3   J Gunther. *Inside Europe* (London: Hamish Hamilton, 1937), 229.
4   Now known as Ethiopia.
5   Mussolini, quoted in J Pearce. *Prevail: The Inspiring Story of Ethiopia's Victory over Mussolini's Invasion* (New York: Skyhorse Publishing, 2014), 139.
6   Mussolini, quoted in Pearce (note 5), 139.
7   A Sbacchi. 'Poison gas and atrocities in the Italo-Ethiopian War (1935–1936)', in R Ben-Ghiat and M Fuller *Italian Colonialism* (New York: Springer, 2005), 48.
8   M Astore and M Fratianni. 'We can't pay: How Italy dealt with war debts after World War I', 2019 *Financial History Review* 26(2): 202, 205, 214.
9   Gunther (note 3) 222–223.
10 DI Kertzer. *The Pope and Mussolini* (Oxford: Oxford University Press, 2014), 20.

11 Kertzer (note 10) 80–82, 166–169.

12 M Power and P Bacchetta (eds). *Right Wing Women: From Conservatives to Extremists around the World* (New York: Taylor & Francis, 2013), 25–26; See also M Gama Sosa. 'Who was Margherita Sarfatti, Benito Mussolini's Mistress?' 3 August 2022. See < https://www.grunge.com/951545/who-was-margherita-sarfatti-benito-mussolinis-mistress/> (Accessed 11 December 2023).

13 L Koorts. *DF Malan and the Rise of Afrikaner Nationalism* (Cape Town: Tafelberg, 2014), 328.

14 C Marx. *Oxwagon Sentinel: Radical Afrikaner Nationalism and the History of the Ossewabrandwag* (Berlin: Lit Verlag, 2008), 434.

15 AM Grundlingh. '"The King's Afrikaners": Enlistment and ethnic identity in the Union of South Africa's Defence Force during the Second World War, 1939–45', 1999 *Journal of African History* 40: 11.

16 National Archives, Kew. Office of the War Cabinet (CAB) 120/474. Inward Telegram from South Africa – Prime Minister's Personal Telegram.

17 DJH Hartnady. 'South Africa's gold production and reserves', 2009 *South African Journal of Science* 105(Sept/Oct): 328.

18 B Nasson. *WWI and the People of South Africa* (Cape Town: Tafelberg, 2014), 159.

19 Nasson (note 18) 162–163.

CHAPTER 1 YOUNG FASCISTS IN ITALY'S AFRICAN COLONIES

1 Pietro Scottu, email correspondence, 28 November 2015.

2 A Fornasin, M Breschi and M Manfredini. 'Spanish flu in Italy: New data, new questions', 2018 *The Infections in the History of Medicine* 1: 101 and 104.

3 G Giro. 'Model of masculinity: Mussolini, the "new Italian" of the Fascist era', 1999 *The International Journal of the History of Sport* 16(4): 27–61.

4 P Corner. 'Collaboration, complicity and evasion under mass dictatorship', in A Ludtke (ed). *Collaboration, Complicity and Evasion under Italian Fascism* (Hampshire: Palgrave MacMillan, 2016), 76.

5 Paolo Ricci interview, Pretoria, 17 February 2016.

6 R Cei. *Seventeen* (Unpublished memoirs, nd), 4.

7 Cei (note 6) 6.

8 Cei (note 6) 5.

9 J Gunther. *Inside Europe* (London: Hamish Hamilton, 1937), 194.

10 G Palermo. We Prisoners: Africa 1941–47 POW 104702 (Unpublished memoirs, nd), 19, 21.

11 Palermo (note 10) 22.

12 Palermo (note 10) 30.

13 Paolo Ricci interview, Pretoria, 17 February 2016.

14 M Gilbert. *Second World War* (London: Phoenix Giant, 1995), 153.

15 P Scottu. Africandiario: The Free Life of an Escaped Prisoner of War in South Africa (Unpublished memoirs, nd), 5.

16 Scottu (note 15) 5.

17 Many years later, Luigi's daughter, Emilia, created a memoir from Luigi's photographs, letters and the timeline he put together: *Chronological Biography of the Period of War and Captivity.*

18 Cei (note 6) 14.

19 DB Katz. *Sidi Rezegh and Tobruk: Two South African Military Disasters Revisited 1941–1942* (Thesis in fulfilment of Master of Military Science, University of Stellenbosch, 2014), 51.

20 Cei (note 6) 15.

21 Cei (note 6) 20.

22 Cei (note 6) 21.

23 N Orpen. *War in the Desert* (Cape Town: Purnell, 1971), 142.

24 R Cornwell. '2 Anti-Tank Regiment, SAA: Tank and anti-tank in the Western Desert, 1940–1942, Part II', 1976 *Scientia Militaria, South African Journal of Military Studies* 6(2): 60.

25 Cornwell (note 24) 71.

26 Orpen (note 23) 151.

27 Cei (note 6) 21.

28 Palermo (note 10) 33.

29 Palermo (note 10) 41.

30 Palermo (note 10) 47.

31 Palermo (note 10) 50.

32 Palermo (note 10) 51.

33 P Ricci. My Story (Unpublished memoirs, nd), 2.
34 National Archives, Kew. War Office (WO) 307/1. HS Hunter to Lieutenant Colonel SJ Cole, Colonial Office, December 1942.
35 DOD AG (POW). Box 61. Personal for General Mitchell Baker from Ross, 19 April 1943.
36 Cei (note 6) 27.
37 Cei (note 6) 27.
38 Cei (note 6) 27.
39 Cei (note 6) 28.
40 Cei (note 6) 30.
41 Cei (note 6) 31.
42 Cei (note 6) 32.
43 Cei (note 6) 33.

Chapter 2 Early days at Zonderwater camp

1 G Palermo. We Prisoners: Africa 1941–47 POW 104702 (Unpublished memoirs, nd), 81.
2 Palermo (note 1) 81.
3 Paolo Ricci interview, Pretoria, 17 February 2016.
4 M Levine. 1985. 'Nova Scotia', in 1985 Global Shark Attack File Database. See <https://sharkattackfile.net/spreadsheets/pdf_directory/1942.11.28-NovaScotia.pdf>.
5 DOD AG (POW). Box 225. South African Red Cross Society, 11 January 1946.
6 Palermo (note 1) 83.
7 P Scottu. Africandiario: The Free Life of an Escaped Prisoner of War in South Africa (Unpublished memoirs, nd), 11. In Italy, the umbrella gesture is used to express contempt and to send someone away in no uncertain terms, most often accompanied by a four-letter word.
8 Scottu (note 7) 11.
9 Next to the POW camp at Zonderwater was a UDF training camp. Both of these camps were located on the Premier Mine grounds in Cullinan. As a result, some referred to the POW camp as Cullinan, while others referred to it as Premier Mine. The most commonly used name, however, was Zonderwater.

10 Palermo (note 1) 85.

11 Climate Data. Pretoria Climate (South Africa). See <https://en.climate-data.org/africa/south-africa/gauteng/pretoria-154/>.

12 Palermo (note 1) 86.

13 P Ricci. My Story (Unpublished memoirs, nd), 3.

14 B Moore and K Fedorowich. *The British Empire and Its Italian Prisoners of War, 1940–1947* (Hampshire: Palgrave, 2002), 55.

15 DOD UWH. Box 275. 'Italians to build Du Toit's Kloof Pass', *Cape Times*, 7 February 1941.

16 DOD AG (POW). Box 158. Lindenberg to Hoffe. Employment of POWs by SA Railways, 13 October 1941.

17 DOD AG (POW). (note 16).

18 Article 31 of the Geneva Convention, of 27 July 1929, relative to the Treatment of Prisoners of War states that 'Work done by prisoners of war shall have no direct connection with the operations of the war. In particular, it is forbidden to employ prisoners in the manufacture or transport of arms or munitions of any kind, or on the transport of material destined for combatant units'. See <https://icrc.org/en/doc/resources/documents/misc/57jnws.htm>. (Accessed 26 July 2021).

19 DOD AG (POW) (note 16).

20 DOD AG (POW) (note 16).

21 DOD AG (POW). Box 158. Notes of Meeting held at Pretoria on 7 October 1941.

22 DOD AG (POW) (note 16).

23 Palermo (note 1) 98.

24 Palermo (note 1) 101.

25 DOD AG (POW). Box 50. OC Troops, Premier Mine to AG, 26 June 1941.

26 DOD AG (POW). Box 91. YMCA, 2 June 1945.

27 DOD AG (POW). Box 91. War Office to Staff Captain Hodges, Military Mission, Pretoria, 14 July 1942.

28 DOD AG (POW). Box 91. Secretary of Defence.

29 DOD AG (POW). Box 91. YMCA, 2 June 1945.

30 DOD AG (POW). Box 81. Directorate of Works to AG, 7 November 1941.

31 Moore and Fedorowich (note 14) 57.

32 Moore and Fedorowich (note 14) 56.

33 DOD AG (POW). Box 81. Directorate of Works, 15 August 1941.

34 DOD AG (POW). Box 87. Special Order by Col G Rennie, VD, 22 August 1941.

35 South Africa and other British colonies were given Dominion status at the Imperial Conference in 1926 when JBM Hertzog was Prime Minister of the Union of South Africa. Hertzog advocated a republic but had to settle with Dominion status.

36 Moore and Fedorowich (note 14) 242.

37 DOD AG (POW). Box 79. DC1472/4/3. Secretary of Defence to Adjutant General, Prisoners of War: Transfers of Artisans to United Kingdom, 7 February 1942.

38 DOD AG (POW) (note 37).

39 DOD AG (POW). Box 79. SAM/AQ/4. Captain PB Carroll to DAG Pretoria, 25 March 1942.

40 R Cei. *Seventeen* (Unpublished memoirs, nd), 34.

41 Palermo (note 1) 110.

42 Palermo (note 1) 118.

CHAPTER 3 CHEAP LABOUR: POWs FOR HIRE

1   DOD AG (POW). Box 61. Inspection of POW Camp: Worcester, 5 December 1942.

2   DOD AG (POW). Box 61. Italian POW – Outside Employment.

3   Anon. 'Italian war prisoners may now be hired', *Rand Daily Mail*, 11 July 1942.

4   DOD AG (POW). Box 55. Under Secretary of Defence, 18 March 1942. DC 1472/20.

5   Anon. 'Statement on Italian war prisoners', *Rand Daily Mail*, 31 July 1942.

6   DOD AG (POW). Box 85. Shortage of Potatoes, PW Camp: Dutoitskloof, 7 May 1944.

7   DOD AG (POW). Box 103. PW/9180/151B. POW Camp: George, 28 June 1943.

8 DOD AG (POW). Box 103. PW/9071/151. George, Du Toitskloof, 25 June 1943.

9 Anon. 'Italian prisoners happy in Union', *Cape Times*, 10 April 1944.

10 Anon (note 9).

11 R Cei. *Seventeen* (Unpublished memoirs, nd), 38.

12 U van der Spuy. *Old Nectar: A Garden for All Seasons* (Johannesburg, Jacana, 2010), 9–10; Una van der Spuy interview, 21 August 2010, Old Nectar, Stellenbosch.

13 DOD AG (POW). Box 37. AG (POW) 8L, 22 May 1942.

14 DOD AG (POW). Box 37. AG (POW) 8(7), 15 June 1942.

15 Una van der Spuy interview, 21 August 2010, Old Nectar, Stellenbosch.

16 DOD AG (POW). Box 37. AG (POW) 8(7). De Wet to Stellenbosch Magistrate, 31 July 1942.

17 DOD AG (POW). Box 37. Report on the Conduct of Prisoners of War (Richards), 1 August 1942.

18 DOD AG (POW). Box 37. Copy of Statement (translated) by No 95744 Bellanthoni Dion. No 138514 Masi Giovan Battista.

19 DOD AG (POW). Box 37. POW/6138/151. De Wet to AG POW, 7 September 1942.

20 DOD AG (POW). Box 37. AG to Van der Spuy, 23 December 1942.

21 DOD AG (POW). Box 37. DAG (o)09/80, 29 August 1942.

22 DOD AG (POW). Box 37. Van der Spuy to AG Ref: POW No 287678 Guisippe Roncello, 29 December 1942.

23 DOD AG (POW). Box 37. Van der Spuy to AG re POW No: 194535 Gualini Guerino, 8 January 1943.

24 DOD AG (POW). Box 37. OE /480/11 Outside Employment Office, 27 January 1943.

25 DOD AG (POW). Box 37. Miller (Worcester Camp Commander) to DAG (POW). POW Employed by General van der Spuy, 29 September 1943.

26 DOD AG (POW). Box 37. Inspection Report on POW Employed by Gen K van der Spuy, Stellenbosch, 19 October 1943.

27 Van der Spuy (note 12) 12.

28 DOD AG (POW). Box 61. Outside Employment of POW, 27 May 1943.

29 DOD AG (POW). Box 38. Prisoners of War: Clothing.

30 DOD AG (POW). Box 38. RCH Enslin to Van Ryneveld, 31 October 1945.

31 DOD AG (POW). Box 77. PsOWAR employed by Col Blumberg.

32 DOD AG (POW). Box 101. Du Toit's Kloof Camp, 3 June 1943.

CHAPTER 4 TROUBLE BREWS AT ZONDERWATER

1 DOD AG (POW). Box 85. Court of Inquiry: Proceedings, 10 October 1941.

2 B Moore and K Fedorowich, *The British Empire and its Italian Prisoners of War, 1940–1947* (Hampshire: Palgrave, 2002), 64.

3 DOD AG (POW). Box 87. Interference with Guards and Sentries by Prisoners of War, 22 August 1941.

4 DOD AG (POW) (note 3).

5 DOD AG (POW). Box 87. Report on Shooting of POW No 97867 Falcinelli, Averando, Block 3 at 1930 on 3 March 1942.

6 DOD AG (POW). Box 87. Death of POW Serrao Antonio Francesco, 21 February 1942.

7 DOD AG (POW). Box 87. Military Liaison Mission to AG, 29 January 1942.

8 DOD AG (POW). Box 87. AEM Jansen to AG, 6 March 1942.

9 DOD AG (POW). Box 87. GA Watermeyer (AG) to Secretary of Defence Jansen, 13 April 1942.

10 DOD AG (POW). Box 87. AG to De Wet, 21 April 1942.

11 DOD AG (POW). Box 87. Death of POW No 199225, 26 March 1943.

12 DOD AG (POW). Box 87. Italian Prisoners of War and their Treatment, 22 April 1943.

13 DOD AG (POW). Box 87. British High Commissioner to AG, re Death of Italian Prisoner of War, 28 May 1943.

14 DOD AG (POW). Box 87. AG to Secretary for External Affairs, 16 November 1943.

15 DOD AG (POW). Box 87. Deaths of Italian Prisoners of War Killed While in Allied Custody, 10 August 1944.

16 DOD AG (POW) (note 15).

17 DOD AG (POW). Box 87. AG to Consul General of Switzerland, 21 August 1943.

18 DOD AG (POW). Box 87. Death of Italian POW No 142891 Faraone Celestino *Rex vs Barend Schoeman*.

19 DOD AG (POW). Box 176. Escapes: POWs, Prinsloo to DAG, 27 April 1944.

20 DOD AG (POW). Box 7. Bi-annual Report, POW Camp: Zonderwater, 23 November 1944.

21 DOD AG (POW). Box 87. AG to Secretary for External Affairs, 10 January 1944.

22 This number excludes those prisoners who were buried at camps such as Worcester and who had been reinterned at Zonderwater since the war.

23 DOD AG (POW). Box 38. Prefect Apostolic to Secretary of Defence, 30 September 1942.

24 DOD AG (POW). Box 38. Secretary for Lands to Apostolic Delegate, 24 November 1942.

25 DOD AG (POW). Box 38. Apostolic Delegate to Secretary for Lands, 27 November 1942.

26 DOD AG (POW) (note 25).

27 DOD AG (POW). Box 38. Secretary of Defence: Release within the Union of Interned Roman Catholic Priests from Kenya, 25 February 1943.

28 G Palermo. We Prisoners: Africa 1941–47 POW 104702 (Unpublished memoirs, nd), 86.

29 Palermo (note 28) 87.

30 Palermo (note 28) 87.

31 Palermo (note 28) 106.

32 Palermo (note 28) 97.

33 Following the Second World War, the 1929 Geneva Convention Relative to the Treatment of Prisoners of War was replaced by another version in 1949. See <https://www.icrc.org/en/document/protected-persons/prisoners-war>. (Accessed 26 July 2021).

34 DOD AG (POW). Box 62. Report on the Prisoner of War Situation
    – South Africa, December 1942.

35 DOD AG (POW). Box 62. Precis Discussion at Office DAG (o) will
    Col Brett War Office POW Liaison Officer,
    1 May 1942.

36 DOD AG (POW). Box 94. Report on the Visit to the Italian
    Prisoner of War Camp, Premier Mine, by Capt GG Hodges,
    16 May 1941.

37 DOD AG (POW). Box 62. Colonel Brett to Brig Gen L Beyers (AG).
    Prisoner of War Matters in the Union, 5 December 1942.

38 DOD AG (POW) (note 37).

39 DOD AG (POW) (note 37).

40 DOD AG (POW) (note 37).

41 DOD AG (POW) (note 37).

42 Moore and Fedorowich (note 2) 60.

43 DOD AG (POW). Box 95. Riot in Block X, 24 November 1942.

44 DOD AG (POW) (note 43).

45 DOD AG (POW). Box 95. Report on Alarms, 31 December 1942–
    1 January 1943.

46 DOD AG (POW). Box 95. Report on Riot in 4 CC (V) BN Lines,
    POW Camp: Zonderwater, 31 December 1942– 1 January 1943.

47 DOD AG (POW). Box 1. Reply to Questions in Parliament,
    25 February 1943.

48 DOD AG (POW). Box 95. Assistance Given by POW: Disturbance
    at Camp, 10 March 1943.

49 DOD AG (POW). Box 95. Preparations to Cope with Anticipated
    Riot among Cape Corps Personnel, 2 January 1943.

50 DOD AG (POW) (note 47).

51 DOD AG (POW). Box 95. Rioting by Personnel of the 2nd Cape
    Corps (V) BN, 19 June 1943.

52 DOD AG (POW). Box 95. Conversation Col Jordan – Col de Wet,
    evening 2–3 January, 4 January 1943.

53 Moore and Fedorowich (note 2) 68.

54 DOD AG (POW) (note 51).

55 DOD AG (POW). Box 62. AG to CGS, 13 January 1943.

56 The Battle of Spioen Kop took place near Ladysmith between British and Boer forces in January 1900.

57 Translated from Afrikaans. JA Ball. Untitled (Unpublished memoirs, nd), 5.

58 The *Croix de Guerre* is a French medal given to soldiers to reward bravery.

59 R Cei. *Seventeen* (Unpublished memoirs, nd), 36.

60 Cei (note 59) 37.

CHAPTER 5 AN 'EPIDEMIC OF ESCAPING'

1 DOD AG (POW). Box 85. Court of Inquiry, Durban, 19 September 1941.

2 DOD AG (POW) (note 1).

3 DOD AG (POW). Box 85. Court of Inquiry: Proceedings, 10 October 1941.

4 DOD AG (POW). Box 51C. 12B2(87). Court of Inquiry, 17 May 1944.

5 DOD AG (POW) (note 3).

6 DOD AG (POW). Box 50. De Wet to AG, 16 July 1941.

7 See, for instance: G Stockings. 'The Anzac Legend and the Battle of Bardia', 2010 *War in History* 17(1): 86–112; See also E Kleynhans. 'The "apostles of terror" South Africa, the East African campaign and the Battle of El Wak', 2018 *Historia* 63(2): 112–137.

8 DOD AG (POW). Box 14. PW/120338/39B.

9 DOD AG (POW). Box 85. Extract of Court of Enquiry Findings RE Escape of POW completed 10 October 1941.

10 AG (POW). Box 9. PW/C/2/13. Reclassification of Italian PsOW as Co-operators or Non-Co-operators. For Italian Routine Order.

11 Colonel De Wet took over the command of the Zonderwater camp from Colonel Rennie in September 1941.

12 DOD AG (POW). Box 158. De Wet to AG POW, 29 October 1941.

13 DOD AG (POW). Box 86. Rennie's last report, POW Administration, 17 September 1941.

14 DOD AG (POW). Box 85. Court of Inquiry; Proceedings, 10 October 1941.

15 DOD AG (POW). Box 37. AG to De Wet, 3 March 1942.

16 DOD AG (POW). Box 51B. 12B2(78). Court of Inquiry: Proceedings, 29 June 1944.

17 DOD AG (POW) (note 16).

18 R Cei. *Seventeen* (Unpublished memoirs, nd), 40.

19 DOD AG (POW) (note 16).

20 DOD AG (POW). Box 1. Clara Urquhart to AG, 23 October 1941.

21 DOD AG (POW). Box 51. PW/L.16040/46/Gen. Courts of Inquiry in Escapes of POWs on Outside Employment.

22 As the cooperators were given priority regarding repatriation after the war, the authorities had to consider the use of non-cooperators by 1946; See DOD AG (POW). Box 9. 34A/1. Employment of Italian Non-cooperators upon Camp Staff, 5 April 1946.

23 DOD AG (POW). Box 51. PW/L.16040/46/Gen. Courts of Inquiry in Escapes of POWs on Outside Employment.

24 DOD AG (POW). Box 51A. 12B2(46). Court of Inquiry, 9 November 1943.

25 DOD AG (POW). Box 51C. 12B2(88). Escapee POW No 334302, Cella Aldo.

26 With thanks to Professor Fransjohan Pretorius for this information.

27 DOD AG (POW). Box 51B. 12B2(74).

28 DOD AG (POW). Box 55. Director of Information to AG, 8 January 1943.

29 DOD AG (POW). Box 51A. 12B2(57). Court of Inquiry, 17 January 1944.

30 DOD AG (POW) (note 24).

31 DOD AG (POW) (note 24).

32 DOD AG (POW) (note 24).

33 DOD AG (POW). Box 51A. 12B2(54). Court of Inquiry, 3 February 1944.

34 DOD AG (POW) (note 28).

35 DOD AG (POW) ES/218/45. Box 14. Statement by No 544193 (V) TCpl Henning KJEN, 19 October 1945.

36 DOD AG (POW). Box 51A. 12B2(47). Police Commissioner, 13 December 1943. WD 10/1/526.

37 DOD AG (POW). Box 51A. 12B2(47). Mrs Forsyth-Thompson to Camp Commandant, Zonderwater, 20 October 1943.

38 DOD AG (POW). Box 51A. 12B2(47). Arturo Pizzie, Sworn Statement.

39 Cei (note 18).

40 Cei (note 18) 43.

41 P Scottu. Africandiario: The Free Life of an Escaped Prisoner of War in South Africa (Unpublished memoirs, nd), 9.

42 Scottu (note 41) 10.

43 Information based on letters between Luigi and Barbara, translated by Emilia Pederzoli.

CHAPTER 6 PRINSLOO TO THE RESCUE

1 HF Prinsloo quoted in C Kruger. 'The Zonderwater Italian prisoners of war 1941–1947: Fifty years down the line', 1996 SA Journal of Cultural History 10(2): 90.

2 JA Ball. 'Italian prisoners of war in South Africa 1941–1947', 1967 Military History Journal 1(1). Available online <http://samilitaryhistory.org/vol011jb.html>. (Accessed 11 October 2016).

3 Ball (note 2).

4 During the First World War, Prinsloo fought with the UDF in the German South-West African Campaign and was again active there to quell protests in 1922 when South West Africa became a mandate territory of the Union of South Africa; See AM Fokkens. 'The suppression of internal unrest in South West Africa (Namibia) 1921–1933', 2012 Scientia Militaria 40(3): 122.

5 Zonderwater Block Association. Zonderwater: A Concentration Camp in South Africa. (Accessed 2 July 2021).

6 It is estimated that a total of 26 251 women and children died in the concentration camps set up by the British to prevent men on commando from getting sustenance from the women on the farms; See E van Heyningen. Concentration Camps of the Anglo-Boer War: A Social History (Johannesburg: Jacana, 2013), 18, 136.

7 British Concentration Camps of the South African War, 1900–1902. Database. See <https://www2.lib.uct.ac.za/mss/bccd/>. (Accessed 2 July 2021.)

8   Anon. Carolina Commando. See <https://www.angloboerwar.com/
    boer-units/1954-commando-carolina>. (Accessed 6 July 2021).

9   Colonel HF Prinsloo addressing the 10th Battalion Middlesex
    Regiment, 2 May 1947. 'Forty-seven years after Spioen Kop', 1967
    Military History Journal 1(1). Available online
    <http://samilitaryhistory.org/vol011mr.html>. (Accessed 5 July 2021).

10 ICRC. Convention Relative to the Treatment of Prisoners of War:
    Article 10. Available online <https://ihl-databases.icrc.org/en/ihl-
    treaties/gc-pow-1929/article-10>.(Accessed 26 July 2021).

11 G Palermo. We Prisoners: Africa 1941–47 POW 104702 (Unpublished
    memoirs, nd), 110.

12 B Moore and K Fedorowich. *The British Empire and its Italian
    Prisoners of War, 1940–1947* (Hampshire: Palgrave, 2002), 69–70.

13 DOD AG (POW). Box 4. Hygiene Officer, POW Camp:
    Sonderwater, Hutment Progress Report For Week Ending
    31 December 1943.

14 DOD AG (POW). Box 86. Disciplinary Command: POW Camp:
    Zonderwater, 1 December 1943.

15 DOD Press and Propaganda (hereafter PP). Box 39. Propaganda
    amongst our own Troops, 8 November 1940.

16 DOD PP. Box 39 (note 15).

17 DOD Archives, Scheepers Collection. Box 6. Medical Services
    during the War.

18 DOD PP. Box 39. PR1, 6 December 1940; See FL Monama. 'South
    African propaganda agencies and the battle for the public opinion
    during the Second World War, 1939–1945', 2016 *Scientia Militaria*
    44(1): 155–156.

19 DOD CGS War. Box 189. Italian POW Welfare Fund; POW Camp:
    Zonderwater, 13 December 1944.

20 H Sonnabend. *About Myself and Others* (Johannesburg, Eagle Press,
    1951), preface.

21 A Levin. 'South African "know-how" and Israeli "facts of life": The
    planning of Afridar, Ashkelon, 1949–1956', 2019 *Planning Perspectives*
    34(2): 298.

22 Sonnabend (note 20) 98.

23 After the war, Sonnabend emigrated to Israel, where he became involved in the establishment of Afridar. His goal there was to help Holocaust survivors become part of a productive society; Sonnabend (note 20), 98, 113.

24 Sonnabend (note 20) 99.

25 DOD AG (POW). Box 61. Progress Report No 3, 17 May 1943.

26 DOD AG (POW). Box 37. PW/700/151(7). Outside Employment of POWs, 2 February 1943.

27 DOD UWH. Box 275. 'Italian prisoners employed at Cape spread propaganda', *Rand Daily Mail*, 13 January 1943.

28 DOD UWH. Box 275. 'Smuts says most Italian prisoners are well-behaved', *Rand Daily Mail*, 26 January 1943.

29 DOD UWH (note 28).

30 DOD AG (POW). Box 61. Office of the High Commissioner for the United Kingdom, 10 May 1943.

31 DOD AG (POW) (note 30).

32 DOD AG (POW). Box 61. Prisoners of War Organisation, Progress Report No 3, 17 May 1943.

33 DOD AG (POW). Box 61. Telegram. Secretary of External Affairs, Pretoria to High Commissioner, London, 16 September 1943.

CHAPTER 7 WELL-BEING THROUGH ART, MUSIC AND EDUCATION

1 P Ricci. *My Story* (Unpublished memoirs, nd), 4.

2 Ricci (note 1) 4.

3 Ricci (note 1) 4.

4 R Cei. *Seventeen* (Unpublished memoirs, nd), 42.

5 Cei (note 4) 42.

6 B Moore and K Fedorowich. *The British Empire and its Italian Prisoners of War, 1940–1947* (Hampshire: Palgrave, 2002), 272.

7 Cei (note 4) 42.

8 The quotation is taken from a prisoner's narrative, 'The story of a violin', in AD Somma. *Mythologising Music: Identity and Culture in the Italian Prisoner of War Camps of South Africa* (Thesis in fulfilment of Master of Music, University of the Witwatersrand, 2007), 11–12.

9 DOD AG (POW). Box 7. PW/9/15. Extended Freedom Scheme, 4 January 1946.
10 DOD AG (POW) Box 13. Alleged Tour of POW Band, 23 December 1943.
11 DOD AG (POW) (note 9).
12 Anon. *Italian POW in the Union of South Africa* (Senior Italian Committee, 1944).
13 Somma (note 8) 72.
14 Raffaello was probably referring to Archbishop Bernhard Adriaan van Gijlswijk (1870–1944); Cei (note 4) 44.
15 Cei (note 4) 46.
16 DOD AG (POW). Box 7. Bi-annual Progress Report. 1 December 1944.
17 G Palermo. We Prisoners: Africa 1941–47 POW 104702 (Unpublished memoirs, nd), 110.
18 Everard Read. Edoardo Villa Biography. See <https://www.everard-read.co.za/artist/EDOARDO_VILLA/biography/>.
19 E Berman, A Crump, V Meneghelli, K Nel, M Sack, K Skawran and A von Maltitz. *Villa at 90* (Johannesburg: Jonathan Ball Publishers and Shelf Publishing, 2005).
20 Berman et al. (note 19).
21 H Sonnabend. *About Myself and Others* (Johannesburg, Eagle Press, 1951), 100–101.
22 Cei (note 4) 40.
23 Cei (note 4) 41.
24 Cei (note 4) 41.
25 DOD AG (POW). Box 7. Progress Report Arts and Crafts Section for Period 1 April–30 September 1944.
26 Palermo (note 17) 111.
27 DOD AG (POW) (note 25).
28 DOD AG (POW). Box 3. PW/14781/2. POW Arts and Crafts Exhibition. 8 December 1944.
29 JA Ball. 'Italian prisoners of war in South Africa 1941–1947', 1967 *Military History Journal* 1(1). Available online <samilitaryhistory.org/volo11jb.html> (Accessed 8 July 2021).

30 Anon. *Mostra d'Arte e Articianato* PDCI (Pamphlet on an art and craft exhibition at Zonderwater), 6 April 1944, 11.

31 DOD AG (POW). Box 4. Hygiene Officer, POW Camp: Sonderwater. Hutment Progress Report for Week Ending 31 December 1943.

32 DOD AG (POW). Box 1. WG Geach. Employment of Italian Prisoners of War on Building Operations at Zonderwater, 23 November 1943

33 DOD AG (POW) (note 32).

34 DOD AG (POW). Box 1. Assembly Debates.

35 DOD AG (POW) (note 34).

36 DOD AG (POW). Box 1. Report of Temporary Organisor. RE Building Construction by Italian Prisoner Labour at Zonderwater, and its Effect on Unemployment in the Pretoria District, 28 February 1944.

37 DOD AG (POW). Box 1. Memo for the Information of Col Pilkington-Jordan, 7 March 1944.

38 L Blumberg. 'Italian POW in South Africa (Medical Services)', 1969 *Military History Journal* 1(4). Available online <samilitaryhistory.org/vol014lb.html> (Accessed 8 July 2021).

39 National Archives, Kew. War Office (WO) 307/2. Secret Cipher Telegram 34456, 24 March 1944.

40 E Spenser. Luigi Perderzoli, POW 18962. (Unpublished memoirs, nd).

41 Spenser (note 40).

42 Spenser (note 40).

43 Cei (note 4) 50.

CHAPTER 8 THE FALL OF MUSSOLINI

1 G Palermo. We Prisoners: Africa 1941–47 POW 104702 (Unpublished memoirs, nd), 120.

2 Eisenhower, quoted in MG St Clair. 'Operation Husky and the invasion of Sicily', in *The Twelfth US Air Force: Tactical and Operational Innovations in the Mediterranean Theater of Operations, 1943–1944* (Montgomery: Air University Press, 2007), 17.

3   J Holland. *Sicily '43: The First Assault on Fortress Europe* (London: Bantam Press, 2020), 125–126.

4   M Zuehlke. *Operation Husky: The Canadian Invasion of Sicily, July 10–August 7, 1943* (Vancouver: Douglas & McIntyre, 2008), 90.

5   Holland (note 3) 83–84, 124.

6   C Duggan. *Fascist Voices: An Intimate History of Mussolini's Italy* (Oxford: Oxford University Press, 2013), 386.

7   The Partisans were resistance fighters who fought on the side of the Allied forces. Most of the resistance members came from the Communist Party in Italy, although all the political parties participated in the effort to rid Italy of German forces.

8   R Packard, quoted in R Moseley. *Reporting War* (New Haven, CT: Yale University Press, 2017), 215.

9   A Beevor. *The Second World War* (London: Weidenfeld & Nicolson, 2012), 608–609.

10 J Holland. *Italy's Sorrow: A Year of War, 1944–45* (London: Harper Press, 2009), passim.

11 R Cei. *Seventeen* (Unpublished memoirs, nd), 56.

12 Palermo (note 1) 120.

13 Palermo (note 1) 119.

14 Palermo (note 1) 119.

15 B Moore and K Fedorowich. *The British Empire and its Italian Prisoners of War, 1940–1947* (Hampshire: Palgrave, 2002), 133–134.

16 DOD AG (POW). Box 4. Proposed Italianization of Services at the POW Camp: Zonderwater, 17 September 1945.

17 DOD AG (POW). Box 5. Status of POW as a Result of the Armistice, 24 September 1943.

18 Palermo (note 1) 122.

19 Palermo (note 1) 123.

20 Palermo (note 1) 121.

21 DOD CGS War. Box 190. Ration Scale: Italian PWs detained in the Union: Onward Telegram No 64: Saving Secret, July 1945.

22 Convention relative to the Treatment of Prisoners of War, Geneva, 27 July 1929.

23 Palermo (note 1) 106.

24 R Cei. *Seventeen* (Unpublished memoirs, nd), 65.

25 Cei (note 24), 39.

26 Palermo (note 1), 130–131.

27 Palermo (note 1), 133.

28 Palermo (note 1), 152.

29 As told to Mark Shaw by Lieutenant Alfred Hugh Spargo, the hospital administrator at Zonderwater. Email correspondence, 29 August 2023.

CHAPTER 9 *OSSEWABRANDWAG* AND FASCIST PRISONERS

1 R Buranello. '*Tra I Reticolati*: The literature of Italian prisoners of war in South Africa', in C von Maltzan (ed). *Africa and Europe: Myths, Masks and Masquerades* (Frankfurt am Main: Peter Lang, 2003), 260.

2 AG (POW). Box 12. Translation of Leading Article in '*Tra I Reticolati*' of 21/10/43. POW Camp: Zonderwater, 2 November 1943.

3 DOD AG (POW). Box 12. Content of Journal '*Tra I Reticolati*' dated 18/11/43. POW Camp: Zonderwater, 22 November 1943.

4 Sonnabend quoted in Buranello (note 1) 260.

5 DOD AG (POW). Box 160. POW Welfare Officer to Prinsloo. Secret, 12 August 1944.

6 DOD AG (POW). Box 160. Extracts from Propaganda Papers Confiscated from POW 332909.

7 DOD AG (POW) (note 6).

8 DOD AG (POW). Box 160. Extracts from Propaganda Papers Confiscated from Civilian, Manoriti Gino.

9 DOD AG (POW). Box 160. Extracts from Propaganda Papers confiscated from POW 379146 Civilian, Ricci Gino.

10 DOD AG (POW). Box 115. Inspection of POW Camp: Kroonstad, July 1944.

11 DOD AG (POW). Box 115. NF Auret to DJ Opperman, Provincial Secretary, United Party, June 1944.

12 DOD AG (POW). Box 160. Secret/Confidential. Translation of Letter in Italian, 24 March 1944.

13 DOD AG (POW). Box 160. Segregation of Blackshirts, 6 September 1943.

14 DOD AG (POW). Box 160. Notes on the Subject of Segregation PS in Block 9.
15 As told by a member of the National Roads Board when asked about Smuts's views on civilians contravening the rules regarding the treatment of POW workers; See B Moore and K Fedorowich. *The British Empire and its Italian Prisoners of War, 1940–1947* (Hampshire: Palgrave, 2002), 179.

CHAPTER 10 ARMISTICE JITTERS
1 AG (POW). Box 5. PW/337/2/2. POW Camp: Zonderwater.
2 AG (POW). Box 5. Special Order No 84/43. Volunteers in Support of House of Savoy and Royal Italian Government.
3 AG (POW) (note 2).
4 AG (POW) (note 2).
5 AG (POW). Box 5. POW 265587 Sub-Lieutenant Majetta, Eugenio Di Guiseppe.
6 AG (POW). Box 67. Memorandum from the Italian Government to its Prisoners of War.
7 DOD AG (POW). Box 12. Summary of Camp Journal '*Tra I Reticolati*' (Weekly publication, 25 May 1944), 2 June 1944.
8 AG (POW). Box 5. Ref O1(W)5/4/3/1. DAG to DAG, 24 September 1943.
9 AG (POW). Box 5. DAG to Camp Commandant, Zonderwater. No 262587 Sub-Lieutenant Majetta, Eugenio Di Giuseppe, 28 September 1943.
10 AG (POW). Box 5. No 1017. Secret (EAS). Telegram. High Commissioner London to Secretary for External Affairs, Pretoria. 23 September 1943.
11 DOD AG (POW). Box 12. For attention A.C.C. (1) What about Ourselves? 22 May 1944.
12 AG (POW). Box 5. Translation, Sergeant Magg Petrosillo 14th Company, Block 9. Zonderwater, 13 May 1944.
13 DOD AG (POW). Box 12. Re: Publication of Newspaper, 7 June 1944.

14 J le Gac. 'From suspicious observation to ambiguous collaboration: The Allies and Italian Partisans, 1943–1944', 2008 *Journal of Strategic Studies* 31(5): 724–726.

15 R Cei. *Seventeen* (Unpublished memoirs, nd), 37.

16 Cei (note 15), 51.

17 A Beevor. *The Second World War* (London: Weidenfeld & Nicolson, 2012), 887.

18 J Holland. *Italy's Sorrow: A Year of War, 1944–45* (London: Harper Press, 2009), 281, 290, 340, 407. Unfortunately, Giovanni Palermo did not mention his place of birth in his memoirs.

19 DOD UWH. Box 275. 'Prisoner of War Information Bureau', *The Star*, 27 September 1945.

20 DOD AG (POW). Box 12. Occupation of Rome by Allied Forces, 5 June 1944.

21 DOD AG (POW). Box 74. Report No 3 on Political Situation in POW Blocks, 19 June 1944.

22 G Palermo. We Prisoners: Africa 1941–47. POW 104702 (Unpublished memoirs, nd), 126.

23 Palermo (note 22) 126.

24 DOD AG (POW). Box 3. PW/7475/2/18. POW Camp: Zonderwater, Public Holiday for POWs, 23 May 1944.

25 DOD AG (POW). Box 3. PW/L. 11108/1/1 POW Camp: Zonderwater, Barrack Damages, 11 September 1944.

26 DOD AG (POW). Box 3. POW Camp: Zonderwater, Commitments to Detention Barracks, 29 May 1944.

27 Cei (note 15) 47.

28 DOD AG (POW). Box 5. Colonel DAG (POW) to Camp Commandants, 20 October 1943.

29 DOD AG (POW). Box 13. Boccardi Onofrio to Prinsloo, 23 April 1945.

CHAPTER 11 FREEDOM AT ANY COST

P Scottu. Africandiario: The Free Life of an Escaped Prisoner of War in South Africa (Unpublished memoirs, nd), 11.

2 Scottu (note 1) 11.

3 Scottu (note 1) 11.
4 Scottu (note 1) 11.
5 At the time, Mozambique was a Portuguese colony. Portugal and its
   colonies remained neutral during the war.
6 Scottu (note 1) 12.
7 Scottu (note 1) 12.
8 DOD AG (POW). Box 51A. 12B2(49). Court of Inquiry:
   Proceedings, 17 November 1943.
9 DOD AG (POW). Box 51C. The Commissioner of the South African
   Police, 23 May 1944.
10 DOD AG (POW). Box 74. RCI/44/11/36. Special Investigation
   Office to Prinsloo, 13 November 1944.
11 DOD AG (POW) (note 10).
12 DOD AG (POW). Box 176. Mr S Compagno to Prinsloo,
   7 March 1945.
13 DOD AG (POW). Box 176. POW 182763 Compagno Sebastiano,
   20 March 1945.
14 A la Grange. 'The Smuts Government's justification of the emergency
   regulations and the impact thereof on the Ossewa-Brandwag, 1939
   to 1945', 2020 *Scientia Militaria, South African Journal of Military
   Studies* 48(2): 49.
15 DOD AG (POW). Box 176. Escaped Italian Prisoners of War,
   25 February 1943.
16 DOD AG (POW). Box 176. JC Ingle to Secretary of Native Affairs,
   8 February 1943.
17 DOD AG (POW). Box 176. Secretary of Defence to AG, 25 April
   1943.
18 B Moore and K Fedorowich. *The British Empire and its Italian
   Prisoners of War, 1940–1947* (Hampshire: Palgrave, 2002), 62.
19 DOD AG (POW). Italian Secret. S11/1/5. Office of High
   Commissioner, Pretoria, to Secretary of Defence, 20 November 1941.
   As early as October 1940, German evacuees from Tanganyika were
   interned in the Union.
20 FL Monama. 'Civil defence and protective services in South Africa
   during World War Two, 1939–1945, 2019 *Historia* 64(2): 89–90.

21 In most cases, large groups of these evacuees were sent to camps in Southern Rhodesia, but others were sent to Koffiefontein, Andalusia and Baviaanspoort. Although they were not POWs, they were heavily guarded on the journey to the Union and also in the Union. In October 1940, 88 Italians and 4 German internees were transported from Kenya to camps in the Union, the Italians to Koffiefontein, the Germans to Pretoria. This group was followed by another of between 600 and 700 Germans from Tanganyika in April 1941. Among them were 330 women and 280 children who would be transported to Southern Rhodesia, while the men remained in the Union at Andalusia. Later the same year, a large group of Italian civilians, who were not regarded as 'voluntary refugees', were also transferred to Southern Rhodesia via Durban. The convoy stopped at the Pietermaritzburg camp, making contact between different groups of POWs possible.

22 GPJ Trümpelmann. 'Die Interneringsjare – Kampleier teen Wil en Dank' (North-West University: OB Argief, 1978). Trümpelmann viewed his time in the camp as an inspiration and believed that the internment camps offered Afrikaners who were opposed to South Africa's involvement in the war a chance to set aside their differences and work out a strategy to capture the minds of the nation. According to Trümpelmann, this contributed significantly to the National Party victory in the 1948 elections.

23 Trümpelmann (note 22).

24 Trümpelmann (note 22).

25 Trümpelmann (note 22).

26 DOD AG (POW). Box 79. SAM/AQ/4/14, April 1942.

27 DOD AG (POW). Box 65. Deputy Director Military Intelligence to AG, 23 September 1942.

28 DOD AG (POW). Box 65. AG to Deputy Director Military Intelligence, 6 October 1942.

29 DOD AG (POW). Box 51A. 12B2(60). Court of Inquiry, 14 February 1944.

30 DOD AG (POW) (note 29).

31 Pietro Scottu, email correspondence, 26 July 2017.

32 Pietro Scottu, email correspondence, 16 November 2015.

33 Scottu, (note 1) 12.

34 Scottu (note 1) 14.

35 Scottu (note 1) 13–14.

36 DOD AG (POW). Box 1. Annexure AG (POW) 1B, 14 March 1944.

37 Scottu (note 1) 14.

Chapter 12 'What are you doing in my bedroom?'

1   B Moore and K Fedorowich. *The British Empire and its Italian Prisoners of War, 1940–1947* (Hampshire: Palgrave, 2002), 138, 199.

2   DOD AG (POW). Box 1. Questions in Parliament, 7 March 1944.

3   DOD AG (POW). Box 103. Office of the Deputy Police Commissioner, Cape Town, 15 December 1942.

4   DOD AG (POW) (note 3).

5   DOD AG (POW). Box 103. Outeniqua Fortress, 27 February 1943.

6   DOD AG (POW). Box 103. RE POW Camp – Montagu Pass, George.

7   DOD AG (POW) (note 5).

8   DOD AG (POW). Box 41. War Measure No 49 of 1942 as amended by 47 of 1943. South African Police, 28 December 1943.

9   DOD AG (POW). Box 41. Office of the Deputy Commissioner, Bloemfontein, 5 January 1944.

10 DOD AG (POW) (note 8).

11 DOD AG (POW). Box 41. South African Police, RCA. No 59.2.44. Paarl, 10 February 1944.

12 DOD AG (POW). Box 115. POW 258442 Pte Calicciuri Giuseppe, 1 May 1945.

13 DOD AG (POW). Box 115. Van Heerden to AG, June 1945.

14 DOD AG (POW). Box 115. Outside Employment Inspector, Lieut vd Westhuizen, June 1945.

15 DOD AG (POW). Box 115. Bruwer to AG, June 1945.

16 DOD AG (POW). Box 115. Report – POWs in the Employ of Mr Bruwer Jnr and Mr Bruwer Snr, July 1945.

17 DOD AG (POW). Box 41. PW/2317/20/1. Prinsloo to AG, 15 February 1944.

18 DOD AG (POW). Box 41. Outside Employment of POW. Police Commissioner to Adjutant General, 23 February 1944.

19 DOD AG (POW). Box 41. Deputy Commissioner SA Police (Witwatersrand) to Commissioner of the South African Police, 18 April 1946.

20 DOD UWH. Box 275. Press cuttings; *Rand Daily Mail*, 5 May 1944.

21 DOD UWH (note 20).

22 DOD UWH. Box 275. Press cuttings; *The Star*, 26 February 1944.

23 DOD AG (POW). Box 1. Questions in Parliament, 24 January 1945.

24 DOD AG (POW). Box 7. Bi-annual Progress Report, 1 April–30 September 1944.

25 DOD AG (POW). Box 41. No 98/44, 14 February 1944; See also TD 16/6915(3), 16 January 1945.

26 DOD AG (POW). Box 120. Military Police Department to Officer Commanding, Standerton, 20 June 1945.

27 DOD AG (POW). Box 77. Affidavit, Corporal van den Berg, 1 March 1945.

28 DOD AG (POW). Box 140A. Station Commander (SAP) to Camp Commandant Miller, 18 January 1946.

29 DOD AG (POW) (note 28).

30 DOD AG (POW). Box 140A. Camp Commandant Miller to AG, 23 January 1946.

31 DOD AG (POW). Box 77. 167666 Nicolini, Gino, 10 April 1945.

32 DOD AG (POW). Box 77. Letter of Information re Farm Rietvlei 17 at Eikenhof, 10 April 1945.

33 DOD AG (POW). Box 140A. *Rex vs POW … and Circuit Court to Local Division*, 3 April 1946.

Chapter 13 Love beyond the rules

1 R Cei. *Seventeen* (Unpublished memoirs, nd), 46.

2 Cei (note 1) 46.

3 G Fiasconaro. *I'd Do it Again* (Cape Town: Books of Africa, 1982), 32–37.

4 Cei (note 1) 47–48.

5   Cei (note 1) 50.

6   Cei (note 1) 61.

7   DOD AG (POW). Box 14. 24813 S/T Gerli Ferdinando, 25 September 1946.

8   DOD AG (POW). Box 14. Gerli Ferdinando to Prinsloo, 17 September 1946.

9   DOD AG (POW). Box 14. 24813 S/T Gerli Ferdinando, 25 September 1946.

10 DOD AG (POW). Marriages of POWs to SA Women. Names are withheld to protect the identities of those concerned.

11 DOD AG (POW) (note 7).

12 Translated from the Afrikaans.

13 DOD AG (POW) (note 7).

14 DOD AG (POW) (note 7).

15 DOD AG (POW) (note 7).

16 DOD AG (POW). Box 74. Assistant Deputy Chief Censor, February 1945. Names are withheld to protect the identities of those concerned.

17 DOD AG (POW). Box 74. POW Camp: Zonderwater, 26 February 1945. Names are withheld to protect the identities of those concerned.

18 DOD AG (POW). Box 74. Fraternisation. PW, 23 May 1944.

19 DOD AG (POW) (note 18).

20 DOD AG (POW). Box 74. Fraternisation. Political Section, 17 April 1944.

21 DOD AG (POW). Box 41. Fraternisation. POW and Public, 20 April 1945.

22 P Scottu. Africandiario: The Free Life of an Escaped Prisoner of War in South Africa (Unpublished memoirs, nd), 14.

23 Scottu (note 22) 16.

Chapter 14 The long wait to return home

1   J Holland. Italy's Sorrow: A Year of War, 1944–45 (London: Harper Press, 2009), 283–284.

2   Holland (note 1) 523.

3   R Moseley. Reporting War (New Haven CT: Yale University Press, 2017), 313–317.

4   A Beevor. *The Second World War* (London: Weidenfeld & Nicolson, 2012), 342.

5   Beevor (note 4) 402–403.

6   DOD AG (POW). Box 11. 2/18: Senior Chaplain, 7 May 1945.

7   Holland (note 1) 528–529.

8   J Pollard. *The Fascist Experience in Italy* (London: Routledge, 2005), 136.

9   CL Leavitt. 'An entirely new land?: Italy's Post-war culture and its Fascist past', 2016 *Journal of Modern Italian Studies* 21(1): 5.

10 DOD AG (POW). Box 67. 15 September 1945. Memorandum for the Italian Government to its Prisoners of War.

11 DOD AG (POW). Box 14. Stanley Smollan to AG POW, 9 September 1946.

12 DOD AG (POW). Box 14. POW 273180 De Lellis Tomaso, 2 October 1946.

13 DOD AG (POW). Box 92. Report on Incident in Fascist Block, 17 May 1946.

14 B Moore and K Fedorowich. *The British Empire and its Italian Prisoners of War, 1940–1947* (Hampshire: Palgrave, 2002), 210–212.

15 DOD UWH. Civil Box 275. File B1.27: Prisoners of War in the Union. Press Cuttings: *The Star*, 15 May 1945, 'Warning to Italian prisoners'.

16 DOD AG (POW), Box 1, File 1.B. Questions in Parliament, 12 May 1945.

17 ICRC. Convention relative to the Treatment of Prisoners of War. Available online <https://ihl-databases.icrc.org/en/ihl-treaties/gc-pow-1929/article-75>. (Accessed 26 July 2021).

18 National Archives, Kew. Foreign Office (FO) 371/49939. From Rome to Foreign Office, December 1945.

19 The country known today as Libya is made up of two former Italian colonies, Cyrenaica and Tripolitania.

20 National Archives, Kew. Dominions Office (DO) 35/1923. Italian Colonies: Note of a Meeting in the Dominions Office, February 1946. Libya (Cyrenaica and Tripolitania) was administered by Britain after the war and became independent in 1951.

21 DOD AG (POW). Box 14. PW118591/2/23. Prinsloo to T Anthony, 4 October 1945.

22 G Palermo. We Prisoners: Africa 1941–47. POW 104702 (Unpublished memoirs, nd), 214.

23 DOD AG (POW). Box 55. Alleged Unseemly Behaviour of Captain Johnson, 16 May 1945.

24 DOD AG (POW). Box 7. Zebediela RCI.9/3/46. Theft of a Motor Vehicle by Italian Prisoner of War, 16 March 1946.

25 DOD AG (POW). Box 51. PW/L.16040/46/Gen. Courts of Inquiry in Escapes of POWs on Outside Employment.

26 DOD AG (POW) (note 25).

27 DOD AG (POW). Box 51. 12B/1/29B. Repatriation of Recaptured POW Escapees.

28 DOD AG (POW). Box 14. SAM/1768/PW/96. Undesirable Aliens.

29 DOD AG (POW). Box 14. B3/388/17. Transfers into Block 3; Escapes from Block 3, October 1945.

CHAPTER 15 THE END – BUT NOT YET

1 DOD AG (POW). Box 52. Prisoners of War Censorship Summary No 48, 31 August 1945.

2 DOD AG (POW). Box 5. Policy in Relation to Fascists. AG to Prinsloo, 13 December 1945.

3 DOD AG (POW). Box 74. POW Correspondence to Fascists in PMB. Political Section, 4 October 1944.

4 DOD AG (POW). Box 52. Prisoner of War Censorship Summary No 42, 1–31 January 1945.

5 J Holland. *Italy's Sorrow: A Year of War, 1944–45* (London: Harper Press, 2009), 528–533.

6 J Pollard. *The Fascist Experience in Italy* (London: Routledge, 2005), 134.

7 DOD AG (POW) (note 3).

8 DOD AG (POW). Box 65. The Secretary for External Affairs, 24 September 1945.

9 DOD AG (POW). Box 65. Circular D. No 1770 SECRET (Dom), 21 September 1945.

10 DOD AG (POW). Box 9. Vaccaro Giuseppe to Camp Command, 28 March 1946.

11 DOD AG (POW) (note 9).

12 DOD AG (POW). Box 9. Re-instatement of POW to Co-operator Status, 1 April 1946.

13 DOD AG (POW) (note 3).

14 DOD AG (POW) (note 3).

15 DOD AG (POW). Box 52. Prisoners of War Censorship Summary No 43, 1 February–15 March 1945.

16 DOD AG (POW). Box 11. PW/11552/2/18. Black Market Activities, 11 May 1945.

17 DOD AG (POW) (note 16).

18 DOD AG (POW). Box 49. Consul General of Switzerland to AG, 8 December 1945.

19 DOD AG (POW). Box 49. AG (POW) 11G/2, 19 December 1945.

20 DOD AG (POW). Box 14. Memorandum, 20 August 1946.

21 DOD AG (POW). Box 14. Secretary for the Interior to AG, 31 December 1946.

22 DOD AG (POW). Box 1. File 1B. Questions in Parliament. Press cutting: *Die Transvaler*, 18 January 1947, ''n Staatsgeheim'.

23 DOD UWH. Civil Box 275. File B1.27: Prisoners of War in the Union. Press cutting: *Rand Daily Mail*, 27 January 1947, 'MOTHS don't want Italian POWs as immigrants, priority suggested for allied nationals'.

24 DOD AG (POW). Box 81. Memorandum Regarding Proposal to Select Italian Prisoners of War as Immigrants.

25 DOD AG (POW). Box 79. Disbandment of POW Camp: Zonderwater. Acting AG to Prinsloo, 23 January 1947.

26 DOD AG (POW). Box 14. Italian POW Escapees, 11 March 1947.

27 DOD AG (POW). Box 51. B Kelly to Commissioner for Immigration, 3 May 1947; DOD AG (POW). Box 51. PW424/46. Secretary of the Interior to AG, 29 May 1947.

28 DOD AG (POW). Box 51. 154/60/7/S.

29 DOD AG (POW). Box 51. TOO. 020859C/July.

30 DOD AG (POW). Box 51. 12B/1. Italian POW Escapees from MT *Dominion Monarch*, 10 July 1947.

31 L Koorts. *DF Malan and the Rise of Afrikaner Nationalism* (Cape Town: Tafelberg, 2014), 349–350, 374.

32 DOD AG (POW). Box 160. Acting AG to Secretary of Defence, 20 December 1948.

33 DOD AG (POW). Box 51. AG (D) 154/60/7S. Italian POW No 321395 Cinito, Vito.

34 DOD AG (POW). Box 14. ES/389/47. POW Records and Returns, 17 March 1947; DOD AG (POW). Box 51. 12B/1. Recaptured Italian POW Nucci Ulderico alias Testa Pietro 379835, 16 October 1948.

35 DOD AG (POW). Box 51. Red Cross to War Records, 1 November 1951.

36 DOD AG (POW). Box 51. AG(D)154/60/7S. District Commandant, Kroonstad, 15 July 1947.

37 E Rankin and RM Scheider. *From Memory to Marble: The Historical Frieze of the Voortrekker Monument* (Berlin/Boston: Walter de Gruyter, 2019), 67.

38 DOD AG (POW). Box 51. Officer in Charge of Records, 12 April 1949. According to Ancestry.com, Tomasso Scarcella died in the Free State in 1978. He was married to Susanna Maria Scheepers.

39 DOD UWH. Civil Box 275. File B1.27: Prisoners of War in the Union. Press Cuttings: *Sunday Times*, May 1947, '86 Italians must surrender by Wednesday'.

40 DOD AG (POW). Box 51. 12B/1.

Chapter 16 'I ALSO NEED SO MUCH TO CRY'

1 R Cei. *Seventeen* (Unpublished memoirs, nd), 54.

2 G Palermo. We Prisoners: Africa 1941–47 POW 104702 (Unpublished memoirs, nd), 202.

3 Palermo (note 2) 205.

4 DOD AG (POW). Box 95A. Affidavit, March 1946.

5 DOD AG (POW). Box 51. Translation of Letter to Headquarters POW/Red Cross, 14 February 1946.

6 DOD AG (POW). Box 12. Il Printo [sic], dated Zonderwater 30.3.XXIV (Year of Fascism, ie 1946).

7 DOD UWH. Box 275. *Sunday Times*, 'Fights as POWs leave to embark at Durban', 5 January 1947.

8 DOD UWH. Box 275. *Rand Daily Mail*, 'POWs print Fascist pamphlets on train', 4 January 1947.

9 DOD AG (POW). Box 66. Repatriation Special Cage, 11 January 1947.

10 Palermo (note 2), 154.

11 Palermo (note 2) 156.

12 Palermo (note 2) 173.

13 Giovanni's use of physiognomy refers to the pseudo-science of Eugenics which suggested that a person's character and/or ethnicity could be determined by facial features and other physical traits. Eugenics was the 'scientific' basis for Fascism, which in Germany's case led to discrimination against Jews and others as a result of their Jewish blood. This in turn led to the Holocaust and the genocide of millions of people.

14 Palermo (note 2) 154.

15 DOD UWH. Box 275. *Rand Daily Mail*, 23 January 1947.

16 DOD UWH. Box 275. *Rand Daily Mail*, 23 January 1947.

17 Cei (note 1) 48–49.

18 Cei (note 1) 58.

19 Cei (note 1) 52–53.

20 Cei (note 1) 56.

21 Cei (note 1) 53.

22 Luigi Pederzoli to Barbara Pederzolli, 29 April 1946 (translated by Emilia Cerasi Pederzoli).

23 Luigi Pederzoli to Barbara Pederzolli, 8 September 1946 (translated by Emilia Cerasi Pederzoli).

24 Pederzoli (note 22).

25 Email correspondence with Emily Spenser, Luigi's daughter.

26 Luigi Pederzoli to Barbara Pederzolli, 20 October 1946 (translated by Emilia Cerasi Pederzoli).

27 Luigi Pederzoli to Barbara Pederzolli, 7 November 1946 (translated by Emilia Cerasi Pederzoli).

28 *Il Rimpatrio* [Repatriation], compiled by Emily Spenser, passim.

29 Palermo (note 2) 162.

30 Palermo (note 2) 185.

31 Palermo (note 2) 186–187.

32 'Up north' referred either to Egypt, where UDF troops were stationed, or to Libya, where they fought against German and Italian forces.

33 P Scottu. Africandiario: The Free Life of an Escaped Prisoner of War in South Africa (Unpublished memoirs, nd), 18.

34 Scottu (note 33) 19.

35 Scottu (note 33) 20.

36 Scottu (note 33) 21.

37 Scottu (note 33) 22.

38 Scottu (note 33) 23.

39 Scottu (note 33) 23.

40 Scottu (note 33) 24.

41 Scottu (note 33) 24.

42 For many years, Emilio Coccia, President of the Zonderwater Block ex-POW Association, looked after the Zonderwater grounds, the cemetery and the museum. The museum contains artworks made by POWs during their captivity. The Zonderwater Block commemorates the fallen on the first Sunday of November every year.

43 P Ricci. My Story (Unpublished memoirs, nd), 6.

44 V Zamagni. The Economic History of Italy 1860–1990 (Oxford: Clarendon Press, 2003), 232.

45 M Giorcelli. Economic Recovery and the Determinants of Productivity and Innovation: Evidence from Post-WWII Italy (PhD Dissertation, Stanford University, 2016), 4.

46 M Legassick. 'Legislation, ideology and economy in post-1948 South Africa', 1974 Journal of Southern African Studies 1(1): 6.

47 Now Lilian Ngoyi Street.

48 Ricci (note 43) 8.

49 Paolo Ricci interview, 17 February 2016, Pretoria.

50 Ricci (note 43).

EPILOGUE

1 AD Somma. Mythologising Music: Identity and Culture in the Italian Prisoner of War Camps of South Africa. (Thesis in fulfilment of Master of Music, University of the Witwatersrand, 2007).

Bibliography

Interviews

Emilia Cerasi Pederzoli (Luigi Pederzoli's daughter), email
   correspondence, 2016–2023.

Emilio Coccia (President of the Zonderwater Block ex-POW Association),
   interview, Zonderwater Camp Museum, 9 February 2016.

Paolo Ricci, interview, Pretoria, 17 February 2016.

Pietro Scottu email correspondence, 2015–2017.

Raffaello Cei, email correspondence, June 2016.

Una van der Spuy interview, Stellenbosch, 21 August 2010.

Memoirs and letters

Ball, JA. Untitled. (Unpublished memoirs, n.d.).

Cei, R. *Seventeen*. (Unpublished memoirs, n.d.).

Palermo, G. We Prisoners Africa: 1941-47 POW. 104702. (Unpublished
   memoirs, nd).

Pederzoli, Luigi, to Barbara Pederzolli, letters translated by Emilia
   Cerasi Pederzoli (Emily Spenser).

Ricci, P. *My Story*. (Unpublished memoirs, n.d.).

Scottu, P. Africandiario: The Free Life of an Escaped Prisoner of War in
   South Africa (Unpublished memoirs, n.d.).

Spenser, E. Luigi Perderzoli, POW 18962. (Unpublished memoirs, n.d.).

Archives

International Committee of the Red Cross (ICRC), Photo and Sound
   Archives, Geneva, Switzerland <https://avarchives.icrc.org>.

National Archives, London. Dominions Office (DO).

National Archives, London. Foreign Office (FO).

National Archives, London. Office of the War Cabinet (CAB).

National Archives, London. War Office (WO).

South African Department of Defence Archives, Pretoria, Adjutant General (AG), Prisoners of War (POW).

South African Department of Defence Archives, Chief of the General Staff (CGS).

South African Department of Defence Archives, Union War Histories (UWH).

South African National Museum of Military History (NMMH).

Ossewa Brandwag Argief, North-West University.

Trümpelmann, GPJ. 1978. '*Die interneringsjare – Kampleier teen wil en dank*'.

PRIMARY SOURCES

Anon. 1944. *Italian POW in the Union of South Africa*. (Published by the Senior Italian Committee).

Anon. 6 April 1944. *Mostra d'Arte e Articianato PDCI*. (Pamphlet on an art and craft exhibition at Zonderwater).

Cape Times

Die Transvaler

Rand Daily Mail

Sunday Times

The Star

SELECTED SECONDARY SOURCES

Astore, M and Fratianni, M. '"We can't pay": How Italy dealt with war debts after World War I', 2019 *Financial History Review* 26(2): 197–222.

Beevor, A. *The Second World War* (London: Weidenfeld & Nicolson, 2012).

Berman, E, Crump, A, Meneghelli, V, Nel, K, Sack, M, Skawran, K and Von Maltitz, A. *Villa at 90* (Johannesburg: Jonathan Ball Publishers and Shelf Publishing, 2005).

Buranello, R. '*Tra I Reticolati*: The literature of Italian prisoners of war in South Africa', in C von Maltzan (ed). *Africa and Europe: Myths, Masks and Masquerades* (Frankfurt am Main: Peter Lang, 2003).

Corner, P. 'Collaboration, complicity and evasion under mass dictatorship,' in A Ludtke (ed). *Collaboration, Complicity and Evasion under Italian Fascism* (Hampshire: Palgrave MacMillan, 2016).

Cornwell, R. '2 Anti-Tank Regiment, SAA: Tank and anti-tank in the Western Desert, 1940–1942, Part II', 1976 *Scientia Militaria, South African Journal of Military Studies* 6(2): 49–71.

Duggan, C. *Fascist Voices: An Intimate History of Mussolini's Italy* (Oxford: Oxford University Press, 2013).

Fiasconaro, G. *I'd Do it Again* (Cape Town: Books of Africa, 1982).

Fokkens, AM. 'The suppression of internal unrest in South West Africa (Namibia) 1921–1933', 2012 *Scientia Militaria* 40(3): 109–146.

Gilbert, M. *Second World War* (London: Phoenix Giant, 1995).

Giro, G. 'Model of masculinity: Mussolini, the "new Italian" of the Fascist Era', 1999 *The International Journal of the History of Sport* 16(4): 27–61.

Grundlingh, AM. '"The King's Afrikaners": Enlistment and ethnic identity in the Union of South Africa's Defence Force during the Second World War, 1939–45', 1999 *Journal of African History* 40, 11.

Gunther, J. *Inside Europe* (London: Hamish Hamilton, 1937).

Holland. J. *Italy's Sorrow: A Year of War, 1944–45* (London: Harper Press, 2009).

Holland, J. *Sicily '43: The First Assault on Fortress Europe* (London: Bantam Press, 2020).

Kertzer, DI. *The Pope and Mussolini* (Oxford: Oxford University Press, 2014).

Kleynhans, E. 'The "apostles of terror": South Africa, the East African campaign and the Battle of El Wak', 2018 *Historia* 63(2): 112–137.

Koorts, L. *DF Malan and the Rise of Afrikaner Nationalism* (Cape Town: Tafelberg, 2014).

Kruger, C. 'The Zonderwater Italian prisoners of war 1941–1947: fifty years down the Line', 1996 *SA Journal of Cultural History* 10(2): 88–104.

La Grange, A. 'The Smuts Government's justification of the emergency regulations and the impact thereof on the Ossewa-Brandwag, 1939 to 1945', 2020 *Scientia Militaria, South African Journal of Military Studies* 48(2): 39–64.

Leavitt, CL. '"An entirely new land?" Italy's post-war culture and its Fascist past,' 2021 *Journal of Modern Italian Studies* 21(1): 4–18.

Levin, A. 'South African "know-how" and Israeli "facts of life": The planning of Afridar, Ashkelon, 1949–1956', 2019 *Planning Perspectives* 34(2), 285–309.

Marx, C. *Oxwagon Sentinel: Radical Afrikaner Nationalism and the History of the Ossewabrandwag* (Berlin: Lit Verlag, 2008).

Monama, FL. 'South African propaganda agencies and the battle for the public opinion during the Second World War, 1939–1945', 2016 *Scientia Militaria* 44(1): 145–167.

Monama, FL. 'Civil defence and protective services in South Africa during World War Two, 1939–1945', 2019 *Historia* 64(2): 82–108.

Moore, B and Fedorowich, K. *The British Empire and Its Italian Prisoners of War, 1940–1947* (Hampshire: Palgrave, 2002).

Moseley, R. *Reporting War* (New Haven CT: Yale University Press, 2017).

Nasson, B. *WWI and the People of South Africa* (Cape Town: Tafelberg, 2014).

Orpen, N. *War in the Desert* (Cape Town: Purnell, 1971).

Pearce, J. *Prevail: The Inspiring Story of Ethiopia's Victory over Mussolini's Invasion* (New York: Skyhorse Publishing, 2014).

Pollard, J. *The Fascist Experience in Italy* (London: Routledge, 2005).

Rankin, E and Scheider, RM. *From Memory to Marble: The Historical Frieze of the Voortrekker Monument* (Berlin/Boston: Walter de Gruyter, 2019).

Sbacchi, A. 'Poison gas and atrocities in the Italo-Ethiopian War (1935–1936),' in R Ben-Ghiat and M Fuller. *Italian Colonialism* (New York: Springer, 2005).

Sonnabend, H. *About Myself and Others* (Johannesburg: Eagle Press, 1951).

Stockings, G. 'The Anzac Legend and the Battle of Bardia', 2010 *War in History:* 17(1), 86–112.

Van der Spuy, U. *Old Nectar: A Garden for all Seasons* (Johannesburg: Jacana, 2010).

Van Heyningen, E. *Concentration Camps of the Anglo-Boer War: A Social History.* (Johannesburg: Jacana, 2013).

Zamagni, V. *The Economic History of Italy 1860–1990* (Oxford: Clarendon Press, 2003).

Zuehlke, M. *Operation Husky: The Canadian invasion of Sicily July 10– August 7, 1943* (Vancouver: Douglas & McIntyre, 2008).

INTERNET

Anon. Carolina Commando. <https://www.angloboerwar.com/ boer-units/1954-commando-carolina>.

Ball, JA. 'Italian prisoners of war in South Africa 1941–1947', 1967 *South African Military History Journal* 1(1). <http://samilitaryhistory.org/ volo11jb.html>.

Blumberg, L. 'Italian POW in South Africa (Medical Services)', 1969 *South African Military History Journal* 1(4). <samilitaryhistory.org/ volo14lb.html>.

British Concentration Camps of the South African War, 1900–1902. <https://www2.lib.uct.ac.za/mss/bccd/>.

Everard Read. Edoardo Villa Biography. <https://www.everard-read. co.za/artist/EDOARDO_VILLA/biography/>.

International Committee of the Red Cross (ICRC). Convention Relative to the Treatment of Prisoners of War, Geneva, 27 July 1929. <https:// icrc.org/en/doc/resources/documents/misc/57jnws.htm>.

Prinsloo, HF. 'Forty-seven years after Spioen Kop', 1967 *Military History Journal* 1(1). <http://samilitaryhistory.org/volo11mr.html>.

Zonderwater Block Association. Zonderwater: A Concentration Camp in South Africa'. <http://www.zonderwater.com/en/>.

INDEX